Geoff G

10 . 11 . 12

M000168208

THE IRVING BERLIN READER

*Puccini, as a money-maker, had nothing
on the Broadway melodist [Irving Berlin].*

Columbus Dispatch, May 7, 1916

His songs sound as though they
were born that way—not written.
Harold Arlen

It is easier to understand Beethoven than Irving Berlin.
Fred Elizade (1907–1979, band leader)

You have to hug him
to hear him [sing].
Unknown

It must be hell being Irving Berlin.
The guy's his own toughest competition.
Anonymous Music Publisher

The Irving Berlin Reader

Edited by Benjamin Sears

OXFORD
UNIVERSITY PRESS

OXFORD
UNIVERSITY PRESS

Oxford University Press, Inc., publishes works that further
Oxford University's objective of excellence

Oxford   New York
Auckland   Cape Town   Dar es Salaam   Hong Kong   Karachi
Kuala Lumpur   Madrid   Melbourne   Mexico City   Nairobi
New Delhi   Shanghai   Taipei   Toronto

With offices in
Argentina   Austria   Brazil   Chile   Czech Republic   France   Greece
Guatemala   Hungary   Italy   Japan   Poland   Portugal   Singapore
South Korea   Switzerland   Thailand   Turkey   Ukraine   Vietnam

Copyright © 2012 by Oxford University Press, Inc.

Published by Oxford University Press, Inc.
198 Madison Avenue, New York, NY 10016

www.oup.com

Oxford is a registered trademark of Oxford University Press

All rights reserved. No part of this publication may be reproduced,
stored in a retrieval system, or transmitted, in any form or by any means,
electronic, mechanical, photocopying, recording, or otherwise,
without the prior permission of Oxford University Press.

Library of Congress Cataloging-in-Publication Data
The Irving Berlin reader / edited by Benjamin Sears.
p.   cm. — (Readers on American musicians)
Includes bibliographical references and index.
ISBN 978-0-19-538374-4
1. Berlin, Irving, 1888–1989—Criticism and interpretation.
2. Musicals—United States—20th century—History and criticism.
I. Sears, Benjamin.
ML410.B499I78   2012
782.42164092—dc22   2011012613

9 8 7 6 5 4 3 2 1

Printed in the United States of America
on acid-free paper

TO BRAD

. . . not for just an hour, not for just a day, not for just a year . . .

*. . . if you don't want as much Berlin in a show
as possible, please leave the room.*

David Ives, *Playbill* for *Face the Music*, March, 2007

~~~~~~

Contents

PART III

The Melody Lingers On: Later Years

PART IV

Irving Berlin in His Own Words

You're the top,
    You're a Waldorf salad;
You're the top,
    You're a Berlin ballad.
Cole Porter, "You're the Top"

Acknowledgments

Many people have helped make this book possible. My parents, Benjamin and Nancy, gave me at an early age a love of music, language, and words; the latter no doubt is a reason that song lyrics have always been a special interest. My sisters, Jennifer and Becca, and my brother, Nathan, have always supported my musical adventures.

Helpful in all sorts of ways with research were Janet Katz of the Harvard Law School Library Reference Department; Betty Auman and Ray White at the Library of Congress; and the staff of the Billy Rose Collection at the New York Public Library.

Irving Berlin's three lovely and gracious daughters, Mary Ellin Barrett, Linda Emmet, and Elizabeth Peters, have been nothing but supportive of this project and all the Berlin projects I have undertaken. Mary Ellin and Linda gave advice and encouragement on the *Reader*. Also supportive and helpful were Ted Chapin, Bert Fink, Nicole Harman, and Robin Walton of Irving Berlin Music and the Rodgers & Hammerstein Organization.

Of special significance are Diana Cole and June Judson, both of whom are in the categories of mentor, colleague, and friend. Others, in no particular order, who helped along the way are Jim Randall; Carol Oja; Lee Orr; Howard Pollack; Margaret Knapp; Charles Hamm; Wayland Bunnell; Jeffrey Magee; Larry Hamberlin; Tom Riis; Amy Asch; Robert Kimball; Caryl Flinn; Ward Morehouse III; Lori Trethewey, Hope College; Karen Rice, West End Collegiate Church, New York; Julia May Jonas, EMI; Elliot Webb, ICM Talent; Carla Jablonski; David Jablonski; Allison Robbins; Anthony Bye, *The Musical Times*; Robert Bonotto; Sheryl Kaskowitz; Robert Tieman; and Ian Whitcomb. Dawn Carson read an early version of the *Reader* and provided her usual words of wisdom.

One person I cannot thank enough is Bradford Conner, with whom I share my life and have researched, performed, and recorded together the music of Irving Berlin for over twenty years. Without him, my Irving Berlin journey would never have started. Others who have been part of the journey are Marilu Nowlin, Martha Goodman, Susan Roberts, Frank Cunningham, Tony Mazzola, Julie Steinhilber, Joanne Barrett, and Andrew Altman.

At Oxford University Press I owe a huge debt to my editor (and friend) Norm Hirschy, who gently nudged me as necessary and often shepherded things along when I was overwhelmed by the reality of producing a book. Music editor Suzanne Ryan supported this project from the start; Katherine Boone also provided assistance. Joellyn Ausanka has shown amazing patience and cheerfully provided endless guidance. To all of them I am truly grateful. OUP sent the manuscript to two anonymous reviewers whose comments (and wit) were invaluable to a novice.

If, as I fear, someone has been forgotten, please know that forgetfulness on my part does not imply any lack of appreciation.

THE IRVING BERLIN READER

Introduction

From Mother Russia to Manhattan's Beekman Place, from "Marie from Sunny Italy" (1907) to "An Old Fashioned Wedding" (1967) for the revival of *Annie Get Your Gun* (with its original star, Ethel Merman, no less), the story of Irving Berlin is fascinating and complex. Jerome Kern's famous quote has passed into cliché, but it is still true that for many "Irving Berlin *is* American music." Two Berlin songs have passed into folksong status ("White Christmas" and "Easter Parade"),[1] and a third has become a second American National Anthem ("God Bless America"). Many more are readily recognized by people who may not otherwise be interested in popular song of the era. No American songwriter had as long a career or is likely to, and few have written as many hit songs or songs that have endured for so many generations. No other songwriter consistently had his name *above* the show or film title, as can be seen even today in "Irving Berlin's *White Christmas*." This was due not only to his prestige but also because Berlin often came up with the original idea for the show. He is among the few songwriters who have outlived their copyrights ("Alexander's Ragtime Band" being the most famous example). No twentieth-century popular songwriter wore his patriotism so openly and proudly, "God Bless America" being the most prominent of many examples. Berlin did not set out to break new dramatic and musical ground in musical comedy as did Richard Rodgers and Lorenz Hart (and later Rodgers with Oscar Hammerstein II), nor did he have the concert hall aspirations of George Gershwin; his goal, as initially a songplugger then as writer of Broadway and Hollywood scores, was to write hits. When asked if he was writing for posterity, he answered simply, "no, prosperity."

---

1. Pete Seeger, as related in Jeffrey Magee's article "Irving Berlin's 'Blue Skies': Ethnic Affiliations and Musical Transformation" (*Musical Quarterly* 84, no. 4 [2000]: 537) accorded "Blue Skies" folksong status by including it in his collection *The Incomplete Folksinger*. Magee considers this inclusion "remarkable because Seeger held such disdain for the commercialism of Broadway and Tin Pan Alley."

Over his sixty years of songwriting Berlin adapted to changing fashions in popular song, often faster than the fashions themselves; yet he was always of his time, reflecting the songs of the moment while setting standards for the songwriters around him. Berlin took the Victorian "waltz ballad" and made it his own, with "What'll I Do?" and "Always" being but two examples of his success with it. He was a culmination of the songwriters before him and a starting point for his contemporaries and successors.

There were several firsts: he was the first Tin Pan Alley tunesmith to move uptown to Broadway with his 1914 show, *Watch Your Step*, and he was the first—and still the only—songwriter to build a theater for his own productions, the Music Box, which is still in use today on Broadway. No other songwriter wrote a show in support of the war effort in each of the two world wars. *And* performed in them along with the army boys. No other songwriter for film recycled his songs as often or as repeatedly (often in two or more films) as Berlin. Until he simply could not adapt one more time in the 1960s, Berlin was consistently producing new songs that appealed to his audiences.

After Berlin's death in 1989 he quickly benefited from the new scholarly interest in the Great American Songbook of the first half of the twentieth century, along with nostalgia for music of that time. Since then major biographies have appeared, books analyzing his songs (including one on "White Christmas" alone), numerous articles, a collection of his complete lyrics, and a scholarly edition of his earliest songs from 1907 to 1914. During his lifetime, however, much of the biographical writing about him was of an adoring nature that offered little or no analysis.

Berlin, who had both a shrewd business ability and a fine sense for public relations, was not averse to some of the legends that sprang up about him, the most prominent being that of musical ignorance. He did learn the rudiments of reading and writing music but did not feel comfortable doing his own notation and always used a musical secretary to transcribe what he played. He had a keen ear, which picked up anything and everything he heard; he knew when his musical secretary had taken down a chord differently from how he had played it; he knew and appreciated opera, occasionally incorporating allusions to the classics in his early songs. The image of musical ignorance was a false one that Berlin felt little need to correct as it created a mystique about him that he found to be to his advantage. Berlin said that his songwriting was not autobiographical, though he did admit some exceptions, such as "Oh, How I Hate to Get Up in the Morning," which he described as particularly heartfelt.

The goal of this *Reader* is to bring together a rich collection of writings on Berlin that may not be readily available elsewhere; much of the current writing on Berlin is easily accessible and so is not reprinted here (which is no judgment on its value). Sorting through the writings about someone who lived to be 101 and whose songwriting career spanned sixty years reveals much about the man, the times, the writers themselves, and changing fashions in art and in reporting. The sort of "fluff" reporting now associated with certain popular magazines was no less prevalent in the early years of the twentieth century. The movements of a successful popular or Broadway songwriter were followed closely, and Berlin was no exception (he even merited a piece in the *National Enquirer* which was short on facts and is not reprinted here). His musical projects and his personal life came to be well documented. Some of these are stories oft-told, such as his courtship of and marriage to Ellin Mackay, and need not be rehashed in these pages. Others, though, shed new light on some of the legends, such as the famous first night of *Betsy*, with its interpolation of "Blue Skies." Jerome Kern's famous quote came from a letter to Berlin's first biographer, Alexander Woollcott, which is reprinted here in its entirety. Magazine profiles of Berlin and writings both contemporary and modern add to the story, as do pieces by Berlin himself on songwriting.

While this *Reader* is not designed to present Berlin's life in a biographical sense, it does present the writings in essentially a chronological fashion. Every effort has been made to use contemporary writings, but the fact remains that much of the best and most insightful writing on Berlin has occurred in the years after his death. Articles generally are placed by when they were written, if contemporary with the events; some post-date the actual period of Berlin's life but discuss an earlier aspect of his career. Recent scholarship has given the early years a great deal of attention, while the four years of the *Music Box Revues* and other Broadway work from the 1920s, 1930s, and 1940s are still waiting for fuller attention, along with some of the lesser-known films.

Because Berlin's career was so long, his work does not divide neatly into periods as do those of Richard Rodgers and George Gershwin, for example. Berlin was his own lyricist, so his work cannot be defined by his collaborators, as with Rodgers; nor did his writing separate as cleanly between Broadway and Hollywood as Gershwin's appears to. There is, though, a clear shift into artistic maturity around 1918 which is complete by the first *Music Box Revue* (1921), and shifts of style and focus occurred at various points in his career. The best defined period of Berlin's work is the early years, roughly 1907–1920, when he produced nearly half of his catalogue, yet even this period easily can be subdivided (using *Watch Your Step* as a dividing line).

The book has been divided into three parts that reflect loose periods in his life, based on the significant output of the years concerned, with a fourth in which the composer speaks. Part I covers the early years of Berlin's youth, his first published song in 1907, the success of "Alexander's Ragtime Band" through the four *Music Box Revues,* ending in 1924. Part II takes Berlin up to his ninetieth birthday. Part III is a summing up of his career in one hundredth birthday salutes, obituaries, and later assessments of his work. The final part is centered on Berlin's own writings and interviews with him on the topic of songwriting and possibly writing an opera in ragtime (an unfulfilled dream), along with a small sampling of his business letters and a brief excerpt from a projected memoir. That the articles on songwriting come from mostly early in his career speaks to an aspect of Berlin's personality in that he knew the value of the publicity gained by them when he needed that publicity. Berlin was not one to look back on his past and in his older years was not likely to give interviews or reflections.

Across the *Reader* certain themes appear. Berlin is often referred to as shy in early articles, a trait overlooked by some of his more critical biographers. In his later years Berlin reverted to that shyness which has led to his late-life reclusiveness being perceived as a sudden change in personality (and he is often portrayed as an unpleasant recluse, too). Berlin was smart enough to know that he needed to become a public figure in order to sell his songs, even if it was against his nature to be such a public figure. When that public profile was no longer needed, he felt he had earned the right to be out of the spotlight.

To see the transformation of Irving Berlin from songplugger to successful songwriter to musical icon, while perhaps not "the journey from here to a star," is to see a special part of American music, indeed to see a reflection of sixty years of the twentieth century in American music.

Part I

Musical Demon
Early Years

You know, it's amazing how often
  you can use the same tunes over again
with a few different twists.
  I've got only seven or eight
really different tunes in my system.
  It's like reassembling furniture.
Irving Berlin

Ward Morehouse: A Trip to Chinatown with Irving Berlin

Irving Berlin never had a press agent, as he was a shrewd public relations (PR) man himself (see "Berlin at 100: Life on a High Note" in Part III for more on Berlin as his own PR agent). Berlin created his own public image, exercising the same control over it as he did over all aspects of his career, thus establishing very early the standard Irving Berlin biography. It was repeated, in essentially the same form, in articles of all types throughout his life with the major variation simply bringing the information up to date in regard to his latest song, show, or movie. The story over more than sixty years startles with its uniformity.

Of the many versions, this one by Ward Morehouse is among the best, in part because of its setting—Berlin, at the age of fifty-eight, leading a tour of his old haunts in Chinatown and reminiscing about his youth along the way. Morehouse (1899–1966) was a leading theater critic in New York and famous for his column *Broadway After Dark* which ran in the *New York Sun* and later the *New York World-Telegram and Sun* from 1926 until his death. Morehouse was of the era when critics had a more personal relationship with celebrities; his friendship with Berlin is evident in his writing.

This article recounts an actual trip taken by Berlin and Morehouse, confirmed by Berlin's daughters Mary Ellin Barrett and Linda Emmet. Curiously, though, when Morehouse reprinted the article almost verbatim in 1958 in the magazine *Theatre Arts* as *The Berlin Baedeker*, he rewrote the opening and ending portions in such a way as to suggest that the event took place in 1958.

Irving Berlin, son of a rabbi and born to the world as Izzy Baline, sipped his coffee at the finish of our elaborate dinner at the Pavilon, a meal inclusive of wild duck and crab meat in pancakes, and said:

SOURCE *New York Sun*, February 24, 1947.

"When I was a kid I never knew there was food like this in the world. But you never miss luxury until you've had it. I never felt poverty because I'd never known anything else."

"We had an enormous family," he continued, "eight or nine in four rooms and in the summer some of us slept on the fire escape or on the roof. I was a boy with poor parents, but let's be realistic about it. I didn't starve. I wasn't cold or hungry. There always was bread and butter and hot tea. I slept better in tenement houses and in lodging houses at 15 cents a night than I do now in a nice bed. Well, shall we get started?"

It was Berlin talking—the slender, swarthy, well-dressed Berlin, now 58, and an erstwhile troubadour from the sidewalks of New York. It was Berlin, composer of 800 songs and the man who earned $10,000,000 for the Army Emergency Relief Fund with his *This Is the Army* show.

He now paid the check, tipped the waiter and several captains, and led the way to his limousine waiting at the curb. We piled in and were off for downtown Manhattan, for Cherry Hill, the Bowery, Chinatown and Nigger Mike's on a sentimental journey that was to keep us prowling until well past midnight.

Our southward course was along Fifth Avenue to Madison Square. We swung over into Broadway and continued to Union Square, once the tumultuous center of New York's theatertown, and stayed on Broadway to Chambers, into which we turned eastward. Berlin spoke with a rush of words:

"I don't know what we're going to find down here; we'll just have to see; it's like going home after you've been away a long, long time. With me, as a kid, it was a case of doing what came naturally. We all came here from Russia in 1893 and my father taught me to sing in the choir. I sang, and later I left home and went on the bum on the Bowery. That way I got to know songs and got to know words. . . . Look! We're getting close."

We were now in the tangle of the lower East Side, streets coming at us from every direction. Our driver, substituting for Berlin's regular chauffeur, and unaccustomed to the complexities of downtown Manhattan, was making his way cautiously. The streets were silent and strangely empty; squares and rectangles of light showed wanly in tenement windows.

We moved northward on Madison Street, turned eastward into Montgomery, and the fidgety Berlin, now wide-eyed with the excitement of rediscovery, leaned toward the driver and said quickly:

"That's Cherry Street at the corner. Stop there. We'll get out."

We got out. Berlin looked around.

"This was my corner," he said. "This was my street. This was the East Side that I knew as a kid. Right down there, at the end of Montgomery Street, we'd go swimming in the river. Right over on that corner"—he indicated the north-west corner building, the ground floor of which is now occupied by a dealer in burlap bags—"was Levy's saloon and on the other corner"—he was looking toward the dingy northeast corner structure, its walls still bearing traces of a Ringling Brothers-Barnum & Bailey twenty-four sheet—"was a German deli-catessen, the Dutchman's, but we kids didn't go there. We went to the Jewish place around the corner. All this looks familiar—but I don't remember any-thing like that!"

He flung out his arm to the north. A tidy, modern, softly lighted apartment building had somehow found its way into the Cherry Street region—intrusively, and with all the appearance of a movie set, put up only that afternoon.

"Come on," he said turning, "and we'll go on down to my house. . . . No, wait a minute. . . . There was a junk shop right around here. I used to go there selling bits and pieces of an old brass samovar that my mother brought from Russia and kept under the bed. I'd get 5 and 10 cents for the pieces and kept selling them until the entire samovar had disappeared."

He began walking southward along Cherry Street, leading the way slowly.

"This was the East Side that a lot of us used to know. Out of all this came the Jessels and the Eddie Cantors and Sam H. Harris. There were tenements right along here. Charlie White, who was a famous referee, lived right in this block. He has a beautiful daughter named Stella and we kids would stand and look at her as she sat on her stoop."

We stopped in front of a remodeled tenement house at No. 330 Cherry Street. Irving Berlin, hat in his hand and excitement in his eyes, backed away to the curb and looked up at the building. He looked southward toward Clinton Street, northward to Montgomery and then stood silent for half a minute, gazing upon No. 330.

"This was my house," he said. "We lived on the third or fourth floor and we had three or four rooms. There used to be a chocolate store on one side of us and on the other side was Kennedy's stable. He buried everybody in the neighbor-hood. When we left here we moved around the corner into Monroe Street. I was in the neighborhood from the time I was 6 until I was 12. It was from another house, one at the corner, that I left home to go to the Bowery. . . . Come on. Let's get back in the car and I'll take you to my old haunts. Then to Chinatown."

Our driver took a northward course, working westward through the East Side maze, and when we finally swung into the Bowery, southbound, we were in front of No. 116, now occupied by the Manufacturers Trust.

"There was a saloon right here," said Berlin, as we got out of the car. "I used to go in there and pass the hat. Blind George was the piano player—I'll never forget him."

He led the way, pausing in front of No. 112, currently the home of A. Kirschner, frames, pictures, antiques.

"This," said the man who wrote "Oh, How I Hate to Get Up in the Morning," "was Steve Brodie's place—Brodie who jumped off the Brooklyn Bridge. There was always a picture around of him doing his stunt.

"These places," he continued, as we walked on, "were bars with back rooms. People who were around here, when I was on the loose, have gone—the bums and the riffraff stayed and died off. Others like myself were only waiting to get-the-hell out of here. . . . Right across there was Diamond Lottie's place—she had a diamond in her tooth, and this place"—we were in front of No. 57—"was the Saranac, run by Biggie Donovan, a bar with a back room. I sang in there, too. Beer was 5 cents a glass. Wilson whisky cost 10 cents. Whisky was called a stack of reds and gin a stack of whites."

Berlin told the chauffeur to pick us up in an hour in front of the Olliffe drug store at No. 6 Bowery, probably the oldest apothecary shop on Manhattan island, and we came to another pause as we reached the intersection of the Bowery and Bayard Street.

"Over there," he said excitedly, pointing to the other side of the thoroughfare "was the Cobdock Hotel, a flop house. . . . No, it would have resented being called that. It was a place to which the gals would take their sailors. . . . I remember a barroom at No. 23 run by a fellow named Sisto and No. 9 was a terrible joint inhabited by the drunkenest sailors, and the oldest hags. I also went there and passed the hat. A lodging house called the Mascot was right near where Bayard runs into the Bowery and I lived there for a year. It was a 15-cents-a-night joint. You got a cubby hole to sleep in, one open at the top, and you were always scared that somebody would reach over and steal your pants."

He stopped at the corner of Pell, glanced about for a moment, and turned into the narrow street, walking very slowly until he was in front of No. 12.

"Now this, Mr. M.," he said quietly, "really brings back memories. This was the Pelham Cafe—Nigger Mike's. I worked right in there forty years ago."

The building at No. 12, now tenantless and forlorn, blinked down upon us through dust-laden lids. The last occupant of the ground floor quarters was the Sun Wah Curiosity Shop; a "For Rent" sign is pasted on the grimy plate glass window. The Quong Sang Yuen Company does business on one side of No. 12, the Lun Wah Company on the other, and directly opposite the Oriental Bazaar and Incense Company, its big window filled with oddities, holds forth. Tiny Pell Street is now garishly neoned as it intersects with Mott at the corner; it is still thronged with sightseers, from night to night, but no longer inhabited by the sinister characters, some of them quite self-consciously so, of the day and time when Irving Berlin was little Izzy, just little skinny Izzy Baline.

Berlin was at the doorway of No. 12, trying to peer in.

"Right in there," he said, "I wrote my first song, 'Marie of Sunny Italy,'[1] on a small table. I did all right working for Nigger Mike, I used to come to work at 8 P.M. and stay on until 6 A.M. I was paid $7 a week and did pretty good in passing the hat. I sang all the popular stuff, a lot of George M. Cohan. Some nights I'd take in $7, and that was terrific. Mike used to get 5 cents for beer, 10 cents for whisky and gin. He didn't sell any food. He was a Russian Jew—very tough and liberal. Spent his money as he got it. They called him Nigger Mike because of his dark complexion. I was very happy here, but I finally got bounced for falling asleep behind the bar. Then I went to work for Jimmy Kelly in 14th Street. That was about 1908. . . . This was my street, all right. The headquarters of the Hip Sing Tong used to be across the way, and one of those buildings was occupied by Chinese with their white women. . . . Come on, let's see what's doing at the Chinese Mission."

We wandered around into the twisting and uncertain alleyway that is Doyers Street and stood for an instant in front of the building of the Rescue Society, 5–7, in the quarters of the old Chinese Theater. Then we entered.

Fifty to sixty old men, slouching and haggard, all looking alike, were huddled together on the rough benches built by Chinese carpenters back in 1893. Some of these broken-down habitués of the flop-houses were listening to the words of the Rev. F. D. Newman, conducting the chapel service; others were asleep, or nearly so. One of them held his head in one hand and his crutches in the other. It was warm inside, but at least half of them sat with coat collars turned up and their hands in ragged pockets.

We seated ourselves on a bench toward the rear of the auditorium, which has space for 118. In less than a minute the superintendent, the Rev. Howard Wade Kimsey having recognized Berlin, came up to us, and asked Berlin if he would say a few words. Berlin went immediately to the rostrum, once the stage of the Chinese theater, and spoke slowly and quietly:

"I spent a lot of time in Chinatown, right around this very street, and that was forty years ago. I'm delighted to see this place coming along so well. I wonder if you fellows would like me to sing a little song."

There was a half-audible murmur of assent from the numbed, white-haired lot. Then, after a slight pause, Berlin stepped briskly to the Steinway grand and in his squeaky voice, and to his own accompaniment, sang his affecting melody, "White Christmas."

He rose and bowed slightly. There was no applause. Something of a stir, but no hand-clapping. His audience just sat there with their glazed eyes and

---

1. The song's correct title is "Marie from Sunny Italy."

expressionless faces in a stunned, but appreciative, silence. A shy grin spread over the unshaven face of a gaunt old man in the very first row; a tear streaked the hollow cheek of a gnarled and shrunken oldster just behind him; the man with the crutches looked up, wide awake for the first time. And then the silence was dramatically and unexpectedly broken by the rasping chant of a sight-seers' guide who, with his party in tow, had entered as Berlin was at the piano.

"Sure, that's him," he quacked. "That's Berlin himself. Didn't I tell you folks you'd get a lot for your money? Didn't I tell you I'd give you a lot of surprises and excitement? Didn't I—didn't I—"

He was at Berlin's heels as we reached the sidewalk of Doyers Street. His group stood a few steps away, staring, fascinated. "Now, Mr. Berlin," said the spieler, aggressively, "won't you give these good people a few words about the old Chatham Club?"

"Go away," growled Berlin. "I've done my act for tonight."

He turned to me.

"Come on. We'll pick up the car and go over to Jimmy Kelly's in the Village."

Our trip to 181 Sullivan Street, the present site of Kelly's, was taken in round-about fashion, including a pause at 212 East 14th Street, formerly the site of Kelly's saloon, in which the up-and-coming song writer who had just taken over the name of I. Berlin, found employment after being fired at Nigger Mike's.

When we reached Sullivan Street Berlin ordered a brandy and relaxed at a wall table.

"Fourteenth Street," he said, "was very swell for me. I was quite a big shot there. I was an entertainer for about a year and then I went uptown and before long I was writing songs with a drawing account of $25 a week. I'd really had an easy time as a kid, honest. My struggles didn't actually begin until after I'd written 'Alexander's Ragtime Band.' It's been a struggle ever since to keep success going.

"I've never been in a tougher spot than I'm in right now. It's easy to do a movie, a package job like *Blue Skies*, but I can't always depend on being able to write the score of an *Annie, Get Your Gun*. . . . Say, I can't forget the faces of those old fellows at the Mission—and wasn't it damn funny for that barker and his gang to come in on cue? . . . Will you have another drink?"

The orchestra, which went into "Alexander's Ragtime Band" the instant Berlin was seen, had now turned to "White Christmas."

"I guess I've gotten to love that song," said Berlin. "And isn't it funny about 'Alexander'? Emma Carus first sang it in Chicago and George Cohan had it introduced in New York at the *Friars Frolic* in 1911. I've heard it arranged every possible way, but it has somehow kept its freshness. And it's now thirty-five years old."

Jimmy Kelly joined us—Kelly, the one-time fighter, who had the combination job of manager and bouncer at Nigger Mike's.

"When I went to work for Jimmy in 14th Street," said Berlin, "he was a damn good boss. Weren't you, Jimmy?"

"Hell," said Jimmy Kelly. "Those were the good old days, all right. I wish they were back. We used to get more for our money and perhaps we kicked around more. When it's quiet down here I get to thinking a lot about you, Izzy, and about Nigger Mike's. He was a peculiar guy. You could have his shirt if he liked you. He was managing me and I was managing the joint. Mike's last name was Salter, but a lot of people never knew it."

It was now past 1 o'clock. Our sentimental evening was nearing its end. We made the trip uptown via Union Square and along Broadway, taking the route that the New York theater has followed as it has marched northward from 14th Street, through the Twenties and Thirties, into the Forties and Fifties. Our final stop was the Stork Club.

"You know," said Berlin, still moved by the explorations of the evening, "if something happened and I found I had to go back to work, to start working at Kelly's all over again, I think I could do it. The change wouldn't be too bad, or difficult to make. I could still sing a little, I guess. My voice has always been a sort of whisky voice—it's just one of those things."

He paused, finished his Cub Room brandy, and said slowly: "America has been good to me. I'm very proud and grateful to live in a country where it's possible to do what you like to do. I'm only 58 and I feel there's a great deal of work still to do. The toughest thing about success is that you've got to keep on being a success. Talent is only a starting point in this business. You've got to keep working that talent. Some day I'll reach for it and it won't be there. . . . Will you have a night cap? I will."

~~~~~~

| 2 |

Rennold Wolf: The Boy Who Revived Ragtime

One of the first major articles on Berlin comes from the *Green Book Magazine*, written by Rennold Wolf (1872–1922), a book writer, reviewer for the *New York Telegraph*, lyricist, and composer. Now forgotten, he contributed to the *Ziegfeld Follies* in 1911, 1915, and 1917 through 1919.

———

SOURCE *Green Book Magazine*, August 1913.

Wolf sets his piece in the context of the emergency writing sessions that so often plague the process of getting a show ready for "the tired business man" (a term in use as early as 1913). In the course of that he provides a first-hand picture of Berlin's all-night writing. The song on which they were working is never mentioned by its title; it appears to be "Answer Me" (now lost), which appeared in the *Hell* segment at the ill-fated Folies Bergère. *Hell* was one portion of the evening's entertainment at which "Alexander's Ragtime Band" failed to make an impression. The now well-set Berlin biography surfaces, but Wolf explores some other areas of Berlin's work including the ragtime opera he hoped to write, a subject often mentioned throughout his early career.

Another unfortunate racially tinged term appears in this piece: "nigger piano" or "nigger key." Many untrained pianists who played by ear found it easy to play primarily on the black keys, which is the key of F-sharp major. The era in which this article was written casually used terms now considered highly pejorative. Away from that era the phrase is offensive (which does not excuse its use in the past) but a historical perspective helps to understand its use.

It is a common mistake to say that Berlin played *only* on the black keys. If he had, his music would be pentatonic and sound very much like the music of the impressionists (e.g., Claude Debussy). Despite the preponderance of the black keys in his playing, Berlin's chords and melodies made full use of the diatonic and chromatic scales.

Finally, note Berlin's generosity with the royalties of the song. This type of gesture was common with him, though his tough business sense and late-in-life reclusiveness have led to a misperception of him as only unpleasantly possessive of his work.

Imbedded in my memory so deeply that it is not likely to be eradicated in this life is the picture of my first contact with Irving Berlin, now beyond all question the world's most consistently successful writer of popular songs. The place, a long sweep of parlors and bedrooms on the second floor of Young's Hotel, Atlantic City; the time, midnight until dawn; the cast, Irving Berlin, Vincent Bryan, Channing Pollock and the writer hereof.

That quartet of more or less rising young literary workers were in the throes of song-building, than which there are no throes more harrowing or elevating. Mr. Pollock and I, in the interest of art and the gross receipts, had written a travesty called *Hell*, with the sub-title, *Everybody Goes There*, The occasion was far more important than our little work, for *Hell* was to be one-half of the entertainment with which the Folies Bergère, New York's most

Irving Berlin in 1912, the year after "Alexander's Ragtime Band." Photo credit: *Photofest*

luxurious and novel resort for the Tired Business Man, was to be opened the following week.

The entire organization, including phalanxes of chorus girls, affluent prima donnas, lugubrious comedians, a large orchestra, various managers, and relatives, friends and chauffeurs of managers, had gone to Atlantic City one week in advance for a preliminary trial of the production at the Apollo Theatre. When *Hell* was opened on Monday night at the Apollo, although it was found to be generally in good condition—if a prejudiced author may be pardoned for saying so—the necessity of one rousing song in the travesty became apparent to everybody concerned.

A song called "The Messenger Boy," upon which we all had relied for the coveted "punch," had "fallen down" to drift into the vernacular of the theatre. The idea of the song was to set forth the various emergencies when a messenger boy and a written lie of excuse or explanation might bring pardon to one who had failed to keep an engagement or who was occupied in clandestine pursuits. Ada Lewis, massively supported by twelve buxom show-girls, rendered the verses and refrains, after which the buxom ones passed through the audience, delivering messages to old gentlemen in the aisle seats, ostensibly receiving the answers, and returning to the stage to read the replies, which the authors previously had written.

Again apologizing as a prejudiced author, may I explain that the costuming of the twelve buxom show-girls did not lend atmosphere to the number. They were frankly exposed in silk tights, over which they wore a sort of mantle, bearing a general resemblance to a lace curtain. The illusion was not there. The spectacle was that merely of twelve overfed young women who might have been drafted from that justly celebrated organization of uplift in popular-price burlesque known as "Billy Watson's Beef Trust." At any rate, the number distinctly did not "go," and, following the performance, the late Henry B. Harris and Jesse L. Lasky, the managers, urged the weary authors to substitute another.

Maurice Levi, the composer of *Hell*, was not in Atlantic City. However, the Boardwalk swarmed with composers, lyric writers and volunteer authors of all descriptions—the usual crowd of minute-men who are always on hand at an out-of-town *première*, eager and ready to answer a call for help. Among them was Irving Berlin. Vincent Bryan, another song writer of established ability, accompanied him, but only in the capacity of court jester. It was decided that we call in Mr. Berlin to supply the tune for another of what my collaborateur, Mr. Pollock, always referred to airily as "our deathless lyrics."

We assembled in Mr. Berlin's imposing suite of parlors, where there was a piano, and then I discovered why that young man must eventually win success. Seated at the instrument, he was not long in conceiving a melody, which immediately he began to pound out. All night, until dawn was breaking, he sat on the stool, playing that same melody over and over and over again, while two fagged and dejected lyric writers struggled and heaved to fit it with words. Berlin must have played that tune two thousand times in the course of the night without leaving the stool once. But never did he by a glance or a word show the least sign of weariness or discouragement.

One cigarette replaced another as he pegged away; a pitcher of beer, stationed at one end of the keyboard, was replenished frequently; and there he sat, trying patiently to suggest, to two minds that were completely worn out by long rehearsals and over-work, a lyric that would fit his melody. Mr. Pollock and I paced the floor; we sat, in turn, in every chair and on every divan in the rooms; we tore at our hair—or, rather, at Mr. Pollock's hair; we fumed, we sputtered, and probably we cursed. And the mountain gave forth a mouse.

My tired brain, almost in a state of collapse, was still sufficiently alert to note the movements of Mr. Bryan. He was constantly in and out of the room, always coming in noiselessly, offering a suggestion and then gliding out noiselessly and mysteriously to seek some fellow nighthawk inclined to late sociability. He moved in and out like a specter, sometimes returning with a fresh pitcher of beer or a handful of cigars, but always denoting by his manner that he felt for us a sympathy born of similar experiences of his own.

I am somewhat ashamed to record the net output of that night's work, and in doing so hasten to state that the fault was in no degree Mr. Berlin's, but entirely that of two aspiring librettists, who had arrived at a state of mental fag which rendered it utterly impossible for them to librett. But here is that chorus, and I blush as I write it down:

Dearie, please keep the taxi waiting;
Dearie, don't be so hesitating—
There'll be just you and me.
And if your wife comes buzzin,'
Tell her that I'm your cousin—
Please keep it waiting, dear, for me.

I am quite willing to concede that the foregoing is the champion long-distance, catch-as-catch-can atrocious lyric of the world.

And yet, all this time, Mr. Berlin had in his possession the words and music of "Alexander's Rag-time Band,"[1] which the management had refused to accept.

The Folies Bergère directly and indirectly lost for the management $400,000. The newspapers have recited at length the merits and deficiencies of *Hell*, and I am quite willing to abide by their verdict. But the scheme in its entirety was so abominably handled that the doom of the pretty little combination restaurant and music hall was sealed from the beginning. No feature of the gigantic failure was so tragic as the lack of judgment that resulted in the

---

1. In early articles about Berlin, this is variously spelled "Rag-time," "Rag time," "rag time," and the now-accepted "ragtime."

declination of "Alexander's Rag-time Band." One number of its ingratiating, popular qualities frequently has "made" a musical entertainment. The Folies Bergère might have had the exclusive rights of this song for nothing, but it was turned aside, only a few weeks later to sweep the country, to be sung in every town and hamlet of the civilized world, and to earn for its publishers alone $150,000.

In the popular mind, Berlin's fame rests largely upon "Alexander's Rag-time Band," and therefore I have mentioned it first among his works. The story of its writing has never before appeared in print. The greater portion of the song was written in ten minutes, and in the offices of the music publishing firm Watterson [sic], Berlin and Snyder, while five or six pianos and as many vocalists were making bedlam with songs of the day.

Berlin was not impressed by it when the melody first came to him. In fact, after playing it over a few times on the piano, he did not take the trouble to note the melody on paper. He might never have completed the song had it not been for a trip to Palm Beach, Florida, which months later he arranged to take with Jean Schwartz and Jack M. Welch. Just before train time he went to his offices to look over his manuscripts, in order to leave the best of them for publication during his absence. Among his papers he found a memorandum referring to "Alexander," and after considerable reflection he recalled its strains. Largely for the lack of anything better with which to kill time, he sat at the piano and completed the song.

During his absence the firm endeavored to introduce the song in current productions. None of the managers or singers to whom it was submitted expressed any faith in it. So Mr. Snyder of the firm continued to peddle it until he too began to lose interest.

Berlin says that the song received its first impetus during the *Friars Frolic* of that year. A big minstrel show had been arranged by the Friars for tour, and Berlin volunteered to sing in the first part. The song he chose was "Alexander." In eight or ten big cities, notably New York, the song scored a sensational success. In a few weeks its melody was being whistled and played all over the country. Over a million and a half copies have been sold, and this song when it reached England had much to do with the rag-time craze which now prevails in every London music hall, one review,[2] for instance. taking its title from a line of the song, "Come over here" [sic].

---

2. The accepted spelling of this type of show is now "revue" but in the early twentieth century both "revue" and "review" were common. A revue often was just that, a review of the recent theatrical season.

Whatever Irving Berlin has accomplished is due entirely to his own efforts. He is now twenty-five years of age, and looks scarcely twenty. Boyish, with coal black hair and eyes, slim of figure and rather sallow of complexion, he might easily be mistaken for a page boy in a big hotel. He is a Russian Jew, the son of a rabbi, and his right name is Isidore [sic] Baline. He came to America when he was two years old,[3] and just as soon as he was able began to shift for himself.

At the age of sixteen he was just a handy boy around "Nigger Mike's," at 12 Pell Street, in the heart of New York's Chinatown. He waited on customers who drifted in, the dope fiends, crooks and drunkards of the slums, and for his compensation received only the pennies which the patrons chose to throw to him. "Nigger Mike's" was one of the resorts visited by the slummers of the sight-seeing automobiles, and Berlin was not long in formulating a plan to win their generosity. He learned a few songs, and upon the arrival of a sight-seeing party would take a conspicuous place on the floor and render one or more of them.

Four years he remained at "Nigger Mike's," and, strangely enough, he now shows no signs of the contact with the scum of civilization that frequented the place. He next went to work for "Jimmie" Kelly, a resort-keeper and prize-fight promoter who held no higher position in the social scale than "Nigger Mike." Kelly's place was in Fourteenth Street, at that time the Rialto of the minor variety actor. Many of them frequented Kelly's back room, and through them Berlin made his first acquaintance with stage folk.

One day young Berlin made so bold as to write a parody on a current popular song and sing it to an actor. The latter liked it and asked permission to use it on the stage. At that moment Berlin chose songwriting for his profession. During the two years at Kelly's he wrote numerous parodies, some of which were occasionally heard on the variety stage, but none of which attained publication.

The consistency of Berlin's success in his chosen field is absolutely without precedent. The average writer of popular songs, like the fortunate playwright, "hits it once." In the language of their own calling, they seldom "repeat." Their fame is established by one number which strikes the public fancy at the moment, and thereafter they usually thrive on past performances and future hopes. But Berlin has completely upset statistics in this respect. Once having demonstrated that he had his melodic finger on the public pulse, he started in to grind out a series of "hits" which have been the marvel of the music-publishing trade.

Dozens of his songs are known to everybody—or nearly so. Many of the readers will be able to whistle a majority of them, and I doubt not that as many more now have copies in the music rack.

---

3. He was five at the time.

The first of his songs to be published was "Marie from Sunny Italy." This was composed to a meter which Berlin calls syncopation, but which he distinguishes from rag-time. His next song, "Queenie," was unqualifiedly of the rag-time variety. These two songs netted him little, and it was not until after the Marathon race in England, when Johnny Hayes, the American, dashed in ahead of Dorando, that he found the inspiration necessary to lift him out of the rut. He then wrote the words and music of "Dorando," which proved most effective as a stage song, a term used to distinguish popular music from the sort sold broadcast to the public.

Then Henry Watterson, a music publisher, gathered him in, subsequently organizing the firm of Watterson, Berlin and Snyder. It is interesting to note that between Mr. Watterson and Berlin there never has been the scratch of a pen to record their business relationship. The two men are close friends and have implicit confidence in each other. Their transactions involve many thousands of dollars, but except for the oral evidence there is no record of an agreement. A side light upon this arrangement is thrown by the fact that six months after Berlin entered into association with Watterson the latter voluntarily increased the song-writer's royalties.

Following "Dorando," the next song was "Sadie Salome, Go Home," a parody on "Meet Me in Rose Time Rosie." The spirit of the parody is to be found in the line, "Go put some clothes on, Rosie." Three hundred and fifty thousand copies of that song were sold, and Berlin's stock continued to boom. Previously Snyder, of the firm, had composed an instrumental number, called "Wild Cherry Rag." It had not attracted much attention, but Berlin added to it a lyric which gave the song a tremendous impetus. In fact, "Wild Cherry Rag" may be said to have inaugurated the revival of rag-time, over which long previously the burial service had been read by carping musical critics. And with the return of rag-time there came also the incidental "business" of snapping the fingers and swaying the shoulders, now the essence of all art in cabaret entertainment.

"My Wife's Gone to the Country," Berlin's next work, proved to be his "biggest seller" up to that point. More than 500,000 copies were purchased by a public immensely pleased with the humor of the lyric. Then came in rapid succession, "Call Me Up Some Rainy Afternoon" and "Next to Your Mother Whom Do You Love?" In all of these songs Berlin was responsible for both words and tune, as he nearly always is nowadays.

His biggest song in a commercial sense, excepting "Alexander," was the one which next left his workshop, "That Mesmerizing Mendelssohn Tune." That was the first of the songs based obviously upon works of the masters, and it started a deluge of that kind of composition.

A complete list of Berlin, songs would be too long for the purpose of this article, but doubtless a few of them are worth recalling, such as "Grizzly Bear,"

"Stop, Stop, Stop," "Yiddle on Your Fiddle," "Mysterious Rag," "Everybody's Doin' It," "Rag-time Violin," "I Want to Be in Dixie," "Take a Little Tip from Father," "Rag-time Soldier Man," "Keep Away from the Fellow Who Owns an Automobile," "When the Midnight Choo-Choo Leaves for Alabam,'" "The Devil's Ball," "In My Harem," "Snookey-Ookums," "San Francisco Bound," and "Old Maid's Ball."

"When the Midnight Choo-Choo Leaves for Alabam'" is a bigger seller even than "Alexander." "I Want to Be in Dixie," at present the rage in London, was written in the Friars Club when Berlin, to use his own expression, was "dubbin' around the piano." Berlin had called at the club to meet Ted Snyder and Tom Penfold, and found them earnestly engaged in game of pool. To while away the time he sat down at the piano, and fifteen minutes later "Dixie" sprang into being.

Curiously enough, Berlin's greatest success is a sentimental balled, entitled "When I Lost You." The song was written shortly after Berlin had suffered a sad bereavement, and a repetition of the words may be interesting to show what this wizard of popular music can accomplish when he endeavors to be serious. Here they are:

The roses each one,
Met with the sun,
Sweetheart, when I met you.
The sunshine it fled
The roses were dead,
Sweetheart, when I lost you.
CHORUS
I lost the sunshine and roses,
I lost the heavens of blue,
I lost the beautiful rainbow,
I lost the morning dew,
I lost the angel who gave me,
Summer the whole winter through,
I lost the gladness, which turned into sadness,
When I lost you.

The birds ceased their song,
Right turned to wrong,
Sweetheart, when I lost you.
A day turned to years,
The world seemed in tears,
Sweetheart, when I lost you.

And yet this young man who has an uncanny insight into the public taste for music has had absolutely no musical education, is unable to read notes, and plays the piano in only one key—and that rather laboriously. That key is what song-writers call the "nigger key," which, to be technical, is F-sharp. Naturally, Berlin labors under a handicap by his inability to compose in more than one key, and he has overcome this deficiency by resorting to a patented device whereby a piece of music is automatically transposed. He has had constructed a piano for his apartments which has a shifting key-board. By moving a lever to a point on a diagram indicating the key desired, and by pressing a button, the keyboard is moved up or down, and, while Berlin strikes the same keys as before, a different set of strings give forth the tones.

Then, too, he derives great help from the most curious combination of secretary and accompanist I have ever met. This *rara avis* is a young man named "Cliff" Hess, who is both an expert stenographer and an accomplished pianist. Hess was playing the piano in a Chicago music publishing house when Berlin first met him. His deftness at pounding out rag-time melodies at once attracted Berlin's attention, and when Hess remarked that he was also a stenographer, Berlin engaged him on the spot.

The two are virtually inseparable these days. Hess resides with Berlin at the latter's apartment in Seventy-first Street; he attends to the details of the young song-writer's business affairs, transcribes the melodies which Berlin conceives and plays them over and over again while the latter is setting the lyrics. When Berlin goes abroad Hess accompanies him.

Hess' position is not so easy as it might at first appear, for Berlin's working hours are, to say the least, unconventional. And right here is to be mentioned the real basis of Berlin's success. It is industry—ceaseless, cruel, torturing industry. There is scarcely a waking minute when he is not engaged either in teaching his songs to a vaudeville player, or composing new ones.

His regular working hours are from noon until daybreak. All night long he usually keeps himself a prisoner in his apartment, bent on evolving a new melody which shall set the whole world to beating time. Much of the night Hess sits by his side, ready to put on record a tune once his chief has hit upon it. His regular hour for retiring is five o'clock in the morning. He arises for breakfast at exactly noon. In the afternoon he goes to the offices of the Watterson, Berlin and Snyder and demonstrates his songs.

One naturally asks why so successful a composer sacrifices himself to such a strain. Let Berlin give his own reason.

"It is harder for me to write songs now than it is for others," he says. "A great deal is expected of me. It is difficult to top my previous efforts. I must keep forever working, for there is so much competition in our business. And then a Chinaman might write a hit.

"There is no such things as 'being in right' in our business, although that is a theory accepted by the unsuccessful writer. A music publisher would accept a hit from the assassin of the Czar. Just show him, that's all. My firm publishes only my songs, and I have to keep hustling."

Berlin turns out an average of three songs a week. The majority of them never are heard by the general public. By a process of elimination about one in ten is finally published. It is upon the basis of that average that Berlin works. He knows that he cannot hit the bull's-eye every time or nearly every time, but he is willing to waste nine efforts for the sake of evolving one good tune.

As with George M. Cohan, the second verse of a song is Berlin's bugbear. With the melody and the first verse and refrain written, Berlin's interest cools, and he is eager to go to work on a new idea. He postpones the writing of the second verse usually until the demands of a professional singer become too insistent for further procrastination.

He has the utmost confidence in his ability to conceive popular melodies until the end of time. He is not so sanguine about the stability of his lyric muse. He foresees the possibility of going stale on lyrics one of these days, but he is positive that tunes will forever be on tap.

"I don't think melody will ever lick me," is the way Berlin expresses himself. "I have a certain number of melody tricks. George M. Cohan has them too. If you will listen to my melodies with this in mind you will note them—that is, you will get on to me. I understand the trick of the thing, and that trick, I am positive, will always work."

Has Berlin any greater ambition than to be the world's most successful popular song writer? Well, rather. He would give it all up if only one dream might be realized—the dream that one of these days he is to write the big American light opera, and an opera in rag-time, if you please. He argues, and argues soundly, that rag-time is our only distinctively characteristic music, and he feels that, treated seriously, the possibilities for a classic in that form of rhythm are unlimited.

In the few years that have elapsed since his escape from "Jimmie" Kelly's, Berlin's royalties have aggregated $225,000. The current year will be his banner one, for his royalties alone will exceed $100,000. In addition, he will get his share of the profits of the publishing firm. He has not managed to save any considerable portion of his great revenues, chiefly because he has not tried to do so. Within the last year he has made a few investments in high class bonds, but the bulk of his income has been frittered away to no especial purpose.

He lives well, without ostentation or show of luxury. A touring car in which he takes trips to Atlantic City and other neighboring resorts affords him his chief recreation. Frequently he participates in sessions of poker, but only as a comparatively inexpensive pastime.

Since "When I Lost You" was placed on the market, Berlin has been the recipient of numerous "mash notes" from sentimental young women eager to console him. This may be the proper place to inform these romantic maidens that Berlin derives much amusement from such manifestations of affection, and does not answer them. Within the year he was married to a charming girl, the sister of another song-writer. Two months later the bride died, and from his bereavement Berlin has not yet fully recovered.[4]

When last I saw him, with the faithful Hess by his side, he was engaged in writing a song somewhat different from his previous themes. The lyric related to the arrival of a baby in the house. By the time these words are in type the song may have reached the market, but the lyrics are well worth reading as showing the development of an idea along popular lines. The song is entitled, "Somebody's Coming to My House," and it is as follows:

Everyone's excited down at my house,
Everyone's delighted there.
Soon you'll be invited down to my house—
Down to a joyous affair.
Can't you see I'm happy—happy and gay?
See the look of joy in my eye.
You'll never guess why I'm feeling this way,
So here's the reason why:
CHORUS.
Somebody's coming to my house,
Somebody's coming to stay.
Father feels so happy, he's jumping with joy,
All he keeps saying is "I hope it's a boy."
Welcome is waiting the stranger,
Who'll come to brighten our lives.
I can hear mother croon,
"He'll be President soon,"
When the cute little stranger arrives.

---

4. His first wife died after five months of marriage. She was Dorothy Goetz, sister of songwriter E. Ray Goetz.

Everything is quiet down at my house,
We must tiptoe through the hall.
Soon there'll be a riot down at my house,
When some one starts in to bawl.
Auntie said, "We'll call it Elizabeth Jane,"
Sister looked at Auntie and smiled;
Dad said, "Elizabeth's fine, but I hope
It's not that kind of a child."

Like the majority of men who are great in their callings, Berlin is as simple as a child. In any gathering where he may be, he is sure to be the most reticent person present. He is ever ready to respond to a call for a song, and will sing until his throat gives out if he finds his hearers are enjoying his efforts. He is quick to volunteer at benefit performances for the needy, is extremely generous in all his conduct, and, to sum up his characteristics, is a fine type of manly, earnest, decorous youth.

A rare unselfishness governs all his dealings. To illustrate, I recall the incident mentioned at the beginning of this article. He had composed an excellent melody that night, and when Mr. Pollock and I—both of us being of sordid dispositions—suggested that we three should agree upon the division of royalties accruing from the song, he replied, "Boys, it is all yours. I wouldn't think of taking any part of it." This prompt relinquishment of all claims to the profits meant something at the moment, for he had not yet heard our dismal lyric.

~~~~~~

Introduction, Chapters 3 and 4

Broadway historian and biographer Edward Jablonski (1923–2004) knew personally Berlin and many of the other songwriters of that era. He wrote extensively about the Gershwins, along with biographies of Harold Arlen, Alan Jay Lerner, and Berlin. In this 1963 article Jablonski traces not only the history of "Alexander's Ragtime Band" but also rounds out some of the early Berlin biography (albeit drawn from the standard version), including a picture of Berlin, a now-famous songwriter, as performer. He also gives a concise history of song plugging and its role in getting a song in front of the public.

Charles Hamm, the leading scholar on Berlin's early years, gives the story as thorough a treatment as it is likely to get in this excerpt from his article, "Alexander and His Band," a fine example of the scholarship that has blossomed since Berlin's death. Hamm addresses the question of whether the song first existed as a piano solo, as Jablonski says in his article (and have many others). A piano solo version was published in an anthology of piano rags, but the anthology is not from Berlin's own publishing house, and does not appear to be Berlin's work. Hamm writes about the only published version clearly known to be Berlin's own, a "March and Two-Step" which appeared some months after the song. Hamm argues quite conclusively that no piano solo preceded the song; Jablonski apparently felt the oft-repeated story needed no confirmation from Berlin. (See the chapter on songwriting for Berlin's comments about this.)

Hamm touches upon his theory that Berlin often was the disguised protagonist in many of his songs about music; a more thorough discussion of that can be found in his book *Irving Berlin: Songs from the Melting Pot: The Formative Years, 1907–1914.* From that same book is a definition of the "coon" song, a genre of song from the early twentieth century which is significant in "Alexander and His Band." "Although the term 'coon' song was sometimes used in the first decade of the twentieth century as a generic label for any song with a black protagonist, it was most often applied to pieces in the tradition of the ethnic novelty song . . . in which protagonists take on stereotypical characteristics and behavior to comic or satiric effect. The chorus, or sometimes even the entire song, is cast in the first person, lending an apparent authenticity to the piece; in performance the black protagonist appears to be speaking for himself or herself and, by implication, for African Americans in general, through the singer." Fortunately the term has disappeared, but it can be jarring when used out of the context of the early twentieth century.

There also was the rumor, as noted by Hamm, that Berlin employed a Negro songwriter to write "Alexander's Ragtime Band," and later the rumor persisted that *all* his songs were the product of this mysterious "little colored boy" as he came to be known. This resurfaced throughout Berlin's life, as will be seen in the articles by Joshua Logan and Johnny Green. The rumor, of course, was nonsense.

Berlin himself made a whimsical allusion to the early history of "Alexander's Ragtime Band," with a musical quote from the song, in the first *Music Box Revue* in a number in which he was interviewed by eight chorus girls (who opened the show as the Eight Little Notes of the musical scale): "For about a year or so / It was laying on the shelf / Nobody liked it / I hated it myself."

Finally, in response to an issue raised in these articles, is "Alexander's Ragtime Band" a rag? It is not about ragtime, per se, but about a *ragtime band.* Therefore, must it be a rag, especially as its theme is "come on and hear" the band?

| 3 |

Edward Jablonski: "Alexander" and Irving

Name one song—if you can—of the thousands hammered out in Tin Pan Alley in 1911. That was the year the New York Public Library was dedicated by President Taft, the socialist magazine *The Masses* was founded, Edith Wharton's *Ethan Frome* was a best seller, George Arliss was appearing in *Disraeli*, and Ty Cobb batted .385. It was also the year of such period pieces as "Little Gray Home in the West," "I Want a Girl Just Like the Girl That Married Dear Old Dad," "The Gaby Glide," "Oh, You Beautiful Doll," and "Jimmy Valentine." These and similar effusions, quaint and charming as flowers of wax, are fondly remembered as evocations of long dead days; the songs are equally dead and dim in the memory.

Also published in 1911, however, was "Alexander's Ragtime Band," the effort of a young former singing-waiter turned song-writer named Irving Berlin. Moderately successful at the time, the 23-year-old song-writer had no idea at the time that, of all the songs published in 1911, his syncopated paean to an already fading popular music style would still be alive fifty years later. Despite the changing musical styles—ragtime, jazz, swing, sweet, hot, cool and rock-and-roll—"Alexander" has managed to attract each succeeding generation and is still being played and sung all over the world today as fresh and as saucy as the day, or rather the morning, it was born.

In the spring of 1911 Irving Berlin was working for the Ted Snyder Company, which he had joined two years earlier as a staff lyricist. Berlin had made some attempts at song writing before he came round to the Snyder office in 1909. "Marie from Sunny Italy," for which he had written the lyric, was published, though the earth had not burned for that song. The young song-writer had another Italian lyric, "Dorando," that he felt might interest Snyder and company. He nervously recited the words to Henry Waterson, manager of the

---

SOURCE *Listen—A Musical Monthly*, October/November 1963. Reprinted by permission of Carla and David Jablonski.

publishing house, who approved but also assumed that the intense, dark young man had a melody to match. He didn't, of course, for he had conceived "Dorando" as a specialty dialect number to be recited. Waterson was willing to gamble a munificent $25 on the song—words *and* music. Well, Berlin admitted, there was a tune; he would be happy to return with it the following day, after he had had a pianist friend write it down for him. Why wait, Waterson countered, when there was Bill Schultz in the next room ready and able to take down the music. Trapped, Irving Berlin could only improvise a melody that fit the lyric. He left the office with $15, not the promised $25—if the song "went over," he would receive the additional ten. He did, and it did. So did his next song go over, "Sadie Salome—Go Home," written in collaboration with Edgar Leslie. It soon became obvious that the shy, young Irving Berlin might prove to be a valuable asset to the firm of Snyder and Co. He was signed up, and the publishing house found that it had been profitably astute indeed. A song written in collaboration with George Whiting, "My Wife's Gone to the Country—Hurrah! Hurrah!" really went over. Berlin's infectious lyrics for this song practically became a national fad. The *Evening Journal* even commissioned Berlin to add verses to the song which, published daily, eventually grew to well over 200.[1]

The Ted Snyder Company was housed, *circa* 1911, in a brownstone at 112 West 38th Street, some ten blocks north of Tin Pan Alley proper. On the top floor there was a room set aside especially for Irving Berlin where he could work away from the usual din in the office. But, as it turned out, Berlin's working habits afforded him all the quiet he needed. After the close of the regular work day Berlin and some of his friends would be out song plugging until after midnight, usually ending up at Maxim's, a cabaret next to the Snyder office. Around one o'clock Berlin would let himself in—for he had a key—climb the stairs, and seat himself at the piano for a night's work that might go on till 3 or 4 in the morning.

Berlin worked at a special Weser Brothers piano which he had bought for a hundred dollars. A self-taught pianist, he could play only in the key of F-sharp; his piano was so constructed that by turning a wheel (later a crank) Berlin could shift to another key. Though still playing in the key of F-sharp, the song would actually come out in another key without Berlin's being bothered with the technicalities of transposition. Pianos with transcribing keyboards were actually common in Tin Pan Alley at the time, for like Berlin many of the busiest pianist played by instinct rather than note. This was especially true of the ragtime and popular pianists who had reputations for tricky playing. They called themselves "fakers."

---

1. Six appear in *The Complete Lyrics of Irving Berlin.*

Though he only paid a hundred dollars for the Weser, Berlin spent thousands in later years taking it with him on his travels. The "Buick,"[2] as he came to call it, travelled all over the world, for Berlin found it an indispensable tool. The "Buick" went with him to the Virgin Islands, to Africa and other ports. Special boltings were devised to keep it from being battered aboard ship. However, in Bermuda it once practically fell apart because of the humidity—the hammers fell out and Berlin was immobilized until a piano repairman could be found. Even in New York he had some trouble with the "Buick," for the neighbors complained of the noise of his playing so that he covered it with pillows and quilts and even silenced the strings with newspapers.

On that morning in March 1911, when he went to work, Berlin had made up his mind to try his hand at an instrumental ragtime number. Those decades from the close of "The Gay Nineties" to the beginning of the First World War have been designated the "Ragtime Years." The true ragtime—that of Scott Joplin and Tony Franklin, for example—had been around long before and was actually a style of playing rather than a method of composing.[3] But the dance crazes of the early 1900s helped to make Tin Pan Alley ragtime profitable. So did such free publicity as came from such as one Dr. Ludwig Gruener of Berlin (Germany, that is).

Said the learned doctor: "Hysteria is the form of insanity that an abnormal love of ragtime seems to produce." Definitions out of the way, and warming up to his subject, the man of science declared with remarkable scientific imprecision: "It is as much a mental disease as acute mania—it has the same symptoms. If there is nothing to check this form it produces idiocy." The good doctor further stated that 90 percent of the inmates in American insane asylums he had visited were "abnormally fond of ragtime." It was not music, he asserted, but a disease.

No less shrieking were the attacks upon popular song itself by Alexander Blume, a newspaper man. America's downfall, he believed, was reflected in our popular song. "What a shiftless, thoughtless and blatantly immoral people we must be if we are judged by our 'popular songs.' . . . 'Popular' music is like drink, in that it goes to the head; and unlike drink in that it goes to the feet." A neatly turned metaphor, indeed. "Did you ever note," Blume queried, "the diabolical grace with which the 'popular' song so readily lends itself to the

---

2. Jablonski implies that there was only one "Buick," but in fact Berlin had a number of them, at home, at his office, and in other locations.

3. Editor's note: Ragtime is both. "True" Ragtime, as expounded by Joplin and others, has a form which tends to be AABBACCDD, roughly similar to a Sousa march. It was usually as strictly followed.

Irving Berlin in later years demonstrating his transposing piano. Photo credit: *Photofest*

sinuous body dance—that didn't laugh openly at the institution of marriage?" The concerned Mr. Blume admitted that he was particularly disturbed by "the disciples of Irving Berlin and company." Hardly the social climate for another ragtime number. But there it was the next day, four pages that had been taken down by the copyist-arranger who was paid his 50¢ a page—just one of the songs Irving Berlin had worked on the night before.

The first objections did not come from pre-Freudian psychologists nor steamed-up moralistic newspapermen. In the Snyder office itself the number was regarded with less than favor: it was too long, running beyond the conventional 32 bars; it was too rangy ("an octave and four," which made it difficult to sing); and besides, it wasn't a real ragtime number anyhow.

When he submitted some songs to Jesse L. Lasky, then preparing to open a lavish nightclub theater called "The Follies Bergere," Irving Berlin included among them the homeless "Alexander," now graced with a lyric. Berlin had written a special number for Ethel Levey, the first wife of George M. Cohan, marking her recent return from Europe after a long absence from Broadway. Her song, "I Beg Your Pardon, Dear Old Broadway," was accepted, but Lasky rejected the ragtime number. Its melody was used, however, at "The Follies Bergere," whistled by Otis Harlin. But it made no mark, lost as it was in the exquisite décor of the theater. The New York *Dramatic News* described the latter as being "finished in pink, gray and turquoise blue, with just enough brown and gold to give charcter [sic] to the lighter shades." The very continental, fleshly proceedings onstage—one act was succinctly titled *Hell*; another, a ballet, was *Temptation*—hardly required the exultant injunction to hear "the best band in the land." So far as Irving Berlin was concerned, "Otie" Harlin could whistle to no avail.

So could, as it eventuated, Jesse L. Lasky, for "The Follies Bergere" was a failure that lost him and his partner, Henry B. Harris, $100,000, an excessively tidy sum in the simpler days of 1911. Decades later, after he had become a leading film producer,[4] Lasky managed to work up a rueful laugh over being a man who "had turned down 'Alexander's Ragtime Band.'"

Almost simultaneously, with the folding of "The Follies Bergere" was the planning for an expanded Friars Club. This leading actors' club annually raised money by holding their gala *Festivals*, or as they came to be called, *The Friars Frolics*. The 1911 *Frolic* was held in order to raise money for a new "monastery" (club house) on 48th Street. (This is incidental, though interesting: A Friars "monastery" was one of the few places from which a piano was stolen in broad daylight.) Abbot and leading light of the Friars as well as the *Frolics* was George M. Cohan—the *Frolics*, in fact, were actually starring vehicles for the popular idol, whose supporting cast was made up of some of the greatest names in show business. The 1911 production was an elaborate minstrel show, and for it Irving Berlin was asked to do a turn. Along with a couple of other songs, he submitted the somewhat tattered and pretty much unsung "Alexander's Ragtime Band." Cohan, no mean judge of a song himself, was the first to respond to it. On hearing its composer sing it, he exclaimed, "Irv,

---

4. In 1913 with Jesse L. Lasky Feature Play Company, then in 1916 with the better-known Famous Players-Lasky Corporation.

that's the song you'll do!" So it was Irving Berlin who introduced "Alexander's Ragtime Band" at the New Amsterdam Theater on May 28, 1911. He was joined by famed lyricist Harry Williams ("In the Shade of the Old Apple Tree") in a double. This introduction of the song was not devoid of energy for, as recalled by the composer, "we sang, did a little dance—and went off with a cartwheel." This vigorous rendition lit the flame that was to sweep the nation, for the *Friars Frolic* went on a cross-country tour.

The Friars appearance had not been Irving Berlin's first upon a stage. The year before (1910) he sang in the revue, *Up and Down Broadway*, at the Casino Theater. In this show were Eddie Foy, Oscar Shaw, Lenore Ulric, and Emma Carus.

Although she sang no Berlin songs in *Up and Down Broadway*, Emma Carus was to affect the fortunes of the hapless "Alexander." One of the great stars of the period, Emma Carus was the outstanding member of that group of "female baritones" (actually contraltos) who pleased the lovers of vaudeville in the early years of this century with their low bass notes and high lung power. Before making a tour of the Midwest in the spring of 1911, Miss Carus had dropped by the Snyder office to pick up a few new numbers for her act. It was at the American Music Hall in Chicago on April 18, 1911 that Emma Carus introduced "Alexander's Ragtime Band." This historic event was merely mentioned in passing by the Chicago *News*. "Emma Carus is there," the reviewer noted, "splendidly dressed and fitted out with a fine repertoire of songs ranging from ballads to ragtime . . ."

Having infected Chicago with the Berlin strain of ragtime (the Chicago branch of the Snyder office began importing sheet music in quantity the week Miss Carus opened at the American Music Hall), she moved on to Detroit and other parts. By late May she was back in New York at the Brighton Theater. The *Sun* reported the event in great detail: "It is in her songs that Miss Carus is most impressive, and she has five new ones that are worthy of the headliner." Of the five, one was singled out for special mention. "'Alexander' has all the swing and metrical precision of 'Kelly,' which Miss Carus brought to this country from England three years ago."

The *Sun* then waxed prophetic with unerring accuracy. "In a few days 'Alexander' will be whistled on the streets and played in the cafes. It is the most meritorious addition to the list of popular songs introduced this season. The vivacious comedienne had her audience singing the choruses with her, and those who did not sing, whistled."

When he made his first trip to London later that year, Irving Berlin was treated to a story-book reception. The newsboy who opened his cab was whistling—"Alexander's Ragtime Band." In Philadelphia, also later in the year, it made the headlines.

RAGTIME MELODY PREVENTS PANIC AT FIRE IN FILM SHOW

The fire had broken out during the course of the film—the pianist was then playing "Hearts and Flowers." Once the cry of "Fire!" was raised the patrons began to stampede for the exits. Whereupon the pianist broke into the strains of "Alexander's Ragtime Band." The rush was stopped and, according to the newspaper report, "all the boys whistled and the women hummed."

There was no radio in 1911, no television, and hardly any phonograph record industry. The only gauge of a song's popularity was its use by vaudeville singers and the subsequent sale of sheet music. That year the Five-and-Ten-Cent Stores put in a sheet music department which greatly expanded the outlet for published music. Song pluggers visited the "Five and Dimes" as well as cabarets and vaudeville houses. In some corner of the store were the racks filled with sheet music and an upright piano for purposes of demonstration. Often as not, the pianist was a local amateur with more nerve than talent, but customers were never very critical. They generally bought a song they already knew, and the far from virtuoso performance, a house courtesy, was good for the ego. The song hardly sounded better in that store than it did when the customer got it home and tried it on his parlor piano. In 1911 most well-appointed "front rooms" came equipped with an upright, across the top of which draped a fringed shawl, and on that, a clutter of family chromos. The sheet music itself was printed on much larger sheets than the songs of today—and it sold for ten cents a copy. Out of this, the composer, if he were a words and music man like Irving Berlin, received one cent. A penny bought more in 1911 than it does today—particularly the pennies that Irving Berlin was to accumulate from his almost orphan, "Alexander's Ragtime Band."

When it was finally published in September, 200,000 copies were scooped up overnight. The sweep was so complete that *Variety* reported that other music publishers were complaining: only "Alexander" was selling; no one was buying any other song. By the middle of November *Variety* reported that the sale had gone over a million. In its half-century "Alexander's Ragtime Band" has sold more than five million copies in America, and an equal number throughout the rest of the world. In 1911 it swept through England, the continent and as far as deep Russia, birthplace of Irving Berlin. It still sells, sometimes 300 copies a day, a good number more than the average old "standard."

"Alexander"'s momentum carried with it not only the career of Irving Berlin—he was soon crowned the "King of Ragtime" by the phrase coiners—but revived Tin Pan Alley as well. Ragtime songs were ground out in profusion, though none ever came up to the prototype. Irving Berlin was the first to point out that "Alexander" was not a rag in the strict definition, but "a song about ragtime." Attempts at writing popular rags had never proved very successful until Berlin invented "Alexander." He revived interest in a waning style. "I didn't originate it," he once declared. "Maybe I crystallized it and brought it to people's attention." This is true. By October of 1911 it was impossible not to have your attention drawn to "Alexander's Ragtime Band." It reverberated from parlors, theaters, and vaudeville houses. In the latter, vaudevillians competed to use the song in their acts. Whoever succeeded in handing it to the band leader first could use it in the show. Not only vocalists, but also jugglers, acrobats, and practically any act tried to use "Alexander" as their "play-off" music—it was almost as sure-fire as using "The Star Spangled Banner."

Berlin himself received a bid from Hammerstein's Victoria, owned by the great showman Oscar Hammerstein I, grandfather, and managed by William Hammerstein, father of Oscar Hammerstein II. Though the Victoria in Times Square booked conventional acts, its major dispensation was the so-called "freak acts," chosen on the strength of their names-in-the-news value rather than the usual marquee pull. If a couple of chorus girls shot a socialite, the Victoria would stand their bail and book them, so to speak, at the Victoria as "The Shooting Stars."[5] One of the biggest attractions was Evelyn Nesbit of the notorious White-Thaw case. (Thaw shot White because of alleged attentions to Miss Nesbit, Mrs. Thaw at the time.)

"The clamor is for novelty," was Willie Hammerstein's philosophy, and he felt that the composer of so astonishing a hit as "Alexander" was worth a thousand dollars a week even if he hadn't shot anyone. And, as for "Alexander," even if it was no shot, it was heard 'round the world. This was enough for the Victoria, which billed him as "The Composer of a Hundred Hits."

Sime Silverman covered the new act for *Variety.* "Next to last [the best spot on the program according to vaudeville tradition] appeared Irving Berlin, who sang two of his newest songs together with a neat medley of his own 'hits' woven into a story. When you can do that," Sime observed, "you can write songs, and to see this slim little kid on stage . . . going through a list that sounded like all the song hits in the world is something to think about. Mr. Berlin," the beloved Sime noted with uncommon formality, "looks so nice on the platform that all the girls in the house fall for him immediately. He did make some hit. They were still applauding after Rayno's Bull Dogs came on to close the performance, but"—Sime reverted to the familiar—"Irving wouldn't return."

---

5. This type of attraction was the source for the film *Roxie Hart* and the subsequent Broadway show and its film adaptation, *Chicago.*

Curiously, the song did not die out, as is usual with a smash hit. Two years later it was introduced in a revue, *Hullo, Ragtime!* by Ethel Levey, she who just missed doing it for the first time in the ill-fated "Follies Bergere." By the summer of that year (1913—the world was but a year away from the loss of its innocence) the management of the London Hippodrome, which housed *Hullo, Ragtime!*, persuaded the persuasive Mr. Berlin to appear in the revue in "a selection from his repertoire." In July of 1913, London seemed ready to change its name, for it went all out for Berlin. The newspapers were filled with stories about the "Rag-time King," or his alternate title, "Song-writing Genius," not to mention the references to the fact that he realized some £20,000 from such activity. Window displays featured life-size posters of the composer and song sheet covers filled the rest. For the occasion Irving Berlin spent a week writing a special song, "That International Rag," which was a hit in England and also in the U.S.

Even by 1914 the ragtime craze was still strong. Producer Charles Dillingham commissioned Irving Berlin to write his first full score for Broadway—the "syncopated musical show" *Watch Your Step*, starring Irene and Vernon Castle. For the popular dance team, Berlin composed another ragtime number, "The Syncopated Walk." But the style itself had just about come full circle, and following the war the related, though new, style called jazz would set the tempos. "Alexander," though, continued to grow. Through the years it has been treated to countless interpretations from symphony to bagpipe band; in 1938 it served as the title of a film that many mistook for a biography of the composer. Unlike the song, the composer was too elusive for them.

George M. Cohan, a life-long friend and admirer of Irving Berlin, summed him up better than anyone else. At a Friars Club dinner the Abbot said, "Irvy writes a great song. He writes a song with a good lyric, a lyric that rhymes, good music, music you don't have to dress up to listen to, but it is good music. He is a wonderful little fellow, wonderful in lots of ways. He has become famous and wealthy, without wearing a lot of jewelry and falling for funny clothes. He is uptown, but he is there with the old downtown hardshell. And with all his success, you will find his watch and his handkerchief in his pockets where they belong."

Irving Berlin is a man completely without pose. Although he is the greatest American *minnesinger* and has "moved uptown," there he is with "the old downtown hardshell" of self criticism, and the completely realistic outlook, "I believe in hits," he will tell you, and by his own hard work and through that secret chemistry that tells him what people will like, he has written, besides "Alexander's Ragtime Band," fifteen more songs that have sold more than a million copies. No other popular song writer has come close to equaling that number. Two of the songs, "God Bless America" (1939) and "White Christmas" (1942) were published long after the day of sheet music sales was over. Jerome Kern, like George Gershwin, Harold Arlen, Cole Porter and others, a great Berlin fan, suggested one clue to Berlin's touch. Kern said, "he honestly absorbs the vibrations emanating from the people, manners, and life of his time, and in turn, gives these impressions back to the world—simplified—clarified—glorified."

Irving Berlin's personal evaluation is not quite so definite, nor as fancy. When, in 1919, he broke away from the Snyder Company to form Irving Berlin, Inc., a close friend recalls that he "was scared to death because he didn't know if he could continue to write hits." He then proceeded to write "A Pretty Girl Is Like a Melody," "Say It with Music," "All Alone," "Always," "Remember," "Blue Skies," "Marie," "How Deep Is the Ocean?," "Easter Parade," "White Christmas," and "God Bless America." Also the *Music Box Revues, As Thousands Cheer, This Is the Army, Annie Get Your Gun, Miss Liberty,* and *Call Me Madam.*

He still gets his biggest thrill when he hears today's performers doing "Alexander's Ragtime Band." When Ethel Merman sings it today on television and it sounds as fresh as it did when Emma Carus sang it in 1911, Irving Berlin is a happy man.

His watch and his handkerchief are still in his pockets where they belong.

| 4 |

Charles Hamm: Excerpt from Alexander and His Band

"Alexander's Ragtime Band" was not Irving Berlin's first commercial hit; a dozen or more of his songs had chalked up substantial sheet music sales before it was published early in 1911. It was not his first song to attract international attention; Bert Feldman had brought out eight of his songs in London, in *Feldman's Sixpenny Editions,* before adding "Alexander" to the series. It is not his best-selling song of all time—"White Christmas" enjoys that distinction—or even his best song in the opinion of most critics. But it did attract more public and media attention than any other song of its decade. It quickly became an icon for the ragtime era, and its popularity has persisted to the present.

SOURCE *American Music* 4, no. 1 (Spring 1996). Reprinted by permission of University of Illinois Press.

Given the amount of attention paid to "Alexander" from 1911 to the present, it is hardly surprising that several controversies have sprung up around it and that some aspects of the song and its history have been misrepresented. A survey of these difficulties will serve as an introduction to a more general discussion of the song and its history.

THE RAGTIME CONNECTION

A recent biographer of Berlin claims that the text of "Alexander" is "the kind of old-fashioned 'coon' lyric that came easily to him," but the protagonist's excited invitation to his "honey" to come along and listen to the "best band in the land" is nothing of the sort. The gesture of the piece, a first-person exhortation to anyone and everyone within earshot to come and listen to a band, has no precedent in earlier "coon" songs or any other songs of the Tin Pan Alley era, or even in British balladry's "come-all-ye" command to heed the words of the bard. Berlin himself was convinced that the song "started the heels and shoulders of all America and a good section of Europe to rocking" largely because of this direct, exuberant, first person outcry: "[Its] opening words, emphasized by immediate repetition—'Come on and hear! Come on and hear!'—were an *invitation* to 'come,' to join in, and 'hear' the singer and his song. And that idea of *inviting* every receptive auditor within shouting distance to become a part of the happy ruction—an idea pounded in again and again throughout the song in various ways—was the secret of the song's tremendous success." His first biographer agrees that the song was unusual and effective because of its "exultant" nature, so unlike many of Berlin's "lugubrious melodies" that betray a heritage of "generations of wailing cantors."

Although there is no exact precedent in Berlin's earlier songs for this "come-and-hear-the-band" gesture, he came close to it in "That Kazzatsky Dance," a Jewish novelty song copyrighted and published in December 1910, in which the female protagonist enthuses to her friend Abie, "Can't you hear very clear, they're playing that Kazzatsky dance, Cohen with his hand leads the band ain't it grand." Once the gesture proved to work so well with "Alexander" however, Berlin used it again and again, in such later songs as "A Little Bit of Everything," "Follow the Crowd," and particularly "Lead Me to That Beautiful Band":

Dear, lend an ear to the finest music in the land,
You'd better hurry and take a hand;
I want to linger beside that grandstand band, and
Hon,' better run, just because I hear them tuning up.
Just hear that slide trombone a-blowin' for me,
Just hear those sweet cornets all goin' for me,

Hear the piccoloer pick a melody,
See the clarionetter clarionetting me,
Hear that cello moan . . .
Lead me, lead me to that beautiful band.

The urgency of this lyric is captured wonderfully in Stella Mayhew's performance on Edison Blue Amberol 2173, recorded in April 1912.

Much of the literature on "Alexander" deals with its relationship, or more often its alleged nonrelationship, to ragtime. Alexander Woollcott rhapsodized that the song made the "first full use of the new rhythm which had begun to take form in the honkey-tonks where pianists were dislocating old melodies to make them keep step with the swaying hips and shoulders of the spontaneous darky dancers," but most later writers have insisted that the song has little or nothing to do with ragtime music. According to Sigmund Spaeth, "it is now an old story that 'Alexander's Ragtime Band' not only had nothing to do with the development of ragtime, but is actually a song with hardly a trace of ragtime in it." Alec Wilder says, "I have heard enough ragtime to wonder why [it] was so titled," and in his curious and clumsy language, Laurence Bergreen writes, "the 'ragtime' melody Berlin devised . . . was actually a march: a safe choice, for a march suggested ragtime without incurring the liability of being ragtime. His melody employed only a brief jumpy phrase of being ragtime."

"Alexander" does have features of ragtime, though. At the most general level it "has to do with the Negro," as contemporary writers insist was one measure of ragtime: its obviously black protagonists make it a "coon" song, a label that was sometimes put on it in advertising copy and in the press. Beyond that, it has structural elements in common with ragtime. The claim that it was the first popular song with a chorus in a key different from that of verse is simply wrong, and pointless in any event, since a shift of key for the chorus never became an important feature of subsequent Tin Pan Alley songs. Three earlier songs by Berlin himself, "Wild Cherries," "Grizzly Bear," and "Oh, That Beautiful Rag," have choruses in the subdominant. All three were written and published as piano rags before being reworked into songs, and this is exactly the point: instrumental ragtime pieces, like marches of the period, usually move to the subdominant for the trio, which became the chorus if the piece was converted into a song. By fitting "Alexander" with a chorus in the subdominant, Berlin made a musical connection with ragtime. The often-noted fact that the chorus to "Alexander" is thirty-two bars in length, rather than sixteen, as in most songs of the period, can be explained in the same way: although most strains in piano rags are sixteen measures long, they are intended to be repeated, with a second ending: thirty-two-bar AA' segments thus are a feature of piano rags, as well as of marches, waltzes, and other dances.

Furthermore, despite assertions to the contrary, Berlin's music for "Alexander" does make repeated if simplistic references to rhythmic patterns associated with ragtime. The chief motif of the verse, repeated a number of times, places an accent on a weak beat in the right hand (and voice), the chorus just as insistently features a short-long-short pattern suggesting the "cakewalk" figure common to proto-ragtime pieces of the 1880s and 1890s and persisting in the early rags of James Scott and his peers, before yielding to more sophisticated syncopations. There is, of course, a difference between the "cakewalk" rhythm (ex. 1) and the rhythm permeating the chorus of "Alexander" (ex. 2), but the listener hears both as short-long-short patterns, and in fact the two are not always clearly distinguished from one another in performance.

Dismissals of "Alexander" from the canon of ragtime music have been based on latter-day notions of what constitutes a piece of ragtime. Edward Berlin has argued forcefully that the ragtime revival's insistence on making the term *ragtime* synonymous with "piano ragtime" has no historical justification, since in the first years of the twentieth century many popular songs and pieces for instrumental ensembles, particularly marching or concert bands, were considered to be ragtime also. If one wishes to understand why "Alexander" was judged to be a piece of ragtime in 1911, one should compare it not just to the piano rags of Scott Joplin and James Scott but also to other ragtime songs of the day and to syncopated pieces played by the bands of John Philip Sousa and Arthur Pryor.

Example 1: James Scott, "Ragtime Oriole" (1911), mm. 72–79.

Example 2: Irving Berlin, "Alexander's Ragtime Band" (1911), mm. 22–29.

When Alec Wilder, after finding "no elements of ragtime" in "Alexander," modifies this pronouncement by adding "unless the word 'ragtime' simply specified the most swinging and exciting of the new American music," he comes close to the real issue—that in 1911 a piece of popular music was judged not by how it looked on paper, in musical notation, but by how it sounded in performance. To understand why period audiences thought that "Alexander" and other songs by Berlin were ragtime pieces, one must listen to the "swinging and exciting" performances by such performers as Stella Mayhew and Blossom Seeley, preserved on period recordings, which are our only aural access to the way in which "ragtime" performers, particularly female "coon shouters," projected these songs. As *Variety* (June 24, 1911) explains in a review of a performance by Seeley at the Brighton Theatre, ragtime performance was as much a matter of spirit, attitude, and stage deportment as of rhythmic patterns: "There is a wild craze on in New York for the 'rag' style of singing and dancing, at which no one has yet shown who can handle this better than she. When Blossom starts those hands agoing, and begins to toddle, you just have to hold tight for fear of getting up and toddling right along with her."

The instrumental accompaniments to period recordings of ragtime songs provide another link to what was perceived to be ragtime then. For instance, several phrases of the last chorus of Billy Murray's recording of "Alexander" (Edison Blue Amberol 2048) are taken by the accompanying orchestra, which sounds like a scaled-down Sousa band playing a ragtime or cakewalk piece, complete with piccolo obbligato and phrase-ending trombone runs; the band accompanying Stella Mayhew in "The Grizzly Bear" (Edison Wax Amberol 479) plays an entire chorus of that song in the same style.

In the end it is pointless to argue over whether "Alexander" draws on specific elements of ragtime or looks like a piece of ragtime on the page. It *was* a piece of ragtime music, and as such it helped to define the genre for its audiences.

WHO REALLY WROTE "ALEXANDER?"

Questions were raised concerning the authorship of the song almost as soon as it became a hit. As Berlin himself tells it, "two years or so ago, when 'Alexander's Rag-time Band' was a big hit, some one started the report among the publishers that I had paid a negro ten dollars for it and then published it under my own name." The real author might have been the black pianist Lukie Johnson, it was whispered, and even though Johnson insisted that he had nothing to do with "Alexander" or any other song by Berlin, and no other likely candidate was identified, the rumors refused to die. Berlin was finally moved to respond: "When they told me about it, I asked them to tell me from whom I had bought my other successes—twenty-five or thirty of them. And I wanted to know, if a negro could write 'Alexander,' why couldn't I? Then I told them if they could produce the negro and he had another hit like 'Alexander' in his system, I would choke it out of him and give him twenty thousand dollars in the bargain. If the other fellow deserves the credit, why doesn't he go get it?"

A similar controversy flared up several decades later, this time with Scott Joplin as the purported composer. Joplin's widow was quoted as saying that "after Scott had finished writing [*Treemonisha*], and while he was showing it around, hoping to get it published, some one stole the theme, and made it into a popular song. The number was quite a hit, too, but that didn't do Scott any good." The piece in question was supposedly "Alexander's Ragtime Band." At about the same time, Rudi Blesh and Harriet Janis interviewed a descendant of John Stark, Joplin's most important publisher, who remembered that "the publication of 'Alexander's Ragtime Band' brought Joplin to tears because it was his [own] composition." Stark's grandson later elaborated on this story: "Joplin took some music to Irving Berlin, and Berlin kept it for some time. Joplin went back and Berlin said he couldn't use it. When 'Alexander's Rag-time Band' came out, Joplin said, 'that's my tune.'" Sam Patterson, Joplin's friend and colleague, reported essentially the same story to Blesh and Janis, adding that Scott identified his "Mayflower Rag" (an unrecovered work) and "A Real Slow Drag" from the opera *Treemonisha* as pieces from which Berlin supposedly stole material.

Attributing these claims to "Joplin's declining mental health," Blesh and Janis downplayed the matter in their book. More recently Edward Berlin has uncovered circumstantial evidence that Joplin and Berlin had contact with one another during the period in question. Although admitting that "there is no information on specific meetings between Irving Berlin and Scott Joplin," he suggests that "they *must* have known each other and that Berlin had the opportunity to hear the score [of *Treemonisha*] prior to its publication," through "the association of both with Henry Waterson and others in the Waterson circle." Waterson was co-owner of Crown Music, a distributor of Joplin's rags and his *School of Ragtime* in 1908–9. He also owned an interest in Seminary Music, which published eight piano pieces by Joplin in these same years, and was manager and treasurer of the Ted Snyder Music Company, which Berlin joined as staff lyricist in 1909. All three publishing companies—Crown, Seminary, and Snyder—shared offices at 112 West 38th Street. "Given Joplin's relationship with the Waterson companies," says Edward Berlin, "he might well have brought them the score for examination, thus giving Irving Berlin the opportunity to hear it." Edward Berlin finds some similarity between several measures of Joplin's "A Real Slow Drag" and the verse of Irving Berlin's "Alexander" but hastens to add that "the resemblance is not extensive and could not, legally or otherwise, be called a theft." He summarizes: "We can be pretty sure that Joplin made the charge of musical theft, that the opportunity for it to occur existed, and that there were rumors that Berlin had stolen his song from a black man. However much this convergence of evidence may fuel our speculations, it does not prove the charge."

The lyrics of several of his songs indicate that Irving Berlin heard and admired the playing of black pianists around 1910. Given Joplin's presence in New York at this time, and given the fact that one of Berlin's functions at the Ted Snyder Music Company was to be on the lookout for publishable music by other composers, Edward Berlin's hypothesis that the young songwriter could have heard Joplin's music in one of the offices, played by a staff musician (since Berlin could not read music) or by Joplin himself, is quite plausible. Even if this did happen, however, and even if a phrase or a melodic fragment of one of Joplin's pieces did find its way into "Alexander," it still does not follow that Berlin "stole" the song from Joplin. "The theme could simply have lodged itself in Berlin's memory, to be drawn out inadvertently a few months later," as Edward Berlin suggests, and even if Berlin did consciously appropriate a bit of Joplin's music into "Alexander," the song did not become a hit because of this. I have suggested elsewhere that one reason for Berlin's unprecedented success in writing song after song that listeners wanted to hear again and again was that he knew all the music his audience knew, and his songs make use of the common melodic, harmonic and rhythmic patterns of this music and frequently offer direct quotations from one familiar piece or another. The same thing could be said of other Tin Pan Alley songwriters, true enough. But Berlin, more effectively than any of his peers, drew on the collective knowledge and memory of his audience to fashion dramatic situations and musical phrases similar to those found in songs they already knew, [but] shaped in slightly unexpected ways. His best songs were almost—but not quite—already known to listeners when heard for the first time. They were old stories with new twists. Like other early Tin Pan Alley songwriters, Berlin deliberately and routinely used rhythmic, melodic, and harmonic patterns similar to those found in other pieces, as well as direct quotation of lyrics and music from other songwriters, for associative or expressive effect. Ian Whitcomb describes Berlin as "a concoctor, almost an inventor. He wasn't stealing anything from anybody." Berlin himself said, "We depend largely on tricks, we writers of songs. There's no such thing as a new melody. There has been a standing offer in Vienna, holding a large prize, to anyone who can write eight bars of original music. The offer has been up for more than twenty-five years. Thousands of compositions have been submitted, but all of them have been traced back to some other melody. Our work is to connect the old phrases in a new way, so that they will sound like a new tune."

If Berlin did quote a fragment of *Treemonisha* in "Alexander's Ragtime Band," it puts Joplin in the company of Georges Bizet, whose opera *Carmen* is quoted in Berlin's "That Opera Rag"; F. Paolo Tosti, whose song "Good Bye" is quoted in "Keep Away from the Fellow Who Owns an Automobile"; Gaetano Donizetti, whose *Lucia di Lammermoor* is quoted in "Opera Burlesque"; Reginald DeKoven, whose "Oh Promise Me" is quoted in "He Promised Me"; Felix Mendelssohn, whose "Spring Song" is quoted in "That Mesmerizing Mendelssohn Tune"; and Harry Von Tilzer, whose "Down Where the Wurzburger Flows" is quoted in "I Was Aviating Around"—not to mention Stephen Foster, whose "Old Folks at Home" is quoted in "Alexander's Ragtime Band," and Irving Berlin himself, whose "Alexander's Ragtime Band" is quoted in "Hiram's Band" and many other later songs by Berlin.

As a coda to this discussion, I would like to toss out the suggestion that, in a most curious way, it could be argued that someone other than Irving Berlin *did* write "Alexander's Ragtime Band" and some of his other songs.

As I have pointed out elsewhere, the lyrics of a number of Berlin's early songs that have black musicians as protagonists could be self-portraits, in that the songs' descriptions of the musical background, piano playing, and songwriting of these protagonists apply equally to Berlin himself. In "Ephraham Played upon the Piano," for instance, "any kind of music he could understand, still he didn't play by ear, he played by hand"; since Ephraham (like Berlin) had no formal musical training, "he had ev'rybody guessin,' how he played with such a lovin' tone." The unnamed protagonist of "Piano Man"

Sits on his stool like a king on the throne,
And plays and plays with ease,
Why, the melody just nestles in his finger tips
And oozes out in the keys.

In "He's a Rag Picker" the protagonist, Mose, "bangs upon the piano keys, in search of raggy melodies," and "makes an ordinary ditty sound so pretty, like nobody can"; in "That Humming Rag" Mose writes a tune that everyone is "simply daffy over" and that sets them humming and "act[ing] like so many lunatics"—just as happened with "Alexander's Ragtime Band."

Several decades later, after the emergence of blues and jazz, some white musicians were drawn so strongly to African American music and were so convinced that only blacks could perform it in an "authentic" fashion that they wished, or even imagined, that they were black themselves. The jazz clarinetist Mezz Mezzrow, born Milton Mesirow in Chicago in 1899, stands as the classic instance of this syndrome. His first contact with blacks and their music came in his teens, when he was serving a sentence in the Pontiac Reformatory for car theft. "It was in Pontiac that I dug that Jim Crow man in person," he writes in his autobiography. "During these months I got me a solid dose of the colored man's gift for keeping the life and the spirit in him while he tells of his troubles in music. I heard the blues for the first time, sung in low moanful chants morning, noon and night." As a result of this exposure, he says, "By the time I reached home, I knew that I was going to spend all my time from then on sticking close to Negroes. They were my kind of people. And I was going to learn their music and play it for the rest of my days. I was going to be a musician, a Negro musician, hipping the world about the blues the way only Negroes can. I didn't know how the hell I was going to do it, but I was straight on what I had to do." Mezzrow accordingly became a jazz musician, befriended black players and performed with them, lived in Harlem, and at times passed himself off as black.

Berlin did none of these things, of course, but he did develop an honest and deep appreciation for black musicians and their music, and in some of his early songs he created black protagonists with whom he identified so closely that these men became his alter egos. At some level the Alexanders and Ephrahams and Moses in Berlin's songs of this period are extensions of the songwriter's own ego.

Public identification of Berlin the songwriter with the protagonist of his "Alexander" ran high. The *Telegraph*, for instance, ran a feature story on October 8, 1911, under the headline "Wherein You Meet Irving Berlin, the Leader of 'Alexander's Ragtime Band.'" And even though at first glance the cover to the sheet music version of the song seems to picture a white band, a closer look reveals that the group seems to be racially integrated. The faces of three musicians—the violinist third from right, another one (the shape of whose head suggests negroid features) just under the conductor's left arm, and most interesting, the "leader man" himself—are hatched, making their skin appear darker than that of the other band members. Alexander also resembles Berlin in physique and hair style, as can be seen from contemporary photographs of the songwriter. It may be that none of this had anything to do with Berlin, since it is not clear that he had input into the design of the covers for his songs. Nevertheless, someone took pains to see to it that Alexander was pictured as black and that he resembled Berlin.

In the last chorus of a recording of Berlin's "He's a Rag Picker" made by the Peerless Quartet in 1914 (Victor 17655), the song's protagonist, Mose, who has been described in third person in the lyric, suddenly makes a first-person appearance: he is heard playing the piano in ragtime style, then engaging one of the other singers in dialogue.

—What you gonna do now, Mose?
—Why I'se gonna loosen up on these ivories, boy. Now watch these . . . [don't] take yo eye off it, you hear . . . (laughter and chuckles)
—Can you play "Alexander's Ragtime Band?"
—Why sure, I'm de man what wrote it! (chuckle)

Berlin may well have coached the singers and supplied the extra material for this recording, including Mose's spoken lines, taken by Arthur Collins, a member of the quartet. Although Berlin was later angered by rumors that a "little black boy" had written "Alexander's Ragtime Band," in this recording a black character, Mose, is allowed to lay claim to the song's authorship. This makes sense only if Berlin regarded Mose as an extension of himself.

WHICH CAME FIRST, THE SONG OR THE RAG?

Another controversy has to do with whether "Alexander" originated as a song or as a composition for piano. The facts seem straightforward. A copyright entry card in the Library of Congress reads, "ALEXANDER'S RAGTIME BAND; words and music by Irving Berlin. Registered in the name of Ted Snyder Co., under E 252990 following publication March 18, 1911." The song was published with the famous cover by John Frew showing Alexander and his men performing in a bandstand. Almost half a year later, after the song had begun to enjoy phenomenal success on the stage, in vaudeville, and as sheet music, another copyright was issued to another piece: "ALEXANDER'S RAGTIME BAND; march and two step, by Irving Berlin; piano. Registered in the name of Ted Snyder Co., under E 265784 following publication September 6, 1911." This piano version, with a cover by E. H. Pfeiffer picturing Pan playing on an archaic double pipe, has a third strain not found in the song itself, a quodlibet combining "Dixie" in the right hand with "Old Folks at Home" in the left.

The claim that the piano piece was written first is based on a passage in the first biography of Berlin, published in 1925, by his friend Alexander Woollcott: "'Alexander' differed, too, in having been fashioned as an instrumental melody with no words to guide it. As such it had gathered dust on the shelf, wordless and ignored, until one day when he himself needed a new song in a hurry. He had just been elected to the Friars Club and the first *Friars Frolic* was destined for production at the New Amsterdam. He wanted something new to justify his appearance in the bill and so he patched together some words that would serve to carry this neglected tune of which he himself was secretly fond." Later writers have taken this passage as evidence that the piano rag was written before the song. Ian Whitcomb, for instance, imagines the following scenario, in typically lively and fanciful fashion:

> Early one morning, in one of the Snyder cubicles, [Berlin] knocked out a lively march with a bugle-call motif in the main strain (the trio) plus a snatch of "Swanee River." It had all the other parts and modulations like any decent march or rag classic form. . . . A leftover from the march (which has the same form as classic ragtime) gave the verse a novel twist to the ear: it modulated at the end into the subdominant key, thus setting the chorus onto a fresh path. No popular song had done this before.

Laurence Bergreen fantasizes that "so intent was Berlin on showing off his newfound expertise as a composer that he chose the risky course of offering the song as an instrumental, though he did endow it with an evocative title,

'Alexander's Ragtime Band.' . . . With its mixed ancestry, the instrumental failed to find an appreciative audience."

This interpretation of the genesis of "Alexander" rests on taking Woollcott's phrase "instrumental melody with no words to guide it" to be a reference to the later-published piano version of the piece. A melody, however, even one without words, is not the same as an extended piano composition. As Berlin once explained, the first stage in writing a song could be, at least for him, finding a tune: "I get an idea, either a title or a phrase or a melody, and hum it out into something definite." A number of contemporary sources support Woollcott's report that "Alexander" began life as a *melody*—but not as a piano composition. Rennold Wolf wrote in 1913, "The greater portion of the *song* was written in ten minutes, and in the offices of the music publishing firm, Watterson [sic], Berlin and Snyder, while five or six pianos and as many vocalists were making bedlam with songs of the day. Berlin was not impressed by it when the *melody* first came to him. In fact, after playing it over a few times on the piano, he did not take the trouble to note the *melody* on paper." Berlin himself was quoted several years later as saying that the piece was "simon-pure inspiration. I had long admired certain of its progressions, but the *melody* came to me right out of the air. I wrote the whole thing in eighteen minutes, surrounded on all sides by roaring pianos and roaring vaudeville actors."

Berlin had never published a piece for piano when "Alexander's Ragtime Band" was copyrighted as a song, nor are any piano pieces listed in the several handwritten inventories, now housed in the Irving Berlin Collection in the Library of Congress, of his unpublished compositions from 1910 to 1913. Two later songs by Berlin were made into more extended piano pieces, some months after their initial publication, by the addition of new introductions and third strains. "That Mysterious Rag," published as a song in August 1911, was reworked by William Schultz into a piano piece subtitled "Characteristic Intermezzo," and "The International Rag," from August 1913, was later converted into a piano piece subtitled "March and Twostep." This pattern is similar to what happened with "Alexander's Ragtime Band": to tap a different market, a successful song was made into a piano piece. There is no evidence that in 1910 Berlin was interested in, or for that matter capable of, writing a complete piano rag; his first published instrumental piece, rather than an arrangement of a song, was the fox-trot "Morning Exercise," copyrighted on October 8, 1914.

Concerning "Alexander," internal evidence supports the argument that the piano piece was an expanded version of the song rather than the other way around. The structure of the piano version is peculiar, to say the least.

"Alexander's Ragtime Band: March and Twostep" (G major)
Intro   A Trio (C major) B   B   C   B   B
4 bars 16 bars   16 + 16 + 16 + 16 + 16 bars

A is the verse of "Alexander," B is the chorus, and C is the strain not found in the song. The first two strains (A and B) of most marches and rags are in the tonic key, with the third strain (C) usually in the subdominant; more than half of such a piece is thus in the tonic, with the third section (C) affording tonal and melodic contrast. Here, however, a mere twenty measures in the key of the tonic, consisting of the introduction and first strain, are overwhelmed by eighty bars in the subdominant. The obvious explanation for this misshapen tonal structure is that the song, with a verse in the tonic and a chorus in the subdominant, was written first:

"Alexander's Ragtime Band" (C major)
Intro   Verse A Chorus (F major) B   B
4 bars 16 bars   16 + 16 bars

When a third stain (C) in the subdominant was added to make a longer piano piece, it was inserted after the chorus (B), which was already in this key.

Michael Freedland takes the myth of the instrumental genesis of "Alexander" a step further by imagining that it was first performed in an instrumental arrangement by the pit orchestra of a show. "The lyricless 'Alexander's Ragtime Band' had its first public performance by the orchestra on the opening night of the Follies [sic] Bergere's International Revue. But it appeared that the audience was much more interested in the décor, the girls, the champagne and the menu than they were in the music. . . . Lasky saw the way it was being treated with a splendid indifference—and ordered it out of the show." Bergreen embroiders this imaginary episode into "the orchestra flailed away at Berlin's instrumental, but the song made little impression."

After this fiasco, Freedland continues, "Berlin tried to forget 'Alexander' and filed the song away" until "the Ted Snyder Company was reorganized with Berlin as a partner," thus putting him in a position to "decide for himself which of his numbers he was going to have published." When invited to join the Friars Club and take part in their annual Frolic, he "took 'Alexander' out of mothballs and wrote a set of words to go with it."

This account of the early history of "Alexander," accepted uncritically by later writers, is filled with factual mistakes and outright fabrications, and it plays loose and free with chronology. To get some sense of the problems with Freedland's story, consider the following facts: "Alexander" was not a "lyricless" piece when it was supposedly played by a pit orchestra, since the show in question—which, by the way, was not titled *International Revue*—opened on April 27, 1911, six weeks after "Alexander's Ragtime Band" had been copyrighted and published as a song, with text. Nor did Berlin write the "words to go with it" when he supposedly "took it out of the moth-balls" for the *Friars Frolic*, which had its first performance on May 28; the lyrics were written before the song's publication in mid-March. Also, the Ted Snyder Company was not reorganized into Waterson, Berlin, and Synder until December of 1911, by which time countless performances of "Alexander" in several shows and on the vaudeville stage, as well as sheet music sales of the song running into the hundreds of thousands, had dictated such a move.

There is a far more important issue involved here than calling attention to shabby journalism posing as biography: most of the early history of "Alexander" is known to us only from this sort of offhand and undisciplined research and writing. A song so important to the history of American popular music deserves better.

~~~~~~

Introduction, Chapters 5, 6, 7, 8

Irving Berlin's first full score for Broadway, *Watch Your Step* (1914), also marks the first time Tin Pan Alley moved uptown. Berlin and Broadway never looked back. *Watch Your Step* was quickly forgotten after it closed, except for its historical importance (which nonetheless has garnered it little more than passing mention in writings on Berlin and Broadway). It is often referred to as a revue, even by its contemporary reviewers, a theater form with no through-story; in my estimation it qualifies as a book musical as it certainly has a plot which requires ultimate resolution, though with many revue-style detours along the way.[1]

---

1. The book was based on *Round the Clock*, which, in turn, was drawn from a French comedy. As was customary at the time, many vaudeville-type performances with no relevance to the plot were added to the show. The portions of the script that survive are from differing versions of the show and do not create a coherent whole, making it hard to discern the plot. Revues in the first decade of the twentieth century often did have a very slim "plot" to tie together the songs and skits, and reviewers and theatergoers often found it hard to distinguish which type of musical they were watching. Nonetheless, *Watch Your Step* definitely has a plot, however flimsy, and should be considered a book musical.

Marie Schrader wrote as "Madam Critic" in the *Dramatic Mirror*. She and her husband, Frederick, were active in the theater, including as playwrights. Initially they lived in Washington where both were drama critics for the *Washington Post*. In the early twentieth century they relocated to New York where they were connected with the director-producer, David Belasco and Marie continued as a critic. Schrader gives a strong feel for *Watch Your Step* and seems to have caught the importance of the moment, without directly saying so. She makes reference to a show running at the same time, *The Garden of Paradise*, which opened November 28, 1914, and ran only seventeen performances. It was an adaption of Hans Christian Andersen's "The Little Mermaid" by Edward Sheldon, produced by Liebler and Company, who were responsible for the American premieres of several George Bernard Shaw plays including *Pygmalion*, *Candida*, and *Mrs. Warren's Profession*.

Harry B. Smith (1860–1936) wrote the book and lyrics for *Watch Your Step* and Berlin's next complete Broadway score, *Stop! Look! Listen!* (1915). Smith is one of the first major lyricist/book writers on Broadway, and certainly one of Broadway's most prolific (though workman-like rather than inspired) writers. One would expect that by the writing of this autobiography in 1931 Smith would feel some sense of the significance of those shows, but gives them scant attention and has little to offer on Berlin himself. Nonetheless, this brief excerpt provides a small window on an important event in Berlin's life and American Musical Theater.

Margaret Knapp, writing in 1981, gives one of the rare scholarly looks at the show in her presentation to the Conference on Musical Theatre in America at C.W. Post (Long Island University), sponsored jointly by the American Society for Theatre Research, the Sonneck Society (now the Society for American Music), and the Theatre Library Association. Knapp considers *Watch Your Step* more revue than book show, and makes a strong argument for that position.

One of the highlights of *Watch Your Step* was the finale of Act II, the "Opera Parody ("Opera in Modern Time")" in which quotes from *Carmen* (Bizet), *Faust* (Gounod), *Pagliacci* (Leoncavallo), *La Bohème* (Puccini), and *Aida* (Verdi) are turned into current dances—the One-step, Maxixe, Tango, and others. Finally the ghost of Verdi is tortured with the ragging of the quartet from *Rigoletto*. "Ghost of Verdi Interviewed: Tells How He Suffers Nightly" is a "first-hand" account of the master's sufferings, done in the same spirit (as it were) of the show itself.

| 5 |

"Madam Critic": Review of *Watch Your Step*

The opening performance of *Watch Your Step* was the noisiest affair I have ever attended. The people on the stage made all the racket they could, and those out front went them one better. Vernon Castle beat a drum, hit a cymbal and other instruments in such rapid succession and combination that it made you dizzy to watch him. He worked both legs and arms at the same time. Then the chorus whooped it up in the first finale by means of dozens of tambourines, while the orchestra did its best to shut out their sound and the audience tried to drown the orchestra by its laughter and applause.

It was a great night for Broadway.

Nothing like it has been heard here within the memory of the oldest theatergoer. And everybody seemed to be enjoying himself beyond all description. The house was packed to the doors. I didn't know that there were so many strong hands in the town. During my experience of attending first nights on some occasions the applause has been such that the critics described it as an ovation. Now if these moments were ovations, what could the *Watch Your Step* effort be called? It was a mighty roar. Without exaggeration I was obliged to put my fingers to my ears. A 42-centimeter gun couldn't have been much more deafening. Niagara at its loudest couldn't compete. I couldn't help making comparisons between the Berlin comedy reception and the half-hearted acknowledgment bestowed upon some more ambitious things. For instance, if *The Garden of Paradise*, the most beautiful production ever done in New York, with a beautiful love story attached, had had one-fourth of the noise bestowed upon lrving Berlin's maiden effort, conditions would be better for Liebler and Company right now. If Liebler and Company had had as many friends and well-wishers as had lrving Berlin on his opening night, maybe the results might have been different. The New Amsterdam was filled with Berlin admirers. They were there to see the thing through to a success, and they did.

SOURCE *New York Dramatic Mirror*, December 16, 1914.

It is wonderful to have such support in one's ambitions. Berlin is a man to be envied.

Every precaution was taken by the composer and plottist that there should be no over-rating of the production. The musical part was described on the programmes as "a syncopated musical show," and the plot was explained by the words "if any" in parentheses. That left the critics not the slightest chance for indignation.

There was ragtime enough to satisfy the most ardent enthusiast on the subject—even the man who frankly admits that he doesn't understand Wagner and has no desire to do so. The Berlin admirers were there to listen to ragtime and nothing else. But lo and behold! an awful awakening awaited them. The hit of the evening was not an original ragtime composition. I was quite shocked when the famous air from poor old *Rigoletto* was dragged forth and given with ragtime vocal accompaniment. Well might Verdi appear in ghostly form and implore from an upper box in the Metropolitan Opera House scene, "Don't rag my Rigoletto." They did rag it, nevertheless, to distraction, and as that particular bit of *Rigoletto* is familiar to almost everybody, since it had so often been murdered in vaudeville and cabaret performances, a ragging was all that it needed to carry it along with other rags into music-loving homes.

Elizabeth Murray with her quiet method of making a hit with ragtime will have to whoop it up a bit if she expects to put one over. The quietest actor in the show was Harry Kelly's dog. He scarcely opened his mouth to yawn, but he kept the audience convulsed every moment he was on the stage.

I wish all the other managers in town might pay a visit to the New Amsterdam. It would save so much pondering over that eternal question which is still distracting them and causing them to waste hundreds of thousands and to go into bankruptcy, viz: "What do they want?" If the opening performance of *Watch Your Step* may be relied upon, it furnishes the answer. But opening performances, as has been proved time and time again, are not always trustworthy. After the first onslaught of ticket purchases is over, then we can tell better whether they really want what they seem to want. Do they?

| 6 |

Harry B. Smith: Excerpt from *First Nights and First Editions*

Mr. Charles Dillingham gave me—in 1914—an old play to convert into a new musical entertainment. It was of French origin and had been produced at the Châtelet Theatre many years before. In his early years as a manager (in 1868) Augustin Daly had produced his own version which he called *Round the Clock*. Mr. Daly localized the play, and one of the scenes was the dance hall of Harry Hill, where a free-for-all fight took place and the police arrived just in time to rescue somebody. Mr. Hill resented this and wrote to the manager saying that nothing of the kind ever happened at his place, which was patronized by the best people. I had written a number of pieces for Mr. Dillingham, *The Girl in the Train*, *The Office Boy*, and *A Madcap Princess*. For Fritzi Scheff, while she was under his direction, I made new versions of *Fatinitza*, *Boccaccio*, and *Giroflé-Girofla*, and with Victor Herbert, wrote her first starring vehicle, *Babette*.

The composer chosen by the manager for the new play was Irving Berlin, whose career, as chronicled by Alexander Woollcott, makes the life of Dick Whittington seem dull and uneventful. Mr. Berlin was, even then, fairly laureled as the writer of "Alexander's Rag-Time Band" and other popular songs. The result of our collaboration was *Watch Your Step*, which was devised to exploit the terpsichorean talents of Mr. and Mrs. Vernon Castle, the popular dancers. Castle afterward became an officer in the aviation service and was killed in a practice flight. In our play, Frank Tinney was amusing as the carriage caller at the Metropolitan Opera House.

Mr. Berlin wrote the lyrics as well as the music of *Watch Your Step*. He is ingenious in inventing unexpected rhymes. Most bards would think it hopeless to attempt to find a rhyme for "Wednesday"; but Mr. Berlin found one. In one of the songs in this piece, a matinée idol describes his persecution by

---

SOURCE Harry B. Smith, *First Nights and First Editions* (Boston: Little, Brown and Company). Copyright 1931 by Harry B. Smith.

women and alludes to the elderly worshippers who attend the afternoon performances:

> "There's a matinée on Wednesday,
> I call it my old hens' day."

At a Hippodrome dress rehearsal, the composer, Raymond Hubbell, defied Berlin to find a rhyme for "orange." A few minutes later the song writer came down the aisle, stopped the orchestra rehearsal, which Hubbell was directing, and said, "I've got it."

> "Brother Bill and I once stole a cellar door;
> And Bill was eating an orange
> He stole the hind hinge
> And I stole the fore hinge."

I quote from memory, but the idea and the rhyme are correct.

Watch Your Step was a good entertainment and a success, though at rehearsals the material did not seem promising. In the cast was a character woman whose specialty was singing Irish comic songs. At the dress rehearsal on a Sunday night, she remarked, "I went to church this morning and burned candles for the success of this piece; but, personally, I think it will be-blank-blanked failure."

In the following season, Mr. Berlin and I wrote *Stop Look and Listen* [sic] which was presented under Mr. Dillingham's management as a starring vehicle for the beautiful Gaby DeLys, to whom a king was a mere advertisement.

~~~~~~

| 7 |

Margaret Knapp: *Watch Your Step:* Irving Berlin's 1914 Musical

An examination of *Watch Your Step* will remind us that although as historians of the musical theatre we tend to focus on the increasing sophistication of the libretto as one of the most important developments in the twentieth-century

SOURCE *Musical Theatre in America: Papers and Proceedings of the Conference on the Musical Theatre in America*, ed. Glenn Loney, Conference on the Musical Theatre in America (1981: C.W. Post Center). Reprinted by permission of Greenwood Publishing Group, Westport, CT.

musical, we should also be aware that shows with little or nothing in the way of a coherent plot have succeeded in winning both critical praise and audience enthusiasm for as long as there has been an American musical stage. By reviewing the circumstances surrounding the production of *Watch Your Step*, and the critical and audience reaction to the show, I shall attempt to demonstrate how a musical can succeed in spite of, and to some extent because of, a weak libretto.

Watch Your Step was the brainchild of Charles Dillingham, who had been a prosperous Broadway producer for several years before startling the New York theatre community by presenting two smash hit musicals in less than two months during the fall of 1914. The first of these was *Chin-Chin*, a vehicle for the beloved comedy team of David Montgomery and Fred Stone, with music by Ivan Caryll. After its opening in late October, *Chin-Chin*'s combination of innocent pantomime and sophisticated humor amused children and adults for the rest of the season and made it the most successful show on Broadway that year. Dillingham's second hit of 1914 was *Watch Your Step*. For this production he engaged composer Irving Berlin to write his first complete score for a musical. Prior to Dillingham's offer, Berlin had been known primarily as the creator of such popular tunes as "Alexander's Ragtime Band" and "Everybody's Doin' It," and for the individual songs he had contributed to various musical comedies and revues. Early in 1914 Berlin told an interviewer that he planned to write an opera completely in ragtime, a project that never reached fruition. It was not until Charles Dillingham asked Berlin to write the score for *Watch Your Step* that the composer had his first opportunity to demonstrate what he could accomplish on a large scale.

Dillingham also hired Harry B. Smith to write the book for *Watch Your Step*. Smith was the most prolific librettist and lyricist in the history of the American musical stage, turning out by his own estimate the books for over 300 shows and the lyrics for 6,000 songs during his long career. The book for *Watch Your Step* was the fourth libretto by Smith to appear on Broadway in a little over a month. The plot revolved around a will, in which a deceased millionaire bequeathed $2 million to the male or female relative who has never been in love. Various family members try unsuccessfully to claim the inheritance before an innocent young man and his equally naive female cousin are discovered to be relatives of the deceased. The other family members quickly side with either the boy or the girl and try to win control of the money by tricking the other cousin into falling in love. Meanwhile, the young cousins discover that they are in love with one another and try to conceal their feelings so that one of them will win the money. Most of this plot is revealed in the first scene, set in a lawyer's office; for the rest of the show the story resurfaces intermittently as the young cousins are introduced to a variety of situations in which one or the other of them might be tempted to fall in love and thereby forfeit the inheritance. They are taken to a stage door where the girl is introduced to a matinee idol, then to a dance palace where the boy is introduced to the Fox Trot, then to the Metropolitan Opera House where bored patrons transform famous arias into ragtime tunes, then to a Pullman car, and finally to a fashionable New York cabaret.

One reason for the episodic nature of the libretto was Dillingham's decision to employ vaudeville entertainers rather than musical comedy performers in most of the leading roles. The stars of the show were to be Vernon and Irene Castle, who were then riding the crest of the ballroom dancing craze that swept the country in the early 1910s. Vernon Castle had previously appeared as a comedian in musicals produced by Lew Fields, but Irene Castle had had no acting experience prior to *Watch Your Step*. Thus, while Vernon was given the role of one of the innocent cousins, Irene portrayed herself,[1] and Smith found it necessary to create situations where she could logically appear in her customary role as arbiter of the latest fads in ballroom dance. Similarly, the popular vaudeville comedian Frank Tinney appeared in blackface in the latter half of the show as a carriage caller at the Metropolitan Opera, as a Pullman porter, and as a coat room boy, but throughout the evening his monologues were drawn from his vaudeville act rather than from the plot of the show. In fact, at one point Tinney addressed the audience directly to explain that he had not been allowed to appear until late in the second act because it was impossible for him to remain within the bounds of a musical comedy plot. Tinney spent most of his time on stage telling jokes, kidding the audience, and doing his vaudeville specialties. Other stars of the variety houses signed by Dillingham to appear in *Watch Your Step* were dancers Elizabeth Brice and Charles King, ragtime singer Elizabeth Murray, and comedians Harry Kelly and W. C. Fields. All of them had carefully worked-out vaudeville routines which they wished to use in the show. Only Sallie Fisher, who played the innocent female cousin, was a veteran musical comedy actress.

Faced with the preponderance of vaudevillians in the cast, Smith was forced to allow a great deal of latitude in his script so that the specialties of the performers could be introduced. At one place in the script a stage direction indicates that at that point in the show Frank Tinney was to perform one of his vaudeville routines. The nature of the act and its relation, if any, to the plot was left unspecified. Smith also allowed Irving Berlin a maximum of freedom in the composition of songs for *Watch Your Step*. A stage direction repeated

---

1. She was listed in the program as "Mrs. Vernon Castle."

several times in the script states, "cue speeches to duet to be written on what-ever the subject of duet may be." In other words, Berlin could write a duet on any subject he chose, and Smith would then create suitable dialogue with which to relate the number to the plot. In light of these concessions to the per-formers and the composer, it is not surprising that the program for *Watch You Step* carried a credit that read, "Plot (if any) by H. B. Smith." What may sur-prise us is that, given the nature of the performers he had hired, Dillingham bothered to have any libretto at all. The reason for the inclusion of a book was to some extent economic. Dillingham had to justify charging his audiences two dollars a ticket to see the same performers who regularly appeared in vaudeville houses where the top seats cost from fifty cents to a dollar. By add-ing a plot to *Watch Your Step* the producer was able to pass his show off as a musical comedy meriting the higher ticket prices. This attempted deception seems to have fooled neither critics nor audiences but was permitted because of the high quality of the performances and the care and expense that went into the other facets of the production.

In November 1914 Dillingham sent *Watch Your Step* to Syracuse and Detroit for two weeks of out-of-town tryouts. Discovering that the show was too long, the producer cut the scene in which W. C. Fields appeared, and since no other place could be found for the comedian, he was fired, only to be immediately signed by Florenz Ziegfeld for the next edition of the *Follies*. As *Watch Your Step* was completing its out-of-town run, its visual impact was enhanced by the addition of newly painted scenery. The word from the road, as reported in *Variety*, was that *Watch Your Step* was a big hit. When it arrived at the New Amsterdam Theatre on 8 December 1914, New York critics and audiences con-firmed the out-of-town opinions. *Variety* reported that the show shattered all of the New Amsterdam's previous records for receipts, with an expected gross of $22,000 for its first week, and a healthy advance sale. "It ran for 171 perfor-mances, a remarkable record when one considers that from an economic view-point the 1914–1915 season was the worst the American theatre had known up to that time."

The newspaper reviewers were enthusiastic about the show, as were the ticket buyers who lined up at the New Amsterdam's box office. The *New York Times* called the show "as gay, extravagant and festive an offering as this city could hope to see," and the *New York Evening Telegram* proclaimed in its review's headline that *"Watch Your Step* Carries Everything Before It." While all of the reviewers had praise for some or all of the elements of *Watch Your Step*, most of them had difficulty in determining exactly what kind of show it was. One critic called it "glorified vaudeville," another termed it a "ragtime opera," a third dubbed it a "musical extravaganza," and the *Times* conceded that "so many things have been called musical comedies that *Watch Your Step* might as well be called one."

This confusion stems partly from the number of well-known vaudeville entertainers used in the show and partly from the show's lack of a well-developed libretto. Although most of the critics noted that the show lacked a strong book, they seemed largely undisturbed by the omission. As the reviewer for the *New York American* cautioned his readers, "Don't vex your mind with idle thoughts about the plot of *Watch Your Step*. Even Harry B. Smith himself seems doubtful if there is one for the mind to fasten on. No. The new show is just a tissue of bright nonsense, as witty as the heart of man could wish it—as unmeaning as the title which it bears." In his review for the *New York Telegraph*, Rennold Wolf observed of the show's plot, "The development is completely lost about the time the characters reach the Metropolitan Opera House, and it is well, because by ignoring the story the company is enabled to bring down the curtain on as rousing and as ingeniously arranged a finale as the musical stage of this town has ever known."

It may strike us as odd that reviewers could be so complacent about the way in which *Watch Your Step*'s admittedly trite story vanished halfway through the evening. The reason for this lack of concern may be found in the extravagant praise that the reviewers heaped upon the other aspects of the show, particularly upon Irving Berlin's score, the dancing of the Castles, the fine performances of the other principals, the elaborate scenery and costumes, and the general spirit of vitality and freshness that enlivened all of the other elements.

By the fall of 1914 Irving Berlin was acknowledged by many to be America's foremost young composer of popular music. Berlin made his own assessment of his contributions to popular music in the period just before World War I in an interview he gave early in 1914. "I would not say that I claim, by any means, to be the originator of modern ragtime. But I can truthfully say that I have accomplished a number of things which were thought impossible. I have established the syncopated balled and I have proven that the metre can be 'chopped up' to fit the words."

Berlin's songs for *Watch Your Step* gave an early hint of his future versatility as a musical comedy composer. He produced such lively dance numbers as "Show Us How to Do the Fox Trot," "The Syncopated Walk," and "The One-Step," but he also created an unusual waltz called "What Is Love," and a winning duet entitled "Settle Down in a One-Horse Town." Another interesting number from the show was the song "A Simple Melody," Berlin's first use of two separate melodies sung in counterpoint to one another. The song did not receive much attention at the time of *Watch Your Step* but became a standard after it was recorded by Bing Crosby and his son Gary in 1950, and sung with an updated verse by Ethel Merman and Dan Dailey in the 1954 film *There's No Business Like Show Business.*[2]

The most critically acclaimed musical sequence in *Watch Your Step* was called "Old Operas in a New Way."[3] In this number famous operatic arias from *Aida, La Bohème, Faust, Carmen, I Pagliacci,* and *Rigoletto* were given new lyrics and a ragtime beat. Even an appearance by the ghost of Giuseppe Verdi could not convince the singers to spare his music from being "ragged."

Taken as a whole, Berlin's score for *Watch Your Step* was not outstanding, but it did exhibit a certain originality and freshness. At the time when *Watch Your Step* opened, the reviewer for the *New York Evening Sun* said of Berlin's music: "The score differs from that of the ordinary musical comedy. It has no love theme. It has no captivating sentimental duet sung by the hero and heroine under the spotlight moon. It is with one or two inconspicuous exceptions the stuff that one-steps are made of. Its motif is the tango. There is no question that Mr. Berlin has written songs individually superior to any of the numbers in last night's piece. . . . But his ensemble was a unique and thoroughly enjoyable achievement." More recently, Alec Wilder in his book *American Popular Song* characterized Berlin's music for *Watch Your Step* as "a very good score for that era" and discussed in detail six of the songs from the show.

Berlin was fortunate in having a talented cast to perform his music. Most notable were the Castles, who were then at the peak of their popularity as a result of the revolution in ballroom dancing, which had begun around 1910 when the more strenuous and difficult styles of dance such as the cakewalk, the polka, and the schottische were replaced by relatively simple "animal" dances such as the Turkey Trot, the Grizzly Bear, and the Fox Trot. It is estimated that between 1912 and 1914 over 100 new dances found their way into ballrooms, and these dances were enjoyed by a wider public than ever before. The Castles, who made their first success as ballroom dancers in Paris in 1912, returned to America just in time to be hailed as the leaders of the dance craze. Their every move was copied. Irene's gorgeous clothes were envied by women across the country, and when she bobbed her hair, thousands followed suit. In one week of vaudeville appearances in the late spring of 1914 the Castles grossed $31,000, an astounding figure for that time. They were thus at the zenith of their popularity when they starred in *Watch Your Step,* and Dillingham made the most of their appeal by giving them ample opportunity

---

2. There is no lyric change in the film.
3. Also called the "Ragtime Opera Medley."

to display the latest steps in their inimitable style. The Castles' dances in *Watch Your Step* included a One-Step, a Fox Trot, and a Tango; Vernon Castle also sang a song called "The Dancing Teacher," in which he made fun of his success as an instructor. The dance craze was a recurring theme in the show—even the lawyer's office in the opening scene was described in the program as a "law office de dance."

In a reminiscence published after Vernon's death in 1918, Irene Castle wrote that they had done their best dancing in *Watch Your Step*. Most of the critics agreed. One review of the show bore the headline "*Watch Your Step* Is a Castles' Night: Trots and Tangoes Shown in All Their 57 Varieties at the New Amsterdam." The show's success at the box office suggests that the public went along with the critical opinion. The attention paid to the Castles' dancing in *Watch Your Step* helped to hasten the end of the waltz as the primary form of musical comedy dance and made the new ballroom steps an acceptable part of the musical theatre. An insight into the influence of the Castles on musical comedy dance may be gained from the fact that Fred and Adele Astaire spent a good deal of their free time while in New York during 1913 and 1914 watching the Castles dance in vaudeville and in such shows as *Watch Your Step*. The Astaires were very impressed with the Castles' unique style.

In addition to the Castles, *Watch Your Step* featured other entertainers who were at the top of their form. Elizabeth Brice and Charles King had been vaudeville favorites for a number of years. The reviewer for *Billboard* actually preferred the dancing of Brice and King to that of the Castles *in Watch your Step*. Harry Kelly was a popular comedian who made a great hit in *Watch Your Step* with a dog who refused to obey his commands. Elizabeth Murray received praise for her rendition of the song "The Minstrel Parade," and Frank Tinney's comedy was well received. The costumes and scenery were described by reviewers as elaborate but tasteful, one critic stating that the setting seemed to be influenced by the style of Leon Bakst.

All of these individual parts, the fresh new music of Irving Berlin, the graceful dances of the Castles, the excellent performances by the other stars, and the rich but tasteful scenery and costumes contributed to *Watch Your Step*'s image of American vitality and modernity. Such Berlin songs as "A Simple Melody" and "Old Operas in a New Way" served notice that the younger generation had grown impatient with old-fashioned, mainly European, styles of music, while the Castles demonstrated with the Syncopated Walk and the Fox Trot that the older, imported styles of dance had to yield their place to the new ballroom steps. Even the hectic pace with which *Watch Your Step* was performed contributed to the general opinion that here was a brash, sleek, up-to-the-minute musical made by, and for, a new generation. Appearing in the late fall of 1914, when many Americans were worried about being drawn into the European war, *Watch Your Step* provided excellent escapist entertainment; at the same time it radiated a typically American self-assurance and confidence in the future. The success of *Watch Your Step* can be attributed as much to this spirit of vivacity as to the individual triumphs of Irving Berlin and the Castles.

It is tempting for us to view *Watch Your Step* from our vantage point as a rather trivial example of how musicals were created in the days before well-ordered and well-integrated books were a commonplace on the musical stage. I would therefore like to conclude with another excerpt from a review. "It's not a perfect entertainment . . . but it rides so high on affection, skill and, of course, stunning music that the lapses don't begin to spoil the fun. What's more, this is the only Broadway revue of recent vintage that operates on a grand scale. There's a lavishness in the show's physical production . . . and in its depth of performing talent . . . that actually squares with current Broadway ticket prices." Those words could very well have been written about *Watch Your Step*, but in fact they come from Frank Rich's review of *Sophisticated Ladies*, published in the *New York Times* in March 1981. Along with the continuing popularity of musicals such as *Dancin'* and *Sugar Babies*, the success of *Sophisticated Ladies* reminds us that shows with little or nothing in the way of a libretto still occupy an important place on the American musical stage and in the hearts of musical comedy audiences.

~~~~~~

| 8 |

Ghost of Verdi Interviewed: Tells How He Suffers Nightly

The curtain came down on the second act of *Watch Your Step* at the New Amsterdam Theatre. From the auditorium could be heard the applause and laughter of a highly pleased audience. On the stage there was a great deal of orderly confusion; principals and chorus people, some of them still humming the closing bars of the syncopated *Rigoletto* which is the act's finale, were hurrying to the elevator which transports them to the dressing rooms; a small

SOURCE Irving Berlin scrapbooks in the Library of Congress.

regiment of stage hands was attacking the scenery, that must be displaced to make room for the third act setting.

Into the atmosphere of light-hearted activity was projected the melancholy figure of Verdi's ghost. A few short minutes before he (or it) had been melodiously protesting against the caparisoned figures stepping modern measures [lifting] up his voice in rhythmic declamation against the violations of the tempo in his masterpiece; he had made a masterly appeal that his brain child should not be expressed in ragtime. But the curtain descended upon his defeat. He was compelled to listen to his music as modernized and gingerized; to watch a stage full of gayly caparisoned figures stepping modern measures to it; worst of all, there beat upon his ears the thunderous expression of approval given such treatment by a theatre crowded with well dressed, intelligent, cultured persons.

He wiped a pallid palm across a clammy brow.

"It's no use," he said. "Every night except Sunday and on two afternoons of the week I go out there to plead my cause. The result is ever the same; they mock me. You were here? You heard them? Ah! then you know. You can realize what they are doing to me. In Ha—well, where I came from—there is no such cruelty. Tantalus himself admits it. He is forever failing just as the goal is about to be achieved, but there is none to laugh at his failure.

"I retire from the battle ground with applause ringing in my ears—the applause of an audience delighted because of my defeat. At each performance I present myself with the revived hope that I shall receive the encouragement and support of the onlookers; but always I am laughed down.

"Like it? Of course, they like it. That's what gets my goat—I beg your pardon, I meant to say that is what grieves me. What is the world coming to, anyway?"

A look of angry determination came into his eyes. He gestured fiercely with his right hand. His beard bristled.

"But it cannot go on forever," he declared. "Already there are rumblings among my friends and contemporaries. There was a mass meeting of the shades of twenty famous composers the other night, held to consider this very matter. The meeting broke up in a row because Heinrich Wagner[1] tried to run it to suit himself, but sooner or later the eminent musical ghosts will sink their own differences and outline a plan to preserve their reputations. Wagner has already asked permission to come back to earth for the purpose of making a personal investigation to learn whether anybody like Irving

---

1. Wagner's name was Richard. Whether this was intended to be a joke is unknown.

Berlin is tampering with his *Tannhaeuser*.[2] You can imagine what Wagner will do if he finds anybody interpolating ragtime into his stuff—pardon, I mean music."

The ferocity left his voice, the fire died from his eyes. His look and tone were again plaintive.

"But I'm afraid there's little hope for me," he said. "I'm not exactly dense. The first and the second time I appeared here I thought the seeming appreciation of Irving Berlin's work and the actions of those people on the stage was only seeming and nothing more. I believed that the audience was simply chaffing me, intending later to take my side and put an end to this profanation. But now I realize they actually prefer my *Rigoletto* done in ragtime. Realizing it, I am done or undone, whichever you prefer.

"Defeated and desperate as I am, there is still no hope for me to retreat. I'd be satisfied now to find some nice, cool spot in—well, where I come from— and sit there remembering better days—days before the word syncopation found its way into the dictionary. Even that solace is denied me. I'm not sure just why, but I must have done something to earn the animosity of the boss, for he has told me that I must continue coming here and making my protest for a year, at least. When I tell him that the people laugh at me he just chuckles and declares enigmatically, 'That's the idea.' If I attempt to argue he tells me that Broadway demands my presence and he will not listen to any further argument.

"And I can't understand that, either. Why should these people demand me? I always understood that most men were satisfied if the ghost walked;[3] why should I have to talk and sing to make fun for audiences who prefer my wonder piece, *Rigoletto*, done in ragtime to the way I wrote it? I tell you Irving Berlin and Charles Dillingham have a lot to answer for."

He was about to proceed, but just then the orchestra out in front broke into the opening bars of a syncopated melody. His face became furious.

" 'Watch Your Step,' 'Watch Your Step,'" he sneered. "They'd better watch theirs if they don't want the Ghosts' Protective Association to get after them."

And then—pouf! he was gone.

---

2. Berlin does make a brief musical reference to *Tristan und Isolde* in the scene.

3. A ghost that never walked, in show business terms, was a touring company that did not get paid. Verdi is asking that if the show is working (and everyone is paid), why is he needed to help the show? Definitely an in joke.

Introduction, Chapters 9, 10, 11

In 1920 Berlin took the unprecedented for a songwriter—and still unique—move of building his own theater for his own shows. The theater, still active in New York, is called The Music Box, an appropriate name for a home of musicals and revues. That name, with respect to Berlin, had further resonance in that he was unusual in the great number of songs he wrote that are in some fashion *about* music. It opened in 1921 with the first of four annual *Music Box Revues*. After 1924 Berlin began renting the theater to other producers, with *Of Thee I Sing* by George S. Kaufman, Morrie Riskind, and George and Ira Gershwin being a notable resident, though subsequent Berlin shows did play there also.

After ending the *Music Box Revue* series in 1924, Berlin went on to write *The Cocoanuts* in 1925 (the first stage hit for the Marx Brothers) and one of his biggest hit songs, "Blue Skies" (1926).

Alec Wilder (1907–1980) in his landmark book, *American Popular Song: The Great Innovators, 1900–1950,* asserts that 1919–1920 was a significant moment in Berlin's work, when a new maturity appeared in his writing. The first full flowering of this maturity was in the *Music Box Revues.* Robert Baral (1905–1980) was a theater historian with a special interest in the revue format; his book *Revue: The Great Broadway Period* is one of the best (and few) texts on the subject. He takes a look into the past, writing a true nostalgia piece on the series for *Variety* in 1958 (later revised for *Revue*). Despite its late date in Berlin's career, it is significant as one of the first overviews of Berlin as a theater writer (as opposed to popular song writer).

Baral has the common misunderstanding about the song "Mandy," one which still persists. For the army show *Yip, Yip Yaphank!* (1918), Berlin wrote a song called "The Sterling Silver Moon," which is an early version of what later became "Mandy" in the *Ziegfeld Follies of 1919*. Because the earlier song also featured numerous repeats of the name "Mandy," audiences thought that was the name of the song. Berlin renamed it and put a new cover on it; he later extensively reworked it into the better, and better-known, "Mandy."

The Music Box Theatre in a picture taken while *Annie Get Your Gun* was playing next door at the Imperial. Photo credit: *Photofest*

Baral also refers to "I Can Always Find a Little Sunshine in the Y.M.C.A." as a "collector's item." Perhaps at one time, but its presence in the film *Alexander's Ragtime Band*—twenty years before this article—suggests that it had more currency than a collector's item.

Alexander Woollcott (1887–1943) was a leading critic in New York and also a performer and director. He is perhaps now best remembered as the model for Sheridan Whiteside in the Moss Hart and George S. Kaufman comedy *The Man Who Came to Dinner.* A close friend of Berlin, he wrote Berlin's first biography; given that friendship, the book hardly qualifies as a critical assessment. However, it does include some interesting items, such as this letter from Robert Benchley (1889–1945) giving an insider's view of the *Music Box Revues.* Humorist Benchley was featured in the 1923 edition performing his "Treasurer's Report," a skit he had written and performed in the 1922 revue *No Sirree!* Benchley refers to the 1924 edition of the *Music Box Revues* in the letter. Whether this was a mistake in date, or he was a guest at early rehearsals for the 1924 edition is not clear, but the scene he describes is no doubt accurate for all four editions.

In the 1923 *Music Box Revue* Berlin wrote a burlesque on the plague-like ubiquitousness of the song "Yes, We Have No Bananas" (Frank Silver and Irving

Cohn).[1] He transforms the song into selections from *Aida, Rigoletto, Il Trovatore* (Verdi), *Lucia di Lammermoor* (Donizetti), *La Bohème* (Puccini), *Tales of Hoffman* (Offenbach), *Lohengrin* (Wagner), *Messiah* (Handel), and another popular song, "La Paloma."

~~~~~~

| 9 |

Robert Baral: Fond Memory: Those *Music Box Revues*

MUSIC BOX REVUE (1921). The cast: Willie Collier, Sam Bernard, Ivy Sawyer, Joseph Santly, Wilda Bennett, Florence Moore, Paul Frawley, Chester Hale, Richard Keen, Hugh Camron, Rosa Rolando, Margaret Irving, Emma Haig, Brox Sisters, Ethelind Terry, Marguerite & Gill, Rene Riano—and Irving Berlin, Sketches: Frances Nordstrom, Willie Collier, George V. Hobart, T. J. Gray. Sets by Clark Robinson. Dances by Bert French. Costumes by Ralph Mullings, Cora McGeachey, Alice O'Neill. Ballet by L. Tarasoff. Songs by Irving Berlin. Staged by Hassard Short. Ran 313 performances.

Broadway's newest legit house at the time—the Music Box (Cost: $617,012), and the first of four memorable revues blazing with Irving Berlin's songs. This first edition cost $187,613 to produce. Next to Berlin's ace music, for which the theatre was built and labeled, Hassard Short emerged as a stage wizard with his magic elevators which brought new excitement to Broadway. Backstage the Music Box was a mass of extra bridges, traps and structural steel gadgets—all geared to exploit "Say It with Music."

Berlin had his music ready a long time before the world premiere, and he got so excited over "Say It with Music" that he loaned the rough manuscript to the jazz orchestra at the Sixty Club for a one night workover, but it proved such an instantaneous hit right from the start that drastic measures were required to prevent it from growing stale before the show actually opened. Wilda Bennett and Paul Frawley introduced it in the revue—later Ethelind Terry and Joseph Santly took over.

SOURCE *Variety*, November 19, 1958. Reprinted by permission of *Variety*.
1. The song was introduced in 1922 by Eddie Cantor in the revue *Make It Snappy*. It became a hit in 1923, including five weeks as the number one song. Berlin was not the only one to respond to it; the "I've Got the Yes! We Have No Bananas Blues" also came out in 1923, with a number of recordings.

Next to "Say It with Music," the syncopated beat of "Everybody Step," which the Brox Sisters whammed home in their modulated piping, proved irresistible. The number was, as the title implies, a command to let go and dance—which the entire company did. However the revue did not stop with the rich musical portions—the choice cast was up to the top-drawer Berlin tunes. Willie Collier was in charge of the laugh department and had expert help from Sam Bernard, Florence Moore and a loose-limbed zany, Rene Riano, who tied herself up in knots in "I'm a Dumbell" (not published). "Dining Out" had an entire dinner served a la musical fare with the chorines appearing in all the courses from salt shaker to demi-tasse. Later "They Call It Dancing" which travestied modern steps then and marathons [now] proved a riot as done by Sam Bernard with Rene Riano. "The Legend of the Pearls," sung by Miss Bennett, utilized rich pearl effects which dazzled patrons. Irving Berlin loved the show and appeared in this first edition along with the Eight Little Notes: Mary Milford, Virginia Dixon, Helen Clare, Betsy Ross, Helen Newcombe, Claire Davis, Jeanne St. John and Miriam Hopkins (later the film star). Sam Harris' unruffled business hand steered the revue efficiently, lending a certain stability to the venture which was missing from many of the other revues during this hectic period. The *Music Box Revue* reflected high polish and taste—stayed clear of Ziegfeld's girlie sumptuousness—and concentrated on eulogizing Irving Berlin's rich songs within a set frame. "Say It with Music" was a potent title for the first hit to come out of the series. It saturated the Music Box—inside and out.

> *MUSIC BOX REVUE* (1922). The cast: William Gaxton, Charlotte Greenwood, Grace LaRue, John Steel, the Fairbanks Twins, the McCarthy Sisters, Clark & McCullough, Ruth Page, Stowitts, Olivette, Amelia Allen, William Seabury, Robinson Newbold, the Rath Bros. Songs by Irving Berlin. Costumes by Ralph Mulligan and Gilbert Adrian. Skits by Frances Nordstrom. George V. Hobart, Waiter Catlett, Paul Gerard Smith. Dances by William Seabury. Sets by Clark Robinson. Staged by Hassard Short. Ran 273 performances.

Comes the second edition and Smash No.2. Berlin's keyboard delivered "Lady of the Evening" (for a long time this was Berlin's favorite song), and the stuttering rhythm, "Pack Up Your Sins and Go to the Devil," and the plaintive "Crinoline Days"—all fresh today. Clark & McCullough debuted in this edition. Again Hassard Short's mechanical effects proved sensational—especially in "Satan's Palace" with the McCarthy Sisters doing rhythmic justice to "Pack Up Your Sins." Charlotte Greenwood presided over the jazzy ritual as the Devil with other performers depicting Gilda Gray, Ted Lewis, Bee Palmer, Frisco and other "sinners" descending to the lower depths midst steam, elevators and shooting flames. Berlin's syncopated voodoo of "Pack Up Your Sins" permeated this volcanic revel. This song was the basis for a plagiarism suit at the time—but Jascha Heifetz, Neysa McMein and Lenore Ulric stepped in and declared they had heard Berlin play it a full year before it came out. The suit was dismissed.

In the "Diamond Horseshoe" number, the Metropolitan Opera won attention in a shimmer of diamond costuming representing the ladies of the opera with Grace LaRue as Thais mounting the stairs and her train finally graduating to the full sweep of the Music Box stage. Met Opera heroines had long served revues in some form or other—but this particular treatment was a 14-karat sensation. The same idea was repeated when Miss LaRue sang "Crinoline Days"—rising slowly via an elevator and her hoop skirt getting fuller and wider until the final yard came out of the trap to engulf the entire stage. "Lady of the Evening" was given a quiet interpretation—John Steel, with rooftops and soft lights accenting the moonlight melody. Stowitts and Ruth Page handled the ballet numbers which were on the exotic side. The Chinese porcelain fantasy, "Porcelain Maid," was a standout with its lavish oriental costumes created by Gilbert Adrian (soon to go to Hollywood).[2] The McCarthy Sisters had "Bring On the Pepper" as another close harmony rendition which fitted their Dutch-bob personalities. Charlotte Greenwood had special material in "I Want a Daddy Long Legs"[3] (to match her own)—and also a skit in which she fell out of an airplane. Bobby Clark stood out immediately as an enduring comic—his chores dominated his partner's, Paul McCullough. This is one team which C. B. Cochran missed out on in London—they were appearing in *Chuckles* over there with marked success but Irving Berlin got to them first. Incidentally Cockie imported the *Music Box Revue* (minus the best stars) to London but it was a flop. The New York press welcomed Clark & McCullough with plaudits. The Music Box hummed and the box office bulged—and Broadway wondered just how Berlin & Harris could keep up the pace. Ziegfeld envied those song hits.

MUSIC BOX REVUE (1923). The cast: Frank Tinney, Robert Benchley, Joseph Santly, Ivy Sawyer, John Steel, Grace Moore, Phil Baker, Solly Ward, Florence Moore, Mme. Dora Stroeva, Florence O'Dennishawn, Columbus & Snow, the Brox Sisters, Lora Sonderson, Hugh Cameron, Dorothy Dilley. Costumes by Charles LeMaire and Ralph Mulligan. Sets by Clark Robinson. Perfume novelty by Edwin Mendelsohn. Songs by Irving Berlin. Staged by Hassard Short. Ran 273 performances.

---

2. Where he was known simply as Adrian.
3. The songs title is "I'm Looking for a Daddy Long Legs."

Not content with hypnotizing the public with songs, Berlin (or Hassard Short) now proceeded to intoxicate them with perfume . . . "An Orange Grove in California" which Grace Moore and John Steel sang in the midst of a California grove soon dissolved into a festive glow of incandescent orange-colored lights which climbed all over the stage—and orange scent sprayed the audience. It was pure novelty of the highest brand. Berlin always worked with meticulous care in casting his revues—having lined up Grace Moore in Europe the summer before when she was first undertaking serious study for opera. She justified the selection (Ziegfeld wanted her for *The Three Musketeers* later on).

While Berlin's music was generous, no real hit seemed to rise—so an interpolated song, "What'll I Do?" was handed to Miss Moore who made it famous overnight. John Steel continued as the most popular tenor of the time and duetted with the rising diva in all the bigger scenes. The Brox Sisters back on the roster continued to belt out the more spirited Berlin songs—this year being "Learn to Do the Strut" with the full company terping on a slanted stage down to the footlights.

"A Fisherman's Dream" was Hassard Short's dazzler with Florence O'Dennishawn as the Star Fish who was caught with a diamond necklace. Short had utilized miles of diamonds and rhinestones on the elevators—now he turned to mesh. Whiting & Davis, leading mesh firm, created gold & silver mesh gowns in modish styles—and Ivy Sawyer and Joseph Santly sang "Maid of Mesh." The girl inside milady's bag was Helen Lyons. Whiting & Davis took out full page ads in the magazines to advertise this scene—one of the first major promotional tie-ups ever made with a Broadway musical. In the comedy department, this third *Music Box Revue* made history.

Robert Benchley, in business suit and bow-tie, brought his drolleries to the footlights with his "Treasurer's Report," a classic for sophisticated nonsense. The so-called report "brought the activities of the choral society up-to-date, except of course for July and August, when his sister got married (ahem!)." Dizzy but riotously funny. After this click there was a streak of platform speakers who tried to imitate Benchley, but this casual humorist remained supreme in the field for charm and belly laughs. Then George S. Kaufman's gem, "If Men Played Cards as Women Do" with Joseph Santly, Hugh Cameron, Solly Ward and Phil Baker indulging in some bitchy femme gossip. For extra novelty, Mme. Dora Stroeva from Russia via Paris, sang plaintive chanteys in sharp contrast to Berlin's simple unadorned melodies. "Yes We Have No Bananas," then the national nuisance, was given operative [*sic*] workover by a sextet including: Florence Moore, Lora Sonderson, Frank Tinney, Grace Moore, John Steel and Joseph Santly—all they chirped about was bananas! It registered. But what haunted Irving Berlin was "What'll I Do?—next?"

MUSIC BOX REVUE (1924). The cast: Clark & McCullough, Fannie Brice, Grace Moore, Oscar Shaw, Claire Luce, the Brox Sisters, Carl Randall, Hal Sherman, Ula Sharon, Joseph McCauley, Bud & Jack Pearson, Tamiris & Margarita, Runaway Four. Costumes by James Reynolds. Sets by Clark Robinson. Songs by Irving Berlin. Staged by John Murray Anderson. Perfume novelty and blackface effects by Edwin Mendelsohn. Ran 184 performances.

John Murray Anderson stepped in with James Reynolds—and Hassard Short moved over [to] the *Greenwich Village Follies*. It was an amicable switch, aimed basically at injecting spark into the revue form which was beginning to slide downhill all over Broadway. This was the last work on a series for both craftsmen. Murray Anderson selected the character of Rip Van Winkle (Joseph McCauley) as a formal link to weld the show together. This was the year Irving Berlin turned out his heaviest *Music Box* score—nearly 20 songs in all—and there wasn't a smash in the lot.

Duncan Sisters, a sensation in London, were originally wanted for this edition—but they had other commitments to fill which necessitated a reshuffling of the cast and book. "All Alone" was dropped into the show as an interpolated song and stood out. Grace Moore and Oscar Shaw at either end of the stage sang it into lighted telephones before a simple drop. This was probably the most conservative treatment Murray Anderson ever uncorked for this plushy revue. Otherwise the show seemed to sag from overweight. Bobby Clark & Paul McCullough were welcomed back as Music Box regulars—and Fannie Brice, free from her brilliant Ziegfeld period, was also present. Her best number was "Don't Send Me Back to Petrograd" (I'll even wash the sheets for the Ku Klux Klan, but don't sent me back . . .). She also teamed with Bobby Clark for the "I Want to Be a Ballet Dancer" bit.[4]

For "Tokio" number, which Hassard Short already had in the works before he exited, the Brox Sisters sang the Nipponese swingy, "Tokio Blues." Adrian dressed the number lavishly. The Brox Sisters obviously inherited the songs originally concocted for the Duncans. "In the Shade of the Sheltering Tree" evolved into a Weeping Willow splash. The girls waved enormous fans of uncurled ostrich and wound up climbing a fancy ladder and forming the graceful tree midstage. James Reynolds' style was predominant in the larger scenes: "Little Old New York" reflected the Father Knickerbocker era—and an "Alice in Wonderland" spread with costumes designed after the famous John Tenniel drawings. Berlin had composed another "Alice in Wonderland" song

---

4. Brice was famous for her Yiddish accent and so this song was heard as "I Vant to be a Belly Dancer."

for the Dillingham & Ziegfeld production *The Century Girl* (1916). For the Music Box presentation the Brox Sisters invited the audience to "Come Along with Alice . . ." then the Wonderland fantasy took form—Before the Looking Glass—and Behind the Looking Glass. Ula Sharon balleted as Alice and Carl Randall was the Mad Hatter. This extended scene marked Reynolds' final chore on an annual revue. It was circusy—but tasteful. "The Call of the South" led into "Bandana Land" with trick blackface effects donned by the chorus.

Claire Luce, about to join the Ziegfeld galaxy, led off a Wild Cat number which is self explanatory. For "Tell Her in the Springtime" more perfume sprayed the air—but it was a worn stunt by now. Then Rip Van Winkle woke up and the show was fini—and so was the series too. Berlin & Harris, alert to the temperamental chart for revues, decided it was time to lower the lid. The *Music Box Revues*, dedicated to "Say It with Music," opened on top—and shuttered—still on top. The needle never wore out!

~~~~~~

| 10 |

Robert Benchley: Letter about The Music Box

BOOST ELEVENTH AVENUE Committee
Headquarters, 599 Madison Avenue

Dear Mr. Woollcott:

It has been called to someone's attention, and he has called it to mine, that you are writing a book about Irving Berlin. I suppose that it is all right for you writers to write books, but I don't see how you can handle such subjects as Irving Berlin's association with the Music Box without some help from us stage-folk. Unless you have seen a rehearsal or have tripped over things backstage, you can't know what a big thing it is in which this little man finds himself each year.

Nothing could be more discouraging than a rehearsal shortly preceding the opening of the Music Box. Out front there are perhaps a dozen men with their hats on, each sitting on as much of an aisle seat as he can uncover from the big sheet that spreads out over all the orchestra chairs. The house is dark except for what crazy lights come from the stage. Someone yells up to the top balcony for Otto to throw on his baby spot. Otto doesn't hear. Someone else yells, and

SOURCE Alexander Woollcott, *The Story of Irving Berlin* (New York: G. P. Putnam's Sons). Copyright 1925 by Alexander Woollcott.

with much sputtering of calcium, the wrong spot appears. Then three people yell. Silence again.

"All right now!" shouts the director. "All the tiger-skin girls on stage, please!" The tiger-skin girls, who have waiting since eleven P.M. (It is now three-thirty A.M.), walk on in their sleep and stand there. Some one plays the first four bars of the music on a piano and is stopped. "Just a minute, please!"

A stage manager walks across the stage and talks to an assistant. "All right with your straws," he yells to somebody. The director climbs up on the stage with the stage managers. "All right, now! Music, please. All ready, tiger-skin girls!"

The pianist plays seven bars and is stopped again.

Then a little man in a tight-fitting suit, with his hands in his pockets, walks on from the wings. He looks very white in the glare from the foots. You almost expect to have him thrown out, he seems so casual and like an observer. They don't throw him out, however, because he is Mr. Berlin.

You are suddenly overcome with a feeling of tremendous futility. "Irving Berlin's Fourth Music Box Revue" it already says in the lights out in front of the theatre. And Irving Berlin is so little. And the Fourth Music Box Revue is so big. And so far from articulation.

Yet on the opening night, not a week from the rehearsal, you won't feel any futility about it. If you are backstage you will, if you can keep your head from being caved in, be impressed with nothing so much as the tremendous accomplishment of something out of what seemed to be nothing, or worse than nothing, chaos. Way up above in the flies there are men set there for no other purpose than to drop things on you. All across the floor are ropes and wires especially constructed to trip you up. Dozens of men, displaying a fine disdain for the show and the performers, manage to work things so that you out front think that the curtains are being drawn back and drops lowered by electricity. And somewhere in the jam of young ladies dressed as the various manifestations of Springtime, and young men in cutaways who throng the entrances, you may see the top of a small head. If you watch the fedora hat move up and down you can tell that its owner is chewing gum. Then he walks out and goes up to the last row of the balcony where he sits with Sam Harris and watches the show.

For four months he has been working day and night, writing music, devising numbers, engaging principals and chorus, and having a terrible time with his digestion. And yet in all that time no one has heard him raise his voice. And in all that time no one has been hurt by him.

Now you know why you can't get it all from the front on opening night, all of the Music Box, or all of Irving Berlin.

Yours,
Robert Benchley

11

S. I. deKrafft: "Yes, We Have No Bananas" in Grand Opera Setting

Grand opera has never been accused of being mirth provoking and it needed an Irving Berlin to take some of the greatest music ever written and use it for a musical setting for the national banana anthem. It is a scream and is unquestionably the musical hit of the Second Annual *Music Box Revue*.

Six famous characters of Grand Opera stalk out on the stage to the strains of the triumphant [*sic*] march from *Aida* and start to sing, "Yes, we have no—." The audiences scream with laughter, Charlotte Greenwood is gowned as Good Queen Bess, crown. scepter, collar, ruff and all the rest; next to her is Sam Ash in the garb of Romeo; while petite Helen Rich, is a fair Marguerite. In the armour of Siegfried, William Gaxton is a striking figure, setting off the stately blonde beauty of Leila Ricard, as Tosca, with the inimitable Bobby Clark in a *Trovatore* make-up.

The music changes, amid shouts of laughter, to the stately quartet from *Rigoletto*, followed by the famous sextette from *Lucia*; by the time the waltz from *La Bohème* is reached the auditors are struggling for air. Mind you, all of these selections are jazzed, to the intense delight of everybody. Nobody but Irving Berlin would take such liberties with Grand Opera. It is delicious!

The prize moment of the affair is when the Barcarole from *Tales of Hoffman* is reached, which is followed by a hit from *Tannhausser.*[1] The final gasp is the "Miserere" from *II Trovatore*, to wind up with the air of the terrible song.

One does not have to understand music to appreciate this gem of satire. While many of the audiences may not know the various operas from which the hits are taken—this is written in answer to numerous requests for information—the infectious laughter is there and the appreciation of the brains which conceived the burlesque.

SOURCE Irving Berlin scrapbooks at the Library of Congress.
  1. Not only is *Tannhäuser* misspelled, but the opera used by Berlin is another one, *Lohengrin*.

Part II

Blue Skies
Middle Years

12

George S. Kaufman: Memoir

George S. Kaufman (1889–1961) worked with Berlin on *The Cocoanuts* and *Face the Music*. He was a playwright, author, wit, director, and sometime actor famous for his collaborations with playwright Moss Hart. The story of his reaction to "Always" is one of the most repeated of show biz tales. Kaufman wrote up the story more than once; this version also has a witty look at the poetic license of lyricists, using a classic Berlin lyric to make his point.

A good many years ago, Irving Berlin and I went to Atlantic City together to work on a musical show for the Marx Brothers—all seventeen of them. We had adjoining rooms at the hotel, and along about the second week Irving woke me up at five o'clock one morning to sing me a song he had just finished. Now, Irving has a pure but hardly a strong voice, and, since I am not very strong myself at five o'clock in the morning, I could not catch a word of it. Moving to the edge of the bed, he sat down and sang it again, and again I failed to get it. Just when it looked as though he would have to get into my bed before I could hear it, he managed, on the third try, to put it across. The song was the little number called "Always," and its easygoing rhythms were just up my street. I learned it quickly, and as dawn broke we leaned out of the window and sang it to the Atlantic Ocean—its first performance in any hotel. It was destined to be sung millions of times after that, and invariably better.

That task done, we then talked about it. At the time, I was woefully ignorant of music, and by dint of hard work over the years I have managed to keep myself in the same innocent state. To this day, I do not quite know the difference between Handel's "Largo" and—well, Largo's "Handel." But I have always felt that I knew a little something about lyrics, and I was presumptuous enough then to question Irving's first line, "I'll be loving you, always." "Always," I pointed out, was a long time for romance. There were almost daily stories to

---

SOURCE *The New Yorker*, June 11, 1960. Reprinted by permission of Anne Kaufman.

that effect in the newspapers—stories about middle-aged husbands who had bricked their wives up in the cellar wall and left for Toledo with the maid. I suggested, therefore, that the opening line be just a little more in accord with reality—something like "I'll be loving you Thursday." But Irving would have none of it. He was, he said, an incurable romanticist—as opposed to my being an obviously curable romanticist. So he went his own way and celebrated the permanent nature of love, and the history of the song business will show that he was darned right.

My interest in lyrics, mistaken though it was in that instance and discouraged though it was by Irving, did not lag. Not long before turning out "Always," Irving had written the song bearing the somewhat implausible title of "When the Midnight Choo-Choo Leaves for Alabam.'" Like "Always," it swept the country. Irving's lyric glorified the enchanted moment when that choo-choo pulled out of the station for Alabam.' With a view to checking up on the facts of the situation, so that I'd be able to make suggestions to Irving about the realism of this lyric, I turned up in Pennsylvania Station at a quarter to twelve one night for that wonderful and glorious departure.

The first thing I found out was that there *was* no midnight choo-choo for Albam'; the choo-choo for Albam' left at twelve-nineteen. Well, I was not too worried about that. Clearly, Irving could not have written a song entitled "When the Twelve-nineteen A.M. Choo-Choo Leaves for Alabam.'" Next I discovered that the platform was crowded with songwriters, slapping each other on the back and uttering shrill cries in praise of Alabam,' "Where the rhyming is easy." Between times, they were bidding tearful farewells to their dear old mothers, who had moved up from Alabam' twenty-five years before and were living contentedly on West Seventy-second Street. Some of the poorer songwriters, who had not yet had a big hit, were sad to behold. Getting a piano into an upper berth is, at best, a difficult job. But I did learn one thing about it— always get the stool up first, so you'll have someplace to sit while you're waiting for the piano to get there. The moment of departure was noisy and gay. The happy songwriters, jauntily singing their songs, could be observed at every window as the train pulled out. The mothers went happily back to Seventy-second Street. I gave a lusty cheer myself, and was delighted to have witnessed the whole happy scene.

I learned afterward that the songwriters all got off at Newark, took the Hudson Tube back to Manhattan, and were safely in Lindy's by one-thirty. I never told Irving about that, but ever since then I have not quite believed everything I heard in a song lyric.

| 13 |

Letter from Jerome Kern to Alexander Woollcott, from *The Story of Irving Berlin*

Alexander Woollcott, in his Berlin biography, is responsible for soliciting Jerome Kern (1885–1945) for his opinion on Berlin, which resulted in the famous quote, "Irving Berlin has *no* place in American music. He *is* American music." Woollcott wrote a short letter to Kern requesting comments for the biography and received a substantial reply. Kern was the logical choice for this task as he was really Berlin's only elder among the songwriters who came to prominence in the early decades of the twentieth century. Kern was an early innovator of the Broadway musical through his famous "Princess Theatre shows" (not all of which were housed at the Princess) which had more substantial books, often by Guy Bolton, than were common at the time, and were created with the intimate space of the Princess Theatre in mind. Lyricist P. G. Wodehouse rounded out the triumvirate of Princess Theatre writers known familiarly as "Bolton, Wodehouse, and Kern." After the Princess Theatre shows, Kern went on to write the ambitious and seminal *Show Boat* in 1927, with book and lyrics by Oscar Hammerstein II.

The famous quote comes at the end of the letter; the entire letter is largely forgotten now and is reprinted here in full.

I once delivered myself of a nifty. It was at a dinner in London, and I was asked what, in my opinion, were the chief characteristics of the American nation. I replied that the average United States citizen was perfectly epitomized in Irving Berlin's music. I remember I got this off quite glibly, just as if I had thought of it on the spur of the moment. Of course, I enlarged upon the notion and went on to explain that both the typical Yankee and the Berlin tune had humor, originality, pace and popularity; both were wide-awake, and both sometimes a little loud—but what might unsympathetically be mistaken for brass, was really gold.

Published 1925 by G.P. Putnam's Sons. Copyright 1925 by Alexander Woollcott.

Since then, columns have been written about Berlin and his music. Learned expressions like "genre," "con alcune licenza," "melodic architecture," "rhythmic pulsations," etc., etc., have been hurled at the head of modest, shy, little Irving, to his utter bewilderment.

He has been called (by myself) a modern disciple of Aristoxenos, who, as you undoubtedly do *not* know, attacked the Pythagorean theory by asserting that the ear was the only authority in determining consonance and dissonance. I must explain that my Grecian dip was in answer to some highly unsuccessful musician, who was bold and foolish enough to criticize, mathematically, and harmonically, a little treasure of Berlin's—"A Pretty Girl Is Like a Melody."

And all the time this highfalutin' bombardment has been going on, Berlin has entrenched himself in a shell-proof, impregnable position as commander-in-chief of all the purveyors of American light music.

Something snappy should be interpolated at this point to the effect that there is but one legitimate aspirant to the heights occupied by Irving Berlin, the maker of music (if, by a metaphorical stretch, a bomb-proof dug-out can be called a height), and that aspirant is Irving Berlin, the maker of verses.

A critical appraisal of his technical ability as lyrist [*sic*], must be left to my literary superiors, but I, here and now, bend the knee in recognition of Berlin's genius in providing himself with his own lyrical inspiration for melodic invention. For, almost invariably, it is *after* his word-phrases and rhymes occur to him, not before, that he tackles his music. Then ensues real composition in the fullest sense of that much abused word; and Berlin has certainly mastered the art of making an integral whole by uniting two different elements. Not, mind you, by aimlessly fingering the keyboard of a pianoforte until something agreeable is, perchance, struck, but by the same means that Richard Wagner employed in fashioning his dual masterpieces of text and music.

Berlin (like Wagner, an inexorable autocritic) molds and blends and ornaments his words and music at one and the same time, each being the outgrowth of the other.[1] He trims and changes and refashions both, many times and oft, but nearly always, strives for simplicity—never elaboration. He is not bothering much with the seats of the Olympians, but he *is* concerned with the lore, the hearts, yes—and the dancing feet of human folk.

The comparison between the craft of Wagner and Berlin is not a heedless one, and in anticipation of indignant protests, I now go further and say that, to my mind, there are phrases in Berlin's music as noble and mighty as any clause in the works of the Masters, from Beethoven and Wagner down.

---

1. Wagner, in fact, did not write words and music together. He wrote the "poem" (as he called it) first, then set it to music.

When you remember how the latter used to sit in a darkened room, for hours at a time, waiting for a fragment of melody, sometimes of only two or three notes, to come to him, you will agree with my notion that even Wagner would have considered the heroic first three measures in the burthen of "That Mysterious Rag" heaven-sent material. My openly expressed enthusiasm for these five or six notes has amused no one more than Berlin himself. He thinks the theme is pretty good, but any suggestion that it possesses a sheer musical magnificence makes him laugh himself to death.[2]

Much is to be said about his amazing ability in the use and manipulation of rhythms. Abler men than I in that interesting field are better equipped to speak authoritatively, but I certainly object to the absurd implication that Irving Berlin is an explorer, discoverer, or pioneer in what is still childishly called "ragtime."

He doesn't attempt to stuff the public's ear with pseudo-original, ultra modernism, but he honestly absorbs the vibrations emanating from the people, manners, and life of his time, and in turn, gives these impressions back to the world—simplified—clarified—glorified.

In short, what I really want to say, my dear Woollcott, is that Irving Berlin has *no* place in American music. HE *IS* AMERICAN MUSIC; but it will be by his verse and his lovely melodies that he will live and not in his diabolically clever trick accents.

I hope to goodness he never asks me what the Pythagorean theory is, because I don't know much about it myself.

~~~~~~

| 14 |

Richard Rodgers: Excerpt from *Musical Stages*

The opening night of Rodgers & Hart's *Betsy*, with the interpolation of Berlin's "Blue Skies," has become a theatrical legend that has taken on a life of its own, with Richard Rodgers being one of the purveyors of the legend. It has appeared

---

Copyright by Richard Rodgers 1975. Published by Random House, 1975. Excerpt reprinted by permission of the Rodgers & Hammerstein Organization: an Imagem Company. All Rights reserved.

2. The published music says only "by Berlin and Snyder" with no indication of the division of labor. Ted Snyder usually wrote only the music, but there is no reason to think he and Berlin did not collaborate on both words and music. The basic thrust of this paragraph is not lessened, in any case.

in many books, in slightly different versions, but it seems fair to use Rodgers's
version here. His frustration with Ziegfeld was shared by many on Broadway.
Betsy opened in New York on December 28, 1926.

A fitting climax to this whole sorry episode [with producer Florenz Ziegfeld]
came opening night in New York. Almost at the last minute, without saying
a word to anyone, Ziegfeld bought a song from Irving Berlin and gave it to
Belle Baker to sing in the show. Not only did the interpolated number get the
biggest hand of the evening at the premiere, but Ziegfeld also had arranged
to have a spotlight pick out Berlin, seated in the front row, who rose and took
a bow.

My mother, whom I took to the opening with me, was too unsophisticated
to understand what Ziegfeld's slippery piece of showmanship meant to me,
but Dorothy [Rodgers's wife], who was there with a friend, was outraged.

It really didn't take a trained ear to appreciate that the Berlin contribution,
"Blue Skies," was a great piece of songwriting, easily superior to anything
Larry and I had written for the production, but at the time I was crushed by
having someone else's work interpolated in our score—particularly since
Ziegfeld had insisted he wouldn't think of doing the show with anyone else.
A few words in advance might have eased our wounded pride, but Ziegfeld
could never be accused of having the human touch at, least not where men
were concerned.[1] He did show consideration for girls, but even there his over-
riding ego, or insecurity, would occasionally take over. I recall one night at a
Betsy rehearsal when, for some minor infraction, he turned on Madeleine
Cameron, a featured member of the cast, and blasted her to bits in front of the
entire company. Even her hysterical tears failed to stop him. No, Ziegfeld was
not a nice man.

---

1. The *Theatrical Notes* section of the *New York Times* on December 23, 1926, had the
   following sentence: "Irving Berlin has written a song for *Betsy* which comes to the
   New Amsterdam next week." This does suggest that the new song was not quite the
   surprise Rodgers made it out to be. Perhaps neither Rodgers nor Hart was reading
   the papers in their rush to get the show to New York. While Rodgers remained
   disenchanted with Ziegfeld, his friendship with Berlin was not damaged by this
   incident.

Richard Barrios: Excerpt from Chapter "The March of Time" in *A Song in the Dark*

The making of the film *Reaching for the Moon* (1931) was one of the unhappiest episodes in Berlin's career. As film historian Richard Barrios notes, in later years the mere mention of the title infuriated Berlin. The episode is a classic example of Hollywood's approach to creating musical films—the songwriter had little, if any, control over matters, a fact of life that distressed Rodgers & Hart in particular along with other Broadway songwriters. It is little wonder that afterwards Berlin insisted on greater control over his films, what songs would be included, and even having his name appear *before* the film's title.

In contrast to his Hollywood disappointments, Berlin on Broadway at this time was a huge success with *Face the Music* (1932) and *As Thousands Cheer* in 1933 (considered one of the two best revues in Broadway history, the other being the George S. Kaufman, Howard Dietz and Arthur Schwartz 1931 show *The Band Wagon*).

[Joseph] Schenck,[1] it must be observed, was never averse to pursuing big names. His Broadway prospects not particularly bright at the moment, Irving Berlin was more eager than ever to follow the comparatively disappointing *Puttin' on the Ritz* with a movie triumph. While Berlin's script ideas for *Ritz* had gone unused, he was able to sell Schenck and UA [United Artists] on a package that included his own story, eight songs and his services as supervisor. Harry Richman had overshadowed his first try, and this time Berlin was determined to do it himself. His none-too-original story detailed the stormy romance, in New York and aboard a transatlantic cruise, of a Wall

Copyright by Richard Barrios, 1995. Published by Oxford University Press, 1995. Reprinted by permission of Oxford University Press.

1. Producer Joseph M. Schenck (1876–1961) was a major figure at United Artists, then later at 20th Century and 20th Century Fox. He was also Irving Berlin's closest and oldest friend, dating from the Pelham Café days, and godfather to his oldest daughter.

Street bigwig and a famous aviatrix; love wins out even as he's wiped out by the Crash. With its essentially dizzy Jazz Age story tempered by somber post–Black Friday touches, this tale required no carbon tests to date it as early- to mid-1930. Berlin titled it *Lucky Break*,[2] then *Reaching for the Moon*, and for the aviatrix he signed one of Hollywood's most prominent musical women, Bebe Daniels. Both Lawrence Gray and Broadway's Jack Whiting were mentioned for the male lead, and after Ruby Keeler was ruled out, the second female lead went to Paramount's Ginger Rogers. Although Busby Berkeley was announced to stage the dances, the job soon passed into the less sparkling hands of Maurice (*The Great Gabbo*) Kusell. Then, in June 1930, the tone of the project was altered decisively when Douglas Fairbanks, one of the founding fathers of United Artists, stepped into the role of the Wall Street man. The screen's most popular swashbuckler was then heading toward his fifties and obviously in search of a change in direction; this was his first modern-dress role in a decade. He had no vocal talent whatsoever, which meant reconfiguring some of the musical chores, and suddenly *Reaching for the Moon* was subtly changing from a Berlin show to a Fairbanks romp. Berlin, while recognizing the financial soundness of this casting, was not particularly pleased—and became less so with the work of writer-director Edmund Goulding, with whom he felt no rapport.

By the time *Reaching for the Moon* went before the cameras in September 1930, the budget had escalated to $1.1 million, including high fees for Fairbanks, Berlin, UA overhead, and some enormous Moderne sets by William Cameron Menzies. No Ginger Rogers, however—she had departed for New York, and her role went to June MacCloy. Despite ongoing audience aversion, the film was shot and initially previewed as a musical, with six Berlin songs, mostly for Daniels and the belter MacCloy, and one reportedly sung by Fairbanks. Then Schenck had second thoughts; few musicals had drawn more than flies over the past few months, and the odd combination of Fairbanks-Daniels-Berlin seemed unlikely to revive the glory days of *Rio Rita*. So all but one song was cut—not even Berlin's attractive title song was spared—and *Reaching for the Moon* became a straight romantic comedy. The sole musical survivor was the indifferent "When the Folks High-Up Do the Mean Low-Down," sung by Daniels, MacCloy, Bing Crosby, and shipboard chorus; despite the vaunted Berlin touch, it sounded like nothing more than a discard from the latest Alice White picture. The deletions only heightened the story's disjointedness and changes in tone—here a giddy romp, there a serious romance, there an opportunity for Fairbanks to show that he was still in physical trim. Despite a critical response that was equally uneven, *Reaching for the Moon*,

---

2. *Love in a Cottage* was also a working title.

Douglas Fairbanks and Bebe Daniels in a publicity still from the ill-fated *Reaching for the Moon*.
Photo credit: *Photofest*

though it could not possibly recoup its ruinously high cost, was not as drastic a money-loser as *Madam Satan* or *New Moon*. The public still liked Fairbanks—although, as with fellow UA stars Mary Pickford and Gloria Swanson, he was hastening the passing of his vogue by losing touch with the tastes of a still-loyal audience. Beyond that, and with its production problems well known within the industry, *Reaching for the Moon* soon became a symbol of what had happened to musicals. For Berlin, it remained one of the most unpleasant and ignominious experiences in a very long life, and in later years he would become incensed at the very mention of the title.

| 16 |

Howard Pollack: Unity of Word and Tone in
Two Ballads by Irving Berlin

Howard Pollack, professor of music at the University of Houston, has written extensively on music of Berlin's era, including a major biography of George Gershwin. He graciously provided this piece for inclusion here. In it he examines "Say It Isn't So" and "How Deep Is the Ocean," combining the best qualities of analyses by Alec Wilder and Allan Forte, and providing new insights into Berlin's songwriting process.

He collected lots of corny little phrases,
Like "I love you dear," and "You're for me."
But he found that when he set them all to music,
They were just as good as poetry. —Irving Berlin, "Once Upon a Time Today,"
Call Me Madam

"Say It Isn't So" and "How Deep Is the Ocean (How High Is the Sky)," Irving Berlin's two big hits of 1932, offer good case studies of the composer-lyricist's abilities as a songwriter, pure and simple. He wrote them as individual numbers, not as part of any film score or stage work. They also complement each other nicely: "Say It Isn't So," largely in the form of commands, requests a confirmation of love; "How Deep Is the Ocean," almost entirely in the form of questions, provides it.

Furthermore, these two songs became standards of the popular and jazz repertory (neither, incidentally, is gender-specific: Rudy Vallee and Constance Binney, among others, recorded "Say It Isn't So" soon after its composition, while Ethel Merman and Bing Crosby recorded "How Deep Is the Ocean" in the fall of 1932 within weeks of each other) and achieved in time

Used by permission of the author.

significant critical stature as well (Allen Forte selected both for study in his book *American Popular Ballad of the Golden Era*), though the composer brought them forth only at the urging of friends, an indication of how self-critical he could be. "I wrote them during a period of my career when I felt I was all through," he explained in 1945. "It was right after I had lost almost everything I had in the market, along with everybody else, and I had gotten rusty as a songwriter. . . . I developed an inferiority complex." Such vulnerability perhaps explains the special poignance and intimacy of these two songs, even if Berlin admitted to writing a lyric "that expressed a personal emotion" in only four songs: "When I Lost You," "Always," "Count Your Blessings," and "God Bless America."[1]

That both songs eventually appeared in two rather significantly different versions complicates analysis, however. In their original versions, published in 1932 by Irving Berlin Music, Inc., they both featured eight-bar introductions (derived from the last phrase of the chorus), repeated two-bar vamps (that anticipate the first half of the verse's first phrase), and sixteen-measure verses, followed by thirty-two measure choruses with two endings. By the 1940s, however, Berlin Music was publishing these songs without their verses and vamps, and with their introductions shortened to four measures, with the introduction to "How Deep Is the Ocean" still derived from the end of its chorus, but the introduction to "Say It Isn't So" newly conceived. The publishers lowered their keys as well, from F Major to E-flat Major for "How Deep Is the Ocean" and from B-flat Major to G Major for "Say It Isn't So." These revised editions featured other changes, notably a thinning and refinement of textures; new, smoother links at the ends of phrases in "Say It Isn't So"; and the removal of hyphens (in the phrases, "deep-is-the" and "high-is-the") from the title of "How Deep Is the Ocean (How High Is the Sky)."

How much Berlin had to do with these revisions, much as to what extent he penned the originals, remains open to speculation. The original publication of "How Deep Is the Ocean" (but not "Say It Isn't So") credits Berlin's long-time secretary, Helmy Kresa, with the "piano and ukulele arrangement." Berlin may well have left the ukulele arrangement (advertised as usable for guitarists and banjoists as well) to others, but the evidence concerning his working method suggests that Kresa at most touched up the composer's piano

---

1. "Oh, How I Hate to Get Up in the Morning" is also in this category. See Part IV.

accompaniment.[2] As for the later revised versions, Berlin might well have initiated the changes, but presumably at the least approved them.

The composer's daughter Mary Ellin Barrett claims that Berlin's omission of verses in certain later reissues of songs "was purely an artistic decision," but Michael Feinstein suspects that the composer did so to "save money." Characteristically Berlin would have considered both sides of the matter. But the absence of the verses in these two songs arguably represents an impoverishment, and the discussion below considers them as viable parts of the whole, while the analyses of the choruses apply equally to the original and later versions.

"SAY IT ISN'T SO"

"Say It Isn't So" forms a little melodrama, giving rise at times to almost tearful passion. In a verse consisting of two couplets, the lover relates that he has heard that his beloved has been "untrue," and although he knows such gossip to be "mistaken," it fills his "heart with fear" and he wants reassurances from the loved one. (For convenience, I will refer to the gender of the protagonists of both songs under review as that of the composer.) The most arresting aspect of the verse is the move to the major mediant for the lover's not entirely confident assertion, "I know that they're mistaken;/Still, I want to hear it from you." Indeed, for all its surface breeziness, the verse conveys some underlying tension, a dichotomy that helps contextualize and frame the chorus.

In the 32-bar AA' chorus, the lover states that he has heard from "everyone" that his beloved does not love him (first phrase); that his beloved's grown tired of him (second phrase); and that his beloved's found somebody new and will soon leave him (third phrase), at which point he asks for the simple assurance that "ev'rything is still okay" (fourth phrase). The chorus thus forms a phrase-by-phrase narrative that moves from the rumor of a new lover and an imminent break-up toward a climactic plea for reassurance. This cumulative structure naturally offsets and enlivens the formality of its binary structure.

---

2. Author footnote: Laurence Bergreen's biography includes a reminiscence of the composer and arranger Johnny Green that throws some light on this matter. As musical director of the film *Easter Parade,* Green transcribed some of Berlin's songs and recalled suggesting, at one spot in a song, a first-, rather than a second-inversion harmony, a relatively subtle refinement. After listening to the harmony both ways a number of times, Berlin told Green, "Leave it the way I wrote it." Green concluded, "Whether it's a word of lyric, a line of melody, a line of countermelody, a harmonic progression, it was written by Irving Berlin." This testimony, made public in 1990, confirmed Alec Wilder's intuitive comment, "So, though it is known that he has for years paid a professional musician to harmonize his songs under his close supervision, it is very nearly impossible, upon hearing some of these melodies, to believe that every chord was not an integral part of the creation of the tune."

The chorus's lyric epitomizes the kind of conversational ease long the hall-mark of Berlin's lyric writing, including slang ("okay") as well as contractions and colloquialisms ("And what they're saying,/Say it isn't so"). In the tradition of such songs as "Always" and "What'll I Do?," this also involves a considerable amount of repetition, with the alliterative "Say it isn't so" uttered, within a very short span, five times, the word "say" appearing an additional two times, and "saying," yet another two times. As a whole, the lyric characterizes Berlin's rule for good lyric writing: "Easy to sing, easy to say, easy to remember and applicable to everyday events."

Each of the chorus's four phrases comprises a couplet, with the first line of each of the first three phrases featuring an internal rhyme as well. The rhymes are so plain as to be practically unnoticeable. In the first phrase, "so" rhymes with itself two times. The second phrase employs the similarly understated rhyme of "go," "know," and "so"—the kinds of simple rhymes Berlin long favored—and more subtly, "growing tired of me," which rhymes with the simi-larly positioned "saying you don't love me" from the first phrase. The third phrase, with its "you," "new," and "true" rhymes, introduces new but still open vowel sounds, while the phrase "be long before you leave me" offers both a reverse rhyme ("be long before") and a pararhyme ("leave me") of the "love me"/"of me" rhyme heard earlier. The final phrase returns to the "know/so" rhyme, exactly as found in the second phrase, here anticipated by the first syl-lable of "okay," whose second syllable resonates with all the many uses of "say." Meanwhile, as with the reappearances of "say" and "saying," the fourth phrase's use of "ev'rything" recalls the "ev'ryone" and "ev'rywhere" found in the first two phrases. All these inner rhymes, near rhymes, and cross-references create no obvious or conventional scheme; on the contrary, they are highly concealed, evoking the kind of artless spontaneity associated with Berlin's work.

Berlin typically began work on a song with either a phrase or title, a musical idea, or some combination of the two, and then worked on both text and music in a kind of give-and-take ("Writing both words and music I can compose them together and make them fit," he once explained). In this case, it is hard to imagine that the main musical idea of "Say It Isn't So" occurred prior to or independently of the words. Five repeated notes, in a simple dotted-note con-figuration leading to a sustained note at the end, seem a fairly inauspicious musical idea for a popular air, were it not for its perfect wedding to the text, and the inspired notion of starting this motive on the sixth scale degree sup-ported by a tonic harmony in root position (or a submediant harmony in the first inversion: some ambiguity exists until the dominant note enters in the second half of the first measure). Indeed, the gesture perfectly reflects both the inflection and the meaning of the phrase, "Say it isn't so."

Berlin has only to reiterate the idea on the lower sixth degree as part of an augmented tonic triad (m. 3), the fifth degree as part of a simple tonic triad (m. 5), and essentially the third in a V/V harmony (m. 9) to provide increasing tension, as well as to create a descending chromatic line that helps impart a sense of pathos. The restrained, downward motion at the same time encloses, as the rhythm broadens, a dramatic ascent by thirds for the first outburst, "Ev'ryone is saying you don't love me," further dramatized by a break in the harmonic rhythm and a move to the mediant, in turn followed by a tremulous leap of a seventh downwards on V/V, causing further suspense.

Like the first phrase, the second phrase comprises four two-bar groups that can be described as *aaba*, but the melodic shape is loosely inverted, with the halting main idea rising and the dramatic revelation now falling. This melodic inversion mirrors the narrative, as the rise of the melody, placed in a higher tessitura, for "Ev'rywhere I go,/ Ev'ryone I know" suggests both the singer's venturing out among places and people, and his growing anxiety as he finds himself unable to escape the hurtful rumors, while the limp descent for "growing tired of me," including the sighing figure for "tired," neatly colors those words. At the return of "Say it isn't so," the melody falls further, reaching, in fact, its nadir.

The third phrase, retaining the *aaba* structure, is a near-exact duplication of the first phrase, except that the final two-bar group (prepared somewhat differently, with a tonic chord as opposed to the mediant) falls an interval of a second against V/IV, a gesture that recalls the appoggiatura on "tired" from the previous phrase, except that the melody more climactically remains suspended on a non-chord tone, aptly accompanying the phrase "Say it isn't true," itself a lyric variation of the earlier "Say it isn't so." Allen Forte finds this development suggestive of "a change in the lover's rhetoric," perhaps indicative of a "more hopeful prospect," as he argues, or, as might be proposed, correspondingly more urgent, two interpretations not mutually exclusive. In any case, this alteration is needed structurally to push the song toward its harmonic resolution, as opposed to setting the stage for the tensions of the second phrase.

A more subtle variation between the first and third phrases concerns the design of the accompanying lyric. In the opening phrase, each of the four units corresponds to a separate line of text, while in the second and third phrases, the first three units, *aab*, comprise one long sentence, articulated at the end by "Say it isn't so" and "Say it isn't true," respectively. Accordingly, these longer lines need to accommodate two rather lengthy sustained notes that continue both the narrative and that rhyme, and Berlin's solutions neatly reveal his mastery: "Ev'rywhere I go, / Ev'ryone I know / Whispers that you're growing tired of me" and "People say that you / Found somebody new / And it won't be long before you leave me."

This growth from the halting utterances of the first phrase to the more elaborate syntax of the second and third phrases culminates in the final phrase, one long statement in two larger units that might be described as *ab*: "Say that ev'rything is still okay, / That's all I want to know, / And what they're saying, / Say it isn't so." Berlin manages to incorporate, nonetheless, the principal motive three times in the course of the phrase: once at the start ("Say that ev'rything"), once at the end of the second phrase with a descending fourth at its end ("all I want to know"), and finally, for the first time, as a pickup that falls, also for the first time, the interval of a third to land on the tonic note on the downbeat.

In the meantime, the chromatically descending idea, previously heard in the opening measures of each phrase, now occurs in both middle and bass voices in the accompaniment ("a type of motivic embellishment," notes Forte, "that we often encounter in the most elegantly realized ballads of the Golden Era") as well as at the start of the phrase's *b* unit ("and what they're"). This fourth phrase also extends that sighing motive with which the third phrase ends ("Say it isn't true"), taking it upwards to the high point of the song, "Say that ev'rything is still okay," with its climactic appoggiatura on "still." This phrase sounds all the more climactic because of its use of a deceptive cadence and the song's only diminished harmonies, both of which effectively prepare the cadential progression that brings the song to an end.

The accompaniment, with its rich extended harmonies and its solid voice-leading, belies the idea of Berlin as a kind of primitive. The introduction to the later version, which superimposes the principal dotted-rhythm idea with the chromatic descent, is especially smart. In both versions, the accompaniment to the chorus's first three phrases features sighing gestures connected by slurred grace-notes that sometimes comprise whole-tone pitch configurations and that provide an instrumental commentary to the singer's melody. Whether or not these gestures reflect the influence of the kinds of call-and-response patterns associated with jazz and the blues, they clearly suited such traditions, as evidenced by the play between singer and trumpet in Billie Holiday's 1957 recording of the song.

"HOW DEEP IS THE OCEAN (HOW HIGH IS THE SKY)"

Although also a romantic ballad, "How Deep Is the Ocean (How High Is the Sky)" is more straightforward and generally less plaintive than "Say It Isn't So." Singers take "How Deep Is the Ocean" at both slow and up tempos (Billie Holiday does both in her 1954 recording of the song), whereas a fast tempo would clearly distort the meaning of "Say It Isn't So."

In some ways "How Deep Is the Ocean" is also more direct in its poetic structure and rhyme scheme. The entire song comprises a series of couplets: two for the verse and one for every eight measures of the 32-bar chorus. The chorus resembles "Say It Isn't So" in its binary form, but the four phrases form a more symmetrical *ABAB* design, as opposed to the sort of *AAAB* design found in "Say It Isn't So" (although in both cases, the final *B* phrase incorporates, as a final gesture, aspects of *A*). Within these four phrases one finds, in contrast to the halting motives of "Say It Isn't So," a more fluid melodic line. All these differences intimate that the conventional 32-bar form of the early twentieth-century popular song could, like the formal constraints of the sonnet, accommodate considerable diversity and experimentation; they also recall Alec Wilder's wondering comment, "Is Berlin's writing experience one of such enormous intensity that the song being written is totally isolated in his mind, to the exclusion of every other song he has written, resulting in a unique form and style for each one?"

"How Deep Is the Ocean" has many points of interest. Except for one key phrase, "I'll tell you no lie," its lyric, both verse and chorus, consists entirely of questions. The opening verse asks how the lover can "measure" "what is in my heart" and "how much I love you." Berlin maintains this focus throughout the chorus, finding in nature imagery—the ocean, the sky, roses, a star—metaphorical ways to take love's measurement. This emphasis on measurement conveys a certain childlike innocence as well as suggesting, perhaps, a connection to modern industrial life, with its predilection for the quantitative.

Berlin alternately frames his answers in terms of space and time. In the first and third phrases, the lover compares his love to the depth of the ocean and the height of the sky, on the one hand, and to the distance "from here to a star," on the other; while in the second phrase, the singer thinks of the beloved as "many times a day" as there are roses "sprinkled with dew," and in the fourth phrase, on asking "And if I ever lost you, How much would I cry?," returns to the ocean and sky imagery, here suggesting the length of grief at the prospect of loss. The ocean and sky imagery resonates throughout the poem, the former connected to "dew" and "cry," the latter related to "the journey, From here to a star." Although the lyric strikes one as casual and unassuming, the tightness of Berlin's argument resembles an anagram.

The self-sufficiency of the chorus—it begins with a concise recapitulation of the question raised in the verse—makes the verse somewhat superfluous, helping to explain why it quickly disappeared from both printed and recorded versions of the song. However, the verse has an important melopoetic function nonetheless, beginning, as in "Say It Isn't So," playfully in the tonic major, but growing more ardent with the move to the mediant and the mention of "love" in the third phrase; and that much more so with the final line, "How can I measure just how much I do?," and the surprisingly doleful modulation to the submediant, in which key the chorus begins. With its regular downbeats, the verse also provides a foil to the many downbeat rests in the chorus. As with "Say It Isn't So," the accepted practice of omitting the song's verse might heighten the song's gravity, but a compelling case could be made for the retention of the verses of both songs as effectively preparing the deeper, more expressive world of the choruses.

Starting the chorus in the relative minor key, with or without the context provided by the verse, creates a certain kind of modal ambiguity associated with Berlin and one that in its own way informs the very start of the chorus to "Say It Isn't So," as suggested above. Discussing this effect in "Blue Skies," Laurence Bergreen notes that its minor-mode opening "imparted poignancy and fragility to the mood of happiness," and the same could be said of "How Deep Is the Ocean," a bittersweet quality intensified in both songs by a chromatically descending bass line long associated with lament (while in "Say It Isn't So," a similar gesture informs not only the bass line at the song's very end, but the principal tune itself).[3]

The minor mode colors this song even more than "Blue Skies." The first phrase moves from the submediant to the mediant. No sooner does the composer arrive in the tonic major in the second phrase than he creates a new kind of modal ambiguity—that between parallel major and minor—by introducing flatted seconds, thirds, and sevenths that point ahead to a half-cadence in the tonic minor. The third phrase returns to the submediant and the mediant, while the last phrase moves via a half-diminished seventh chord (the Tristan chord, which prompted Allen Forte to ask, "Did Irving listen to Richard? How deep is tradition?") to a clear cadence in the tonic major, neatly providing a new resonance and resolution to the opening lyric, reiterated here.[4] Only in the second half of this last phrase does a clear cadential pattern in the tonic major appear, thereby offering a resolution to the "poignancy and fragility" that infuse this haunting song.

As in "Say It Isn't So," the musical and poetic ideas form an indissoluble whole. Again, the principal musical idea, an expansive one with triplets, surely derives from the natural rhythm of the phrase "How much do I love you?," with the melodic leap up of a third and the move to an unsettled augmented chord matching the raised inflection of the question. The rhetorical response,

---

3. Author footnote: Forte argues that this descending line "is the pictorial representation of the lyric's forthcoming question: 'How deep is the ocean,'" but this would hardly explain its occurrence in "Blue Skies" and numerous other songs.

4. Author footnote: Forte illuminatingly notes that the Tristan chord occurs at some other crucial junctures at the end of four-bar phrases, namely, accompanying the words, "lie," "sky," "are," and "star," so that this appearance at "cry" "represents the terminal intensification" of this "putative Tristan chord."

Editor's note: Berlin did know Wagner and, as shown in earlier articles, did quote him.

which roughly transposes the phrase up a third, dramatically reaches (for the first time in the chorus) the dominant on the word "sky," causing Forte to observe, "One senses a contrast between the short tentative interrogatory rhetoric of the lyric of the first period (C minor) and the more assertive and longer interrogatives of the second period (E-flat major). The lover *qua* singer is definitely trying to make a point." The dominant harmony's unresolved ninth makes this gesture seem all the more skyward.

The second phrase, in contrast, constitutes one long descending sigh, reflecting the "many times a day" the lover thinks of his beloved, its whimsy depicted by its syncopations and downward leaps, its intensity sustained by the string of four dominant seventh chords and a turn toward the tonic minor. For the third phrase, which musically is exactly the same as the first, Berlin puts forth an equally apt lyric, with the arrival of the dominant and the extended high note on the word "star" rather than "sky." As with "Say It Isn't So," the song climaxes at the start of the fourth phrase, with a similar appoggiatura on the downbeat of the phrase's second measure, although the interval falls not by a major second, but by a more pained minor second, and the harmonic context—the move to V/ii—carries greater fervor than found in the corresponding measures of "Say It Isn't So," as appropriate as the singer's shuddering recognition of eventual loss and separation, and as illustrative of the difference between the former's "And if I ever lost you" and the latter's "Say that ev'rything is still okay."

Berlin uses similar cadential formulae in the final phrases of both songs, including the move from the supertonic and a half-diminished seventh chord to a tonic 6/4 chord, but he does so at different points in the phrase, as dictated not only by the structure of the melody, but by the poetic intent and rhetoric of the lyric, although the half-diminished chord arrives at a similarly climactic point: at the words "still okay" and "cry," respectively.

CONCLUSION

Although "How Deep Is the Ocean" resembles "Say It Isn't So" in its formal control of harmony and voice-leading, the latter song features a more articulated shape: a rather classical antecedent-consequent structure for the first two phrases (I to V/V, V to I), followed by a similarly balanced two-phrase structure to round things off (I to V/IV, ii to I). In contrast, "How Deep Is the Ocean" forms a longer line because ends of phrases tend to be both melodically and harmonically unstable; consider the sustained note on the dominant ninth that concludes the first and third phrases, and the move from V to V/vi that accompanies the word "dew" at the juncture between the second and third phrases. How these large-scale structures serve Berlin's poetic idea is open to interpretation, but it would seem that the symmetrical articulation of "Say It

Isn't So" provides some restraint and poise to its requests for emotional reassurance, whereas the more unstable cadences of "How Deep Is the Ocean" impart a certain vulnerability and breathless romanticism to the expressions of love so ineffable that they can only take the form of questions.

Both "Say It Isn't So" and "How Deep Is The Ocean" demonstrate the effective and trenchant lyrics that Philip Furia and William Hyland find typical of Berlin, along with the original and artful melodies, felicitous harmonic progressions, and well-shaped formal climaxes that Alec Wilder and Allen Forte also perceive as characteristic. But above all, it is Berlin's intricate and inspired unity of word and tone that most decidedly reveals his brilliance as a songwriter. Jerome Kern, himself a master songwriter, emphasized just this aspect of Berlin's achievement:

> . . . Berlin has certainly mastered the art of making an integral whole by uniting two different elements. Not, mind you, by aimlessly fingering the key-board of a pianoforte until something agreeable is, perchance, struck, but by the same means that Richard Wagner employed in fashioning his dual masterpieces of text and music.
>
> Berlin (like Wagner, an inexorable autocritic) molds and blends and ornaments his words and music at one and the same time, each being the outgrowth of the other.

Berlin's great gift lay in his ability to take "lots of corny little phrases" and "set them all to music" in such a way that they become "just as good as poetry."

～～～～～～～～～～～～～～～～～～～～～～～～～～～～～～～～

| 17 |

Benjamin Sears: The Origins of "Easter Parade"

The creation of the song "Easter Parade" and its relation to the earlier "Smile and Show Your Dimple" is a misunderstood episode in Berlin's career. Over time, it came to be believed that Berlin merely wrote new lyrics for an extant song, which was not quite the case. Berlin said in an article in the *New York World Telegraph* (October 1, 1933), "I wanted an old-fashioned type song, but I couldn't come up with anything. The most difficult thing to do is to consciously create an old-fashioned tune." The "old-fashioned type song" he used as his

---

Used by permission of the author.

Example 3: "Smile and Show Your Dimple" chorus, showing the tune later used in "Easter Parade."

model was "Put On Your Old Grey Bonnet," but he ultimately turned to an old song of his own.[1] Berlin himself did contribute to the confusion. In a *New York Times* article of January 7, 1934 he said that he "wrote a new set of lyrics, changed the end of the tune a little and let it go at that."[2] As late as 2005 an article on the history of "Easter Parade" in the *New York Daily News* asked "What if he just tweaked it ever so slightly and gave it new lyrics?"

A comparison of the two songs shows that he did far more than merely "tweak" the old song. In fact, the music taken from the earlier song consists of only three-and-a-half measures. The tune accompanying the words, "smile and show your dimple, you'll find it's very simple" became "in your Easter bonnet, with all the frills upon it"; otherwise the latter song was completely new.

It is interesting to speculate that perhaps the line in the second verse of "Smile," "look into my camera/ I'm going to take your photograph" may have been what drew him back to the song when he was developing the rotogravure sketch in *As Thousands Cheer*.

---

1. "Berlin is the last man to deny that he steals from himself. He once estimated that about twenty of his 800 published songs were new ideas. The rest have been variations. Berlin believes this adaptability has seldom produced anything but good for him. For one thing it helped pave the way for his career as a writer of show music." Gordon Allison, *New York Herald Tribune*, May 16, 1948

2. See also his letter to Abel Green in Part IV.

Introduction, Chapters 18, 19, 20

After the attacks on the United States of September 11, 2001, "God Bless America" experienced a revival of popularity. Many drew comfort from its direct sentiments and allusions to storm clouds gathering, while others saw its renewed popularity as politicizing a national disaster. This was by no means the first time "God Bless America" stirred controversy, including periodic calls for it to become the national anthem of the United States, which Berlin staunchly resisted. A small sampling of an earlier controversy follows.

In 1940, as U.S. participation in the world war was uncertain but becoming quite possible, Dr. Edgar Franklin Romig, minister of the West End Collegiate Reformed Church in New York City, gave a sermon denouncing the song as doggerel.[1] The *New York Times* printed a brief article about the sermon which prompted quick replies in defense of Berlin in the Letters to the Editor section. A more extensive article, "G-A-W-D Bless A-M-E-R-I-K-E-R" quotes Romig and takes his position even further. This was written by Cleve Sallendar for an American Nazi publication which took a decidedly anti-Semitic stance on Berlin.[2] Sallendar gets Berlin's name wrong, calling him Izzy Balinsky. Later that year James Alden Barber of radio station KGVO in Missoula, Montana, called for Berlin to forego all royalties to the song (Berlin had turned the royalties over to the Boy and Girl Scouts of America thus, in fact, foregoing royalties) because "it rightfully belongs to the American people as a whole." In 1941 no less a figure than conductor Leopold Stokowski weighed in with his favorable opinion of the song.

---

1. Attempts to locate this sermon for inclusion in this book were fruitless. However, enough of it is quoted to get a sense of Dr. Romig's opinion.
2. See Sheryl Kaskowitz, "As We Raise Our Voices: A Social History and Ethnography of 'God Bless America,' 1917–2009," Ph.D. dissertation, Harvard University, 2010, for more information on this aspect of the song's history.

| 18 |

Cleve Sallendar: G-A-W-D Bless A-M-E-R-I-K-E-R!

About a year ago, a Tin Pan Alley songwriter, one Irving Berlin, nee Izzy Balinsky [sic], ex Singing Waiter, wrote a jingling little tune with decidedly trite lyrics and sentiments, which he called "God Bless America," and which did not arouse any particular attention for some time.

Some months after, "knowing" items began to appear in the "inside" press—items about G-B-A. For instance, the now defunct magazine *Ken* paragraphed: "Idea—not fully developed yet—to make G-B-A the new national anthem; constant plugging by Kate Smith gives additional fillip to what once sounded like the mad notion of a publicity agent. You'll hear more of this later."

And so we did. Items regarding G-B-A began to appear with increasing frequency: The California World's Fair was opened with G-B-A. Both the national conventions were to have G-B-A as their theme song; and, as a matter of fact, G-B-A was very much in evidence during the Democratic Convention, to the visible annoyance of some of the reporters. It was sung by a Jewish night[club] singer and his troupe, with an accompanying audience that sounded pretty thin and squeaky. One commentator refers to "that song again" by the organist, who keeps up G-B-A in season and out. One reporter stated that when the "Star-Spangled Banner" was played it was coupled with G-B-A and people didn't seem to know whether to continue standing or not, although most of them "sat down, proclaiming their membership in the school of thought that thinks the tune is wearing as thin as a popular song too often played."

Also on last Decoration Day, the veterans marched up to the Soldiers and Sailors Monument on Riverside Drive to the whining strains of G-B-A, and so on.

SOURCE *The Free American and Deutscher Weckruf und Beobachter*, September 5, 1940.

But the plugging for the new Tin Pan Alley Anthem ceased to be just a "gag" last month when the new 35,000-ton United States battleship "Washington" was launched. There was great interest in this occasion, and 30,000 people were present at the ceremony, as this was the first battleship launched since 1921. In reporting it for the *New York Sun*, Mr. Ben Andrews spoke of the . . . "sixty minute ceremony which included speech-making by notables of the Navy and civilian life and which for some reason nobody seemed to know, did not include the playing or singing of 'The Star-Spangled Banner,' although that newer patriotic song 'God Bless America' appeared to serve all right as a substitute."

The flood of letters of protest on this "substitution" which were sent to the *Sun* and to Senator David I. Walsh. Democrat, of Massachusetts, chairman of the Senate Naval Affairs Committee, who was the principal speaker at the launching, served as pretty conclusive proof that G-B-A was NOT considered to "serve all right" as substitute for our national anthem! One letter, a copy of which was sent to this writer, read as follows:

"Surely, Senator, you or some other of the Navy and civilian 'notables' present must have noted and resented this insult to our national anthem, upon the occasion of the first battleship launched since 1921, and bearing the name of our greatest American? And if so, doubtless you have taken, or will take steps to investigate the substitution of this Tin Pan Alley opus for the national anthem on an official Navy occasion? No one cares tuppence how much money Kate Smith may get for coming over the mountain with the Berlin songs, but a lot of people will care mightily if there is any suspicion of official connivance or trafficking in the matter of substituting by fraud or trickery of the national anthem by any G-B-As."

So brazen has become this "boring in" of the "Alley Anthem" that one of New York's leading clergyman, Dr. Edgar Franklin Romig, of the West End Collegiate Church, took cognizance of it one Sunday, in such splendidly apposite words that I give them in full: Under the heading "Patriotic Pretense," the *Herald-Tribune* quotes Dr. Romig thus:

The great national anthems that have survived, and that will outlive most contemporary doggerel, came out of the hearts of men who knew what it was to sacrifice for America.

Dr. Romig also decried "the strange and specious substitute for religion (and patriotism?) held by many persons today," which, he said, found expression "in the MAWKISH iteration of snatches of song like 'God Bless America.' Today, as audiences from coast to coast croon some of the modern equivalents of the

old patriotic airs," Dr. Romig said—"without pausing to accompany the sentimental wish for the country's good with a solemn dedication to that ideal, one
cannot escape the feeling that the whole experience has a large element of
unreality and self-deception in it."

If only all of our leaders had the brilliant insight and penetration of this
high-minded American clergyman! Dr. Romig truly applies the word "croon"
to the singing of G-B-A. One does not "croon" the "Star-Spangled Banner"!

The writer does not consider G-B-A a "patriotic" song, in the sense of
expressing the real American attitude toward his country, but considers that it
smacks of the "How glad I am" attitude of the refugee horde, of which Theo-
dore Roosevelt said:

"We wish no further additions to the persons whose affection for this country is merely a species of pawnbroker patriotism—whose coming here represents nothing but the purpose to change one feeding trough for another
feeding trough."

Meantime, we shall be "ware and waking" against any attempts to take over
our national anthem and our equally beautiful "America" either openly or un-
derhandedly, by plugging or propaganda! Once we clearly know and understand
what is behind a movement, it is an easy thing to take effective action against it.
"The people that doth not UNDERSTAND shall fall." (Hosea 4:14)

| 19 |

"No Right to a Personal Interest in 'God Bless America,'" Berlin Is Told

Irving Berlin views a letter from James Alden Barber, program director of
Station KGVO, Missoula, Mont., with frank suspicion. The latter wrote the
songsmith an "open letter" with the suggestion that "God Bless America" be
thrown into the unrestricted class. In Berlin's reply, the songwriter openly
stated that "your letter so obviously has for its true purpose an attack upon the
American Society of Composers, Authors and Publishers, which represents
the songwriters of the world against stations such as yours which seem willing
and anxious to confiscate for their free use all music, that it does not merit any
reply in respect of the suggestions made and intended as a peg upon which to
hang your attack."

SOURCE *Variety*, August 14, 1940. Reprinted by permission of *Variety*.

Long before Barber's proposal, Berlin states he weighed the idea of ultimately making his "God Bless America" free for all usages, but under his scientifically mapped plan to preserve the longevity of the song, especially in view of its economic benefit to the Boy and Girl Scouts of America, to whom all royalties are given outright, he has been rigidly restricting the number and types of performances. Eventually, however, he will have to take off all limitations but the fact that the song has now gone over 500,000 in sales which, at the 8c. royalty, plus accruing mechanicals, has already earned some $50,000 for the Scouts substantiates his judgment, Berlin believes.

Right now Harry Richman is pouting at Berlin, Inc., for curbing the song's performance because Berlin took exception to a chorus-girl routine while the singer was at the Chez Paree, Chicago, recently. That's precisely the way Berlin doesn't want the ballad handled, hence the strict ASCAP restriction.

Due to the increasing American defense problem the song has taken a tremendous jump in recent weeks, the last three especially being abnormal. Some 8,000 copies a week have moved out of the stockroom to dealers, as against the average 3,000–4,000 copies per week.

Berlin's brushoff to radioman Barber is preluded by "I try always to be courteous and it is for that reason alone that I acknowledge receipt of your 'open letter' of July 22. The suggestions contained therein as to the disposal which I should make of the song 'God Bless America' would I think be in much better taste if advanced by an executive of a radio station which had not been a party to defrauding composers and authors of their royalties for a period of years, under legal machinations which made it possible for them so to do."

Barber's original letter to Berlin follows:

AN OPEN LETTER TO IRVING BERLIN

Dear Mr. Berlin:

We have noted with approval and applause your magnanimous gesture in turning over to the Boy and Girl Scouts of America the royalties derived from your patriotic hymn, "God Bless America," and the stirring, if somewhat unnecessary defense of your actions in the matter, by *Variety*. If more of the revenue derived by ASCAP and its favored few composers was put to some charitable and worthwhile use, perhaps broadcasters would not protest so much at the bleeding they have suffered from that organization.

Your gesture in turning over the "God Bless America" royalties to the Scouts is a patriotic one, Mr. Berlin, but it is not enough. I respectfully submit that you are in the position of having written a song that no longer belongs to you, to Miss Kate Smith, or even to ASCAP; it rightfully belongs to the American people as a whole. You have a duty to the nation to retrieve this song from the

ASCAP grip, and make it available to the American people without restriction—
even without the restriction that no one can sing it over the air but Miss Smith.

You have surpassed yourself in writing "God Bless America," Mr. Berlin.
Oh, I'll grant you that you've written great songs before—but they were Tin
Pan Alley songs, Mr. Berlin, and they rarely rose above the tawdry sentimen-
tality that makes a Tin Pan Alley song a success. When you, out of a heart
full of gratitude to the country whose people's acceptance of your ditties
made you a success, wrote this hymn, you won for yourself an acclaim and
an immortality that will far outlast the catchy little rhythm of "Alexander's
Rag-time Band." 500 years from now some scientist may unearth a copy of
one of your Tin Pan Alley effusions, play it over and wonder why on earth it
ever achieved any success. But if he comes across a copy of "God Bless America," he'll sense the genuine emotion of its lyrics, the moving simplicity of its
melody, and he'll call you great because of it, not because of anything else
you may have achieved. And that, Mr. Berlin, is or should be, your only
reward for having written "God Bless America." Even ASCAP can't change
the fact that the greatest deeds men do rarely bring them more than the glory
of having achieved greatness.

If you were one of the "starving composers" whom ASCAP claims it sus-
tains against the predatory instincts of the broadcasters, it might be unjust to
ask you to give up your personal rights in "God Bless America." But since you
are obviously not in need of the royalties from this song, we suggest that you
give this song to the American people with no strings attached. In return, and
because such action on your part would take those royalties away from the Boy
and Girl Scouts, the American people will pledge themselves to continue to
support those two grand organizations with all the money they need, just as
they have always done.

You, Mr. Berlin, have no more right to a personal interest in "God Bless
America" than the descendants of Abraham Lincoln have a right to a restricting copyright on the Gettysburg Address. That great document passed into the
public domain as the words fell from his lips.

I dare to suggest, Mr. Berlin, that you present your song to the United States
Government, so that it may be played and sung everywhere, at any time, without the possibility that an ASCAP could assess punitive measures against a
musician, a singer, a hotel, a barroom, a church, or a radio station, whose patriotism led to an infringement of your, and ASCAP's, doubtful rights in the
performance of the song.

Patriotically yours,
Radio Station KGVO
James Alden Barber
Program Director.

Excerpt from Stokowski, Here for Concert Tonight, Praises Martial, Folk Songs; Likes to Play for Soldiers

"God Bless America" is good music.

That's what Leopold Stokowski, eminent American symphony conductor, said here yesterday afternoon after his arrival with his 86-member All American Youth Orchestra, which will be heard in concert tonight at 8:15 o'clock at Sulphur Dell baseball park.

"We frequently play 'God Bless America' on our programs," said the 57-year-old musician. "It is what you might say very singable—that is, can be carried along handsomely by a great number of people—and it has dignity, simplicity and a wonderful sincerity: and it's not surprising that people all over the nation love to sing it."

Kate Smith, who introduced "God Bless America" in 1938, singing it in the 1943 film *This Is the Army*. Photo credit: *Photofest*

SOURCE *Nashville Tennessean*, June, 1941. Reprinted by permission of the *Nashville Tennessean*.

| 21 |

Irving Berlin Orders Song Word Change

Of the songs written for *Holiday Inn* (1942), only "White Christmas" had a life beyond the film. Berlin viewed "Be Careful, It's My Heart"[1] as the film's potential big song, and certainly "You're Easy to Dance With" has a charm deserving of more popularity. "Abraham" is now largely forgotten, though it did reappear, without singing, in *White Christmas* as a dance number for Vera-Ellen and John Brascia.

When *Holiday Inn* was released, however, "Abraham" caused some controversy. In it Berlin used the term "darky" in a context which, one must assume, he saw as positive: the song tells of Lincoln's emancipation of the slaves. When the Afro-American community reacted negatively, Berlin immediately withdrew the word from the song. This is a clear example of how Berlin was ahead of his time on social issues (even while being a man of his time). One need look no further than his song "Suppertime," written for Ethel Waters in *As Thousands Cheer* (1933), to know how he stood on racial issues. He also stood by Waters during that production when white cast members found themselves uncomfortable taking bows with a black colleague. Earlier he had written a song, "There's a Corner Up in Heaven" (1921), which scandalized because it posited that black folk go to the same heaven as white folk. In Berlin's early years, terms such as "coon" and "darky" were common currency, with the former appearing quite often in his early songs. However, Berlin pictured blacks, and other ethnic minorities, in a positive light, making them the heroes of his songs, especially in songs about music. Berlin's social progressiveness and sense of fair play are reflected in the article about "Abraham."

SOURCE *Richmond Afro-American*, November 14, 1942. Reprinted by permission of the *Richmond Afro-American*.

1. Laurence Bergreen in *As Thousands Cheer* and Jody Rosen in *White Christmas: The Story of an American Song* discuss Berlin's uncertainty about "White Christmas" and his attempt, on the film's release, to promote "Be Careful, It's My Heart."

Irving Berlin wired his New York office Monday to delete the epithet applied to colored people from all future printings of his song titled, "Abraham."

The man who wrote "What'll I Do," "Remember," "All Alone," "Always," "Alexander's Ragtime Band," "Oh! How I Hate to Get Up in the Morning," "When I Lost You" and dozens of other popular numbers that America has whistled and sung for a generation was genuinely affected that after so many years he had offended colored people whom he called his friends.

It was not intentional, he told E. B. Rea, theatrical editor, in the AFRO office Monday.

"No song is important enough to offend a whole race. I should never have released it had I known the epithet was objectionable."

Mr. Berlin is in Baltimore with his new show, *This Is the Army*, which has grossed a million dollars for war charities.

"There are colored people in my show," he said, "and everybody is treated alike. Sometime ago in New York there was a question as to whether Bill Robinson would be permitted to go on in a benefit. I said if Bill couldn't I couldn't; and Bill went on."

In Washington when the new Berlin army show was presented, Mr. Berlin said protests opened theatre ticket sales to all citizens.

He did not explain how after a score of years of publishing music free from offense to any race, he used an epithet applied to colored people in "Abraham."

The piece is sung by Bing Crosby in the Paramount picture, *Holiday Inn*, and came to the attention of the AFRO after it was blatantly rendered in its naked aspect by Fred Waring Wednesday night of last week.

What will we do with the Stephen Foster melodies like "Old Folks at Home?"

"Throw them out the window," was Rea's advice. "You sing no songs applying epithets to Jews."

"You're right," was the Berlin comment. "In the old days, I could push a derby down on my head to the ears and rub my hands as though a sale were in prospect, but it doesn't go now."

The late George M. Cohan, Jack Benny and Irving Berlin constitute a trio of Jewish comics who are nation-wide favorites.

Mr. Berlin, who married Ellen [*sic*] Mackay of the Postal Telegraph millions, without the parental blessing, knows too what it means to belong to a minority group.

In the Rea interview, Mr. Berlin had the last word, "I have advised my New York office to change the word to Negroes."

Shown above [in the original article] is a reproduction of the second verse of Irving Berlin's song, "Abraham," now being featured on the air, in a movie, and

Bing Crosby and Marjorie Reynolds performing "Abraham" in blackface in *Holiday Inn*. Photo credit: *Photofest*

on records.[2] When informed by the AFRO that the term "d—y" was offensive to colored people, Mr. Berlin, who paid a personal visit to the AFRO office on Monday, said he had instructed his New York publishing firm to substitute the word Negroes in place of the offending term.

Introduction, Chapters 22, 23, 24

Nineteen years after *Betsy*, Berlin and Richard Rodgers were collaborating again, though this time by mutual consent. Jerome Kern had been signed to write the songs for *Annie Get Your Gun* with lyricist Dorothy Fields (his favorite collaborator). Before work could begin on the show Kern suddenly died, leaving producers Rodgers & Hammerstein needing a composer, as they did not want to produce *and* write the show.

---

2. "When black folks lived in slavery, / Who was it set the darkey free? / Abraham. Abraham."

Annie Get Your Gun was the first stage show that Berlin wrote for Ethel Merman (1908–1984), though he had worked with her on the film *Alexander's Ragtime Band* in 1938. While she was provided with two new songs in the film (one of which was cut), *Annie* really was Berlin's first opportunity to fashion songs and a show to her talents. The story of how Berlin came to write *Annie Get Your Gun* is an oft-told tale; here it is given in a rare first-person account by Rodgers, including his take on the creation of "There's No Business Like Show Business." Merman wrote two autobiographies, each with a different collaborator; only one gives any real information about Berlin. Merman and Berlin had a warm relationship, which often expressed itself in ribald banter backstage.

Brooks Atkinson (1894–1984) for thirty-five years was the major theatre reviewer for the *New York Times*, which referred to him as "the most important reviewer of his time" in his obituary. If not the most important, he certainly was highly influential and a good review from Atkinson was a likely guarantee of a good run. He was hardly infallible, as his famous quote about Rodgers and Hart's *Pal Joey* has proven ("can you draw sweet water from a foul well?"). In this article (from the Sunday Arts Supplement) on *Annie Get Your Gun* he seriously underestimates Berlin's music (comparing it to that of Franz Léhar and Victor Herbert, two composers whose fame has dwindled compared to Berlin's), while nonetheless enjoying the show overall, especially Merman's contribution.

~~~~~~

| 22 |

Richard Rodgers: Excerpt from *Musical Stages*

Once the shock of Jerry's death had faded, Oscar and I were faced with the problem of finding a composer to replace him on the Annie Oakley musical. Having already chosen Kern, we felt it was extremely important to get another composer of equal stature, and this could only mean Irving Berlin.

"We're aiming awfully high to try to get Berlin," I said to Oscar.

"What can we lose?" he answered. "The worst that can happen is that he'll refuse."

One hurdle would be Dorothy Fields's reaction, since she had already been signed to write the lyrics and Berlin wrote both words and music. Dorothy,

Copyright by Richard Rodgers, 1975. Published by Random House, 1975. Excerpt reprinted by permission of the Rodgers & Hammerstein Organization: an Imagem Company. All Rights reserved.

however, was enthusiastic about bringing in Berlin, though like the rest of us, she was afraid that he would feel miffed at being our second choice.[1]

Apparently this never played any part in Berlin's thinking. When he came to see us, we outlined exactly the kind of show it was going to be and what we wanted him to do, but our enthusiasm barely made a dent. Irving was simply not interested in writing the score for a book show. His latest had been about six years earlier, and many changes had taken place in the theatre since then. As a result of *Oklahoma!*, everyone was upholding the importance of "integration" in creating musicals, and he feared that sticking closely to the story line would inhibit him. We argued that just the opposite would be true: a good libretto could offer tremendous help in stimulating ideas for songs and in showing exactly where they would be the most effective. Still, Berlin remained unconvinced. Finally I said, "Irving, there's only one way to find out. Here's the script. Take it home, write a couple of numbers and then see how you feel about it."

That was on a Friday. On Monday morning Berlin came bounding into the office with a big grin on his face and handed over three songs. They were "You Can't Get a Man with a Gun," "There's No Business Like Show Business" and "Doin' What Comes Natur'lly."[2] They were all brilliant, and there was no further need to convince him that he could write the songs for *Annie Get Your Gun*. In fact, he was so grateful to Dorothy and Herb for the help their script had given him that he insisted that they receive part of his percentage of the show. Generosity such as this is an exceedingly rare commodity.

Although he was justifiably proud of all the numbers he wrote for the score, Berlin was extremely sensitive about their reception. In the early days of preparation, we had a series of evenings in which his pianist played the score for all the staff connected with the production. Everyone adored the songs, of course, but at one performance I noticed that one of them had not been played. When I asked Berlin what had happened to it, he said, "I dropped it because the last time it was being played I didn't like the expression on your face. I didn't think you were happy about it and I decided not to use it."

"My God, Irving," I said, "don't ever pay any attention to the expression on my face. I love that song. I looked sour only because I was concentrating on where it should go."

---

1. Dorothy Fields did stay on to write the book, with her brother Herbert.
2. In the later piece by Joshua Logan, he states that Berlin wrote *four* songs over that weekend; he and Rodgers mention only "Doin' What Comes Natur'lly" in common. The truth is that it is not clear which songs Berlin wrote first.

That's how "There's No Business Like Show Business" almost got cut out of *Annie Get Your Gun*.

My relationship with Berlin during the preparation of the show couldn't have been better, perhaps because everything worked without a hitch almost from the very start. Everything, that is, except for the orchestrations. We were in New Haven for the tryout, and with opening night just a few days away, we spent one morning listening to the first orchestra rehearsal. I was not satisfied with what I'd heard, and I was sure Irving wasn't either.

During the lunch break, the two of us walked across the street to Kaysey's restaurant. Berlin didn't say a word until we sat down. "Well, Mr. Rodgers," he began—and I knew that when he called me "Mr. Rodgers," he was deeply troubled, "I'm very unhappy about the orchestrations." I confessed that I was, too, and after lunch I telephoned Max Dreyfus. "Max," I said, "I need Russell Bennett immediately." Russell was out of town with another show, but the next morning, promptly at ten, he was at the Shubert Theatre in New Haven. He reorchestrated the entire score, did his customary superlative job, and soon Irving was again calling me by my first name.

~~~~~~

| 23 |

Ethel Merman, as told to Pete Martin: Excerpt from *Who Could Ask for Anything More*

Cole Porter has written some fantastically good songs for me (so did the Gershwins), but it was Irving Berlin's lyrics that made a lady out of me. They showed that I had a softer side. It was about time that I had a softer side, because my hard-boiled Tessie type had become a cliché character. The gangster moll, the hey-hey girl, was good in the twenties and thirties but people didn't care about her any more. She'd gone out.

The right approach today is to make fun of that period and kid it good-naturedly as is being done in New York right now in a production called *The Boy Friend*, and on the *Anything Goes* television show I did a gay twenties doll and she came out fine because we were ribbing the whole thing.

According to Dorothy [Fields], Irving was also skeptical about taking on the job because he thought it was out of his line. It called for hillbilly songs,

Copyright Peter B. Martin, 1955. Published by Doubleday, 1955. Reprinted by permission of Peter B. Martin.

ballads, and fast songs as well as comedy songs—and Irving wasn't sure he had that much variety. I don't have to tell anyone he proved that he had.

The whole thing from the first rehearsal to the last performance was a joy.

You never know when Irving is going to get nervous about a song. Sometimes he's right to be nervous and sometimes he's wrong. When we were in Boston breaking in *Annie* he got shaky about "Doin' What Comes Naturally" for some reason. The song was going fine, and Oscar Hammerstein told him, "Why don't you leave it alone?" But Irving thought he could improve it by shortening it. He worked like a dog.

I worked like a dog too, for there's nothing harder than to give a performer *part* of a new lyric to learn, so she has to remember part of the old and part of the new all at the same time. And not only was the song made shorter but there were different lines in Irving's new version. He gave me the new short version on Tuesday. Then when he came to my dressing room just before the Wednesday matinee, I had his new lyric stuck on the mirror in front of me. I'd typed it out and I was studying it as I slapped on my make-up. That afternoon I sang it letter-perfect.

So guess what? Irving decided that it wasn't as good as the one he'd thought up in the first place. "The audience reaction isn't as good," he said.

If you change a thing, the audience will tell you whether or not you've made a smart move. Even if they applaud, you can tell by the *quality* of their applause—by whether it's thin or full-bodied—how you're doing. We went back to Irving's original lyrics.

| 24 |

Brooks Atkinson: On *Annie Get Your Gun*

Possibly America has contributed something to the world theatre that is at once profound and elevating. That at least, should be the pious wish of every virtuous American, because profound things that are also elevating get into the schoolbooks and breed culture. But the only theatrical achievement that you can be sure is basically American is the large, noisy, lavish, vulgar, commercial musical show, like *Annie GetYour Gun*, with Ethel Merman blaring undistinguished tunes by Irving Berlin and everyone in the audience looking dazed and happy.

source *New York Times*, September 29, 1946. Reprinted by permission of the *New York Times*.

London produces expansive musical shows, though, if one may be permitted to be smugly isolationist, the London carousels have less animal gusto than ours. Before the war Paris used to produce luxuriously bedizened girl shows for the tourists and footloose males, but there was very little fun in them. No country except America seems to have the tradition, the organization, the equipment and the audiences for these knockabout capers that blow you out of your seat with explosions of brassy music and whack the funny bone with the slapstick.

From any genteel point of view we ought, perhaps, to have better taste. Although the new season has not yet manufactured a heavy duty musical show for the exhausted business man and his sagging customer from out of town, it has raised a well-bred curtain on *Yours Is My Heart*, with elegant music by Franz Lehar, and *Gypsy Lady*, with two or three memorable melodies by Victor Herbert. None of the songs in *Annie Get Your Gun* can compare in quality with the music of these two old-fashioned operettas, for Irving Berlin's latest score is routine composing. "Sun in the Morning" is as close as he comes to imaginative music writing. Although he wrote the score only last year, none of it has the freshness of Lehar's "Yours Is My Heart, Alone" or Herbert's "Gypsy Love Song." By any of the accepted standards of skill and good taste, Lehar's and Herbert's are superior works worth all proper reverencing.

But are books so unimportant after all? There used to be a showman's maxim that the intelligence quota of books for musical shows did not matter. Since the function of the book is to get the performers on and off the stage and to establish the mood for musical numbers, it used to be said that no harm was done if the book was mentally deficient. But this is no longer the case. *Show Boat* has an intelligent romantic book, and it is a classic; and the same blending of book and music has made a classic of *Oklahoma!* The imaginative book for *Carousel* is another case in point.

None of these books asks you to go back to infancy and play paper dolls or bean bag. They do not require you to swoon with idyllic rapture over the love affair of an actress and a prince, as in *Yours Is My Heart*, nor do you have to be devastated by the practical society joke of betrothing a proud marquis to a low-born gypsy princess, as in *Gypsy Lady*. If the music and dancing are good perhaps you should be ingenious enough to ignore a hackneyed book for the sake of a pleasant evening in the theatre. But the decayed snobberies, the coy, mincing jests and the fundamental old hat of *Yours Is My Heart* and *Gypsy Lady* cannot be ignored by anyone who has learned to read without moving his lips.

Since musical shows are produced for the crowd, Herbert and Dorothy Fields, bookmakers for *Annie Get Your Gun*, see no objection to making books vulgar. (Vulgus, Latin, meaning "common people," as the dictionary points out reassuringly.) Show business is one of show business's favorite subjects; and

Ethel Merman, the star of *Annie Get Your Gun*, singing "Everybody Step" in the 1938 film *Alexander's Ragtime Band* with Tyrone Power as Alexander. Photo credit: *Photofest*

Mr. and Miss Fields accordingly have put a backwoods female target shooter into a razzle-dazzle Buffalo Bill show of a half century ago. For honest enjoyment in a theatre their Annie Oakley is worth a million Marquis de Roncevalle or Princess Sou Chong, although she cannot count above twenty and distinguishes herself for the most part by "Doin' What Comes Naturally." Recognizing the practical limitations of target shooting as a method of getting a husband she bellows: "You can't shoot a male in the tail like a quail," in Mr. Berlin's most inspired lyric. Yes, Annie is a mighty fine subject for musical comedy fooling.

For she is played by Ethel Merman who has developed into a rowdy clown, dragging the guffaws out of the audiences' boots. She has always been a vastly enjoyable music-hall performer—acting in a forthright, swagger style, singing like a persistent trombone player and doin' what comes naturally. In the place of conventional stage beauty she has always substituted an amazing self-confidence. By the time she is finished with either a song or a part she possesses it completely, and very nearly possesses all the other performers and has, at least, a lien on the scenery.

In *Annie Get Your Gun* she adds a sense of low comedy that is blunt and tremendously entertaining. Although, according to tradition, performers are not supposed to act in musical comedies any more than librettists are supposed to write intelligent books, doesn't La Merman make a coherent low comedy character out of backwoods Annie? Like all good dramatic characters, Annie develops in the course of her musical rumpus; and, apart from the fun along the way, you feel that something has been accomplished when, in the last scene, Annie gets her man without having to shoot him down like a quail.

Excuse the libretti of *Yours Is My Heart* and *Gypsy Lady* on the score of old age and changing manners, if you want to. But still the fact remains that the whole approach to audiences of a bespangled carnival like *Annie Get Your Gun* is more sensible and entertaining. Add to the dispensation of Miss Merman, Ray Middleton, who has become a racy performer as well as an admirable singer, and Harry Bellaver, whose Sitting Bull is a gem of character acting, and you have a lively and bountiful show. In spite of its size *Annie Get Your Gun* is continuously gay. That is the basic genius of the American commercial stage.

~~~~~~

| 25 |

Harold Arlen and Ralph Blane: Verse to "Halloween"

When Harold Arlen was working on the score for the film *My Blue Heaven*, it struck him that Irving Berlin had written a song for almost every American Holiday, except Halloween. To fill in the missing holiday Arlen wrote "Halloween," which was featured in the film. To Arlen's chagrin there was not much interest in Halloween's lack of a song. The verse tells the story.

Once upon a time in the long, long ago,
Man's courage was high, but his spirit was low.
People grew tired of all work and no play,
They felt the need of a jolly holiday.
Then along came Christmas,
Along came Easter,
Along came Fourth of July,

SOURCE The motion picture MY BLUE HEAVEN; Lyric by Ralph Blane and Harold Arlen; Music by Harold Arlen; Copyright © 1950 TWENTIETH CENTURY MUSIC CORPORATION; All rights controlled by HARWIN MUSIC CORPORATION; All rights reserved. *Reprinted by permission of Hal Leonard Corporation*

Then along came a man by the name of Berlin
Who took every holiday that ever has been,
He wrote about Christmas,
He wrote about Easter,
He wrote about Fourth of July.
His mind was fertile and his pen was keen,
But he never wrote a word about Halloween.
And to this very day we've been wondering why
This very able man let this holiday go by.

Introduction, Chapters 26 and 27

Fred Astaire (1899–1987) was a favorite of the songwriters of his time; in fact, of the major writers only Rodgers and Hart never wrote a score for him, though *On Your Toes* was originally conceived as an Astaire project. Of those songwriters Astaire was probably closest to George Gershwin (who wrote four scores for him) and Berlin, who wrote six film scores for Astaire, more than he wrote for any other performer.

Much has been written on the influence of Astaire on his songwriters and their influence on him. John Russell Taylor and Arthur Jackson in *The Hollywood Musical* examine this in the context of Berlin's work overall. They are perhaps overly critical in assessing Berlin's melodies and lyrics as compared with his contemporaries. Certainly they miss the deceptive simplicity of Berlin's music that disguises some often very sophisticated musical gestures, all of which he learned unconsciously by ear rather than through study. They also have the same frustrated response to Berlin's style as did Alec Wilder, saying that he "really has no personal style that one can put one's finger on."

Astaire wrote his autobiography, *Steps in Time*, in 1959. Surprisingly he has very little to say about Berlin, considering their fond friendship. Nonetheless, one anecdote does show the Berlin that Astaire knew, and takes place in the week after the birth of Astaire's son.

| 26 |

John Russell Taylor and Arthur Jackson: Chapter Excerpt from *The Hollywood Musical* on Fred Astaire

[N]early all the major American popular composers have been able to make an important contribution to the Hollywood musical—or, to look at it another way, Hollywood has been able to make an important contribution to their over-all careers, from all points of view, financial and artistic. At least one of the great names, Irving Berlin, has indeed done his very best work for the cinema, to which he devoted his energies exclusively between his stage success *As Thousands Cheer* (1933) and his next Broadway show *Louisiana Purchase* (1940). Berlin, born in 1888, was nearly the oldest of a group of great song-writers born in the last few years of the nineteenth century, and musically he was one of the most conservative. Though his first all-time success, "Alexander's Rag-time Band" had revolutionized the popular music scene by really selling as nothing else had done the idea of ragtime, he was fundamentally most at home with very straightforward romantic ballads or comedy songs which would have offered little which was musically unfamiliar to the average Victorian drawing-room. And as Berlin always wrote his own lyrics (indeed, he was a lyric-writer before he was a composer), he never found himself being pushed slightly out of his natural bent by the challenge of having to match some other lyric-writer's verbal intricacies with similarly complex music.

And, of course, the almost infallible common touch of Berlin's melodies, which could produce songs like "White Christmas," "Easter Parade," "How Deep Is the Ocean," "All Alone," "Remember" and "God Bless America" (not to mention "Always," his wedding present to his second wife, estimated on royalty earnings to date to be the most valuable wedding present on record), is not to be sneered at. On the other hand, it is not finally at all as exciting as the special gifts of, say, Cole Porter, Jerome Kern or George Gershwin: the melodies are

Copyright John Russell Taylor and Arthur Jackson, 1971. Published by McGraw-Hill, 1971.
Excerpted and reprinted by permission of pfd

unforgettable, certainly, but somehow ordinary, and the words are adequate but little more. Moments of real musical ingenuity, like the contrapuntal combination of two distinct themes in the "You're Just in Love" number of *Call Me Madam*, are infrequent, and Berlin really has no personal style one can put one's finger on. He takes colour so completely from his surrounding—witness the folksy homespun of *Annie Get Your Gun*, much closer to Rodgers and Hammerstein than to his other work—or from the performers he has in mind—surely it was the presence of Ethel Waters in the cast of *As Thousands Cheer* that inspired the memorable but totally uncharacteristic "Harlem on My Mind" and "Suppertime."

Similarly, three of his most compelling scores were written for Fred Astaire films: *Top Hat* (1935), *Follow the Fleet* (1935) and *Carefree* (1938). For Fred Astaire is one of those performers with a style so personal to himself that composers seem to find themselves automatically adopting or exploiting its salient features as a positive source of inspiration. The essence of Astaire's singing style is that he sings as he dances—lightly, swiftly, with a buoyancy which seems to defy gravity and chafe at confinement to the ground. Think, for example, of the melodic line of "Cheek to Cheek": the way it plunges *in medias res* with "Heaven, I'm in heaven," the voice being forced to cherish the words lovingly, as perhaps only Fred Astaire's can really do, before tripping lightly, almost breathlessly up to the high point of "and my heart beats so that I can hardly *speak*." Equally, Astaire the dancer, and the necessity for the songs to be also music he can dance to, encourage rhythmic subtlety of a kind not elsewhere to be much observed in Berlin's songs. The overall structure of songs like "Isn't This a Lovely Day to Be Caught in the Rain" from *Top Hat*, or "I'm Putting All My Eggs in One Basket" from *Follow the Fleet*, or "Change Partners" from *Carefree*, with their collocation of sections in different rhythms, their restless changes of key, reflects the demands of Astaire the dancer as much as it exploits the particular qualities of Astaire the singer.

Not that Berlin's golden period in the 1930s was entirely confined to his contribution to Fred Astaire films. "Puttin' on the Ritz," which we nowadays think of as an Astaire number par excellence, was originally written for Harry Richman in the 1930 film of the same name. Dick Powell's bland, even tenor inspires two first-rate songs in *On the Avenue* (1937): "I've Got My Love to Keep Me Warm" and "This Year's Kisses." *Second Fiddle* in 1939 saw Berlin agreeably spoofing himself and "Cheek to Cheek" in "Back to Back," and matching Sonja Henie's grace on skates with a classic tango-bolero "When Winter Comes." But, perhaps unfortunately, this period of dedication to the cinema was only temporary. In 1940 Berlin was back on Broadway with *Louisiana Purchase*, after which came his long involvement with the American war effort and the big patriotic army show *This Is the Army*. His only film score during this time was for *Holiday Inn* (1942), which provides a perfect demonstration of his sensitivity, over-sensitivity even, to the performer he was writing any particular song for. The two stars were Bing Crosby and Fred Astaire, and while Astaire inspired Berlin to a characteristically spry and limber song, "You're Easy to Dance With," Crosby, the "old groaner" whose slack, easy-going delivery nearly always seems to bring out the worst in song-writers, produced only "White Christmas" and "Be Careful, It's My Heart." "Only" may seem an unlikely word to apply to the best-selling, biggest money-making popular song of all time, but whatever the sentimental and other merits of "White Christmas," I would gladly swap a hundred of them for one more classic Berlin-Astaire number.

For the most part thereafter Berlin's involvement with the cinema has been in a poorish screen version of *Annie Get Your Gun* (1949), a respectable but unexciting screen version of *Call Me Madam* (1953) and a succession of old-and-new mixtures like *Easter Parade* (1948), where new predominated and one more great Astaire number, "It Only Happens When I Dance With You," made its appearance, and *White Christmas* (1954) and *There's No Business Like Show Business* (1954), where old predominated. Plus for the record, the title song to

Berlin with Fred Astaire, for whom he wrote six film scores, during the filming of *Easter Parade*. Photo credit: *Photofest*

the Marlon Brando vehicle *Sayonara* (1957), which at least informed the world decisively what the Japanese for "goodbye" was. Looking back over Berlin's whole career, there is one thing, I think, that no critic could tax him with, and that is lack of variety. What one might complain of, though, is lack of that underlying consistency beneath apparent diversity which marks the really great composer, in the popular song quite as much as in any other field of musical endeavor. It is hard to like all the numerous Irving Berlins which have been presented to us through the years, impossible to dislike them all: one can only take one's pick. For me the best Irving Berlin is Fred Astaire's Irving Berlin, and it is in the Fred Astaire films he has written for that Berlin has made his distinctive, indeed irreplaceable contribution to the film musical. Perhaps the elegance and sophistication of Astaire's screen personality has proved a unique challenge to Berlin's native directness and simplicity: perhaps it is as native to the chameleon Berlin as "God Bless America" or "White Christmas," But in the six films which allowed Berlin to write for Astaire, they somehow between them produced something individual and in its way definitive: a perfect amalgam of the singer and the song, the song and the dance, the dance and the film.

| 27 |

Fred Astaire: Excerpt from *Steps in Time*

A couple of nights Irving Berlin came down and played gin rummy with me for hours. Irving is always thinking up new song ideas, and in the middle of our gin games he would often sing and throw lyric ideas and rhymes at me to test them out. At this time Irving was working on the picture [*Follow the Fleet*] and his mind was particularly occupied when he left me at about three. He got into a taxi and told the driver to take him to Joe Schenck's house in Beverly Hills, where he was staying. It happened that he got a driver who didn't know much about Beverly Hills and proceeded to drive Irv around all over the place, out into Malibu or somewhere. Irving told me the next day, "I wasn't paying any attention to the driver—my mind was on a tune. When I looked at my watch I found I'd been riding around for two hours."

Copyright Fred Astaire, 1959. Published by HarperCollins, 1959. Reprinted by permission of HarperCollins Publishers.

Part III

The Melody Lingers On
Later Years

| 28 |

Joshua Logan: A Ninetieth-Birthday Salute to the Master of American Song

After *Annie Get Your Gun* Berlin wrote two Broadway scores, *Miss Liberty* (1949) and a second hit starring Ethel Merman, *Call Me Madam* (1950). He followed that with two "catalogue" films (both 1954), *White Christmas* and *There's No Business Like Show Business* (which gave Merman a chance to sing the song on film, after she was passed over for the film version of *Annie*), plus the film versions of *Annie* and *Call Me Madam*. He worked on many projects throughout the 1950s that did not reach fruition, culminating in one that did, his last Broadway score, *Mr. President* (1962).

Berlin effectively retired after *Mr. President*, though he did re-emerge to write "An Old Fashioned Wedding" for the 1966 revival of *Annie Get Your Gun*. He continued writing songs occasionally, but mainly spent his time with a new hobby, painting, and overseeing his publishing business. When "significant" birthdays came along the tributes poured in; in this instance a fond one by director Joshua Logan (1908–1988), who worked closely with him on *This Is the Army* and as director of *Annie Get Your Gun* and *Mr. President*. Logan's loving tribute to Berlin provides a strong contrast to the angry profile he wrote of another Broadway songwriter he worked with, Richard Rodgers [reprinted in the *Richard Rodgers Reader*]; Logan's experiences with the two men were markedly different.

One thing to note in this piece is that as late as 1978 the "little black boy" myth surfaces again, though this time staunchly refuted by one who knew. Berlin mythology was strong, even with the stories that Berlin would have preferred dying.

I first knew him as a disembodied voice on the telephone. The year was 1942.

SOURCE *High Fidelity Magazine*, May 1978. Reprinted by permission of Hachette Filipacchi Media US.

I had been inducted into the service only hours before, and I was sitting on a beer crate at Ft. Dix peeling potatoes and feeling forlorn. Someone tapped me on the shoulder: "Your name Logan? You're wanted on the telephone."

Wondering how anyone in the world could have found me, there among my spuds, I went to the phone. "Hello, Josh?" a hoarse and unfamiliar voice said. "This is Irving Berlin."

Now you must understand that then his name, to my mind, belonged in the pantheon that includes Bizet, Mark Twain, Molière, and Moses. Imagine, then, my shock and excitement—not to mention a touch of fear—on hearing the name on the phone.

"Yes, Mr. Berlin," I must have said. "What can I do for you?"

"You've got to come and help us out," he replied. "My show *This Is the Army* opens in eleven days, and it's in terrible shape. I need somebody to pull it together. I've seen your work, and you're the one I want."

To work with Irving Berlin! A young director's dream! "But Mr. Berlin," I said, "what about the Army? I just got to Ft. Dix."

"Don't worry about that," he said with brisk assurance. "I've already got the wheels in motion. You'll be here this afternoon."

And incredibly, I was. I walked down the aisle of a darkened Broadway theater and saw a smallish, wiry man with a thin Mediterranean face and black, black hair—a face I knew well from photographs in magazines. He was pumping my hand, as excited as a schoolboy, telling me where to sit. It seemed they were going to put the show on for me immediately.

From the moment the curtain went up, I thought the show was marvelous and spectacular. With a cast of 300 members of the armed forces, it had been directed by Ezra Stone and Bob Sidney, and beautifully, I thought. There was, I told Berlin, very little anyone else could do to it except hurt it. But he was adamant. He wanted me to take full charge.

To please him, more than anything, I stayed on and reorganized the show a bit, with a snip or two of the scissors here and a little glue there. Actually, I contributed very little to that wonderful show.

It opened to rave reviews, and I soon asked to be transferred out, so that I could stop playing gin rummy in the wings and join some part of the fighting forces. Berlin at last agreed to let me go. I joined the Air Corps, becoming a lieutenant and an intelligence officer in the 50th Troop Carrier Wing under the command of Col. George Chappell. I imagined that I would not work with Berlin again until after the war, if at all. How wrong I was, and how little I understood his energy and tenacity.

Our unit was sent to England sometime before D-Day. We were to drop parachutists on the French coast the night before the long-awaited landing on the Continent. We were stationed at a little town named Cottesmore, and on my first weekend I went to London, which was all blackout shades and lineups for buses and food. In Trafalgar Square, I ran into a soldier whose face I vaguely recognized from *This Is the Army*, and he told me Berlin was looking for me. *This Is the Army* had crossed the ocean before me and was being readied for a London opening, but Berlin wanted to talk to me first.

I went immediately to his hotel, the Savoy, and found him a bundle of nerves. He wanted to add a new sketch before the show left London to play to military personnel around the world. The sketch was on the bawdy side. It was about a private desperate to sleep with his wife, a lieutenant in the WACs. But to get to her, he had to go through channels, and standing in his way was a ferocious woman, her first sergeant who also happened to be his mother-in-law. Hardly highbrow, but surefire stuff for a GI audience. I thought the sketch was hilarious; Berlin thought I had an evil enough mind to stage it properly—this was his ultimate accolade. But—

There was my C.O., Col. Chappell. Berlin told me not to worry about him. With a flourish he picked up the phone and called Eisenhower—Gen. Dwight Eisenhower, supreme commander of the Allied forces in Europe, who was preparing the most massive invasion in history and could be presumed to have a couple of things on his mind other than the problems of an Army show and the destiny of one Joshua Logan. Eisenhower assured Berlin he would take care of it, and an order came down through channels to the desk of Col. Chappell. Now, with the invasion imminent, unit commanding officers had the absolute and final say about any shifts of personnel. And Chappell was a good combat commander. So what he said to the request was, "No!"

Berlin was incredulous and in a frustrated rage—not at Chappell, mind you, but at Eisenhower. Until now his requests for talent had always gone through unchallenged. He grabbed the phone and put in a transatlantic call to the Pentagon and Gen. "Hap" Arnold, then chairman of the Joint Chiefs of Staff; above Hap there was only the President and maybe the Statue of Liberty. Gen. Arnold promptly approved Berlin's request and dispatched a cable to that effect, which duly arrived on the desk of Col. Chappell, who wrote on it, "Request disapproved."

Berlin by now seemed on the verge of apoplexy. He denounced Arnold and Eisenhower as a pair of "weaklings," then demanded Col. Chappell's phone number from me. Hesitantly, I gave it to him. Berlin called while I listened nervously on an extension.

"Col. Chappell," he said, "this is Irving Berlin." A long silence, and Berlin said, "Hello? Hello?"

Chappell's voice, taut and strangled, came back: "Did you say Irving Berlin? Not *the* Irving Berlin!"

"Of course," Berlin snapped. "Now, listen, colonel, I want Logan for three weeks, and no more crap!"

"But—but certainly, Mr. Berlin. You can have him as long as you want. Longer than that!" Chappell evidently was so rattled that he did not realize he still held an open telephone in his hand, because I heard him say, "Sergeant, do you know who just called me? And *personally*, for Christ's sake! Irving Berlin!"

It has always seemed to me that that story says something not only about Berlin and his stature in the public mind, but about Americans. Col. Chappell was utterly unimpressed by brass. But Irving Berlin? That was a different matter.

When someone asked the late Jerome Kern what place he thought Berlin held in American music, he replied, "Irving Berlin has no place in American music. He *is* American music."

Berlin more than any other man defined the very character of the popular song. Before him, popular music in this country, particularly that of the theater, was dominated by the influence of Viennese operetta and Gilbert and Sullivan. Victor Herbert was in his heyday. Although Rudolf Friml and Sigmund Romberg were still to come, it was Berlin's 1911 hit, "Alexander's Ragtime Band" that was the catalyst of a revolution in popular music.

Legends have grown up about Berlin, some of them malicious and some of them contradictory. One is that he can't read a note of music. It's true.[1] Neither could Ezio Pinza, one of the greatest musical talents with whom I ever worked. Neither could Frank Loesser. Another legend is that Irving can compose only in the key of F sharp and has a special piano on which there is a crank that shifts the keyboard for him so that he can play in other keys. That piano does indeed exist: He calls it his Buick.

It is perhaps time to confront the slander that Irving did not write his songs and, if I can, lay it to rest permanently. There used to be a joke that he employed a little black boy from Harlem who wrote all his songs.

I have directed three Berlin shows, if you include my advice on *This Is the Army*. After the war, I directed *Annie Get Your Gun* and, later, *Mr. President*. I have watched him work and seen his incredible creative energies in operation. He wrote songs profusely. No one else *could* have done that work for him.

Annie Get Your Gun was my first show after the war, and my first smash hit. Richard Rodgers and Oscar Hammerstein II produced it. Kern was supposed to write the score, but he became fatally ill while I was still at Ft. Dix waiting to get

---

1. He did, in fact, learn to read and write music, but still preferred to utilize a musical secretary as he had done in the past.

out of service. Rodgers, Hammerstein, and I began considering other composers. Irving's name was at the top of the list. He had not been asked, as no one thought he would work on a show he had not conceived himself. Oscar said, "I don't believe in scratching anyone's name until we at least ask him." To everyone's amazement, Irving said he'd consider it. But first he wanted to go off by himself to see if he was able to write songs in the hillbilly Americana style that the show required. During that weekend he wrote four. What were they? "They Say It's Wonderful," "Doin' What Comes Natur'lly," "You Can't Get a Man with a Gun," and "Moonshine Lullaby." Only then did he say, "Okay, I'll do the show."

At one point, he threw out "There's No Business Like Show Business" because he thought that Dick and Oscar and I had not reacted with sufficient enthusiasm when he first sang it for us. We set up such a howl that he soon put it back. (He always stands very close when he sings you a new song, and sings right up your nose, putting you under some sort of magnifying glass so that he can judge your reaction. And it's a good thing, too, because as someone once said, "You have to hug him to hear him.")

Just before we went into rehearsal with *Annie*, we had a final meeting to discuss scenery and costumes. Irving was off at the other side of the room. I whispered to Oscar that I thought there ought to be another song between Annie and Frank in the second act. Oscar said, "Keep your voice down. I don't want to make Irving nervous when he's still working on the score. If you start talking about a new song at this point, it's liable to worry him."

At that moment, Berlin, who seemed to have *smelled* that we were talking about him, leaned over Oscar's shoulder and said, "Another song?" His eyes were gleaming.

I stuttered, "Well, uh, yes, Irving, if it's not too much trouble."

"What kind of song?"

"I don't know," I said. "But don't worry about it yet."

Irving called for silence and announced, "There's been talk of a new song for Annie and Frank. Question: What kind of song should it be?"

Someone said hesitantly, "Could it be a love song, Irving?"

"Of course not," he said impatiently. "They hate each other at this point. They are competitors, they're rivals, they're getting ready for a shooting contest."

Rodgers said, "What about a challenge song?"

"A challenge song!" Irving said. "Right! G'bye, everybody, we can all go home now." The important problem—his—had been settled.

My wife and I immediately took a cab from Oscar's house at Sixty-third and Madison to our hotel, the Lombardy, at Fifty-sixth and Park, a trip of no more than six minutes. As we entered our room, the phone was ringing. It was Berlin. "Josh," he said, "listen to this." And he sang, "Anything you can do,

I can do better. I can do anything better than you. . . ." And he finished singing the whole first chorus of the song.

"When the hell did you write that?" I asked in amazement

"In the taxi."

"But so *fast.*"

"I had to do it fast. We go into rehearsal day after tomorrow!"

No doubt the myth that Irving did not write all his songs grew out of not only their number (about 850 *published*), but their incredible variety. But anyone who has examined his life's work in chronological sequence would never for a moment entertain the thought that they were not all his. From "Alexander's Ragtime Band" through the simple "Easter Parade" to the highly sophisticated "Piccolino" and "Change Partners," there is a direct, consistent, and steady evolution of his style. As the music of America changed and grew more sophisticated, Irving changed with it and, indeed, usually led the change. And the lyrics, too, forthright and almost naive, have a total consistency and a recognizable personal imprint.

I worked again with Irving in 1962 on *Mr. President.* Before the New York opening, we played a gala benefit in Washington for the Kennedy Foundation, attended by all the sisters and in-laws as well as Jack and Jackie. No one in the audience dared laugh at a joke until they looked first to see if the President was laughing. The atmosphere was chilly, to say the least. I ran into Irving at intermission. He said, "They didn't come to see a show, they came to be a show."

He has always been a bit jealous of big successes by other people. When Dick Rodgers and Oscar Hammerstein and I were trying out *South Pacific* in New Haven, Irving was working with Moss Hart on *Miss Liberty. South Pacific* was already the hottest news in show business, and it disturbed and rankled Irving that someone had a bigger hit than he might have.

One day, when he and Moss were pacing up and down the living room of his house overlooking the East River, Moss looked out and saw a little tug towing a long chain of barges piled high with waste paper, heading up the river. He pointed out the window and said, "You know what's piled on those barges, don't you? Mail orders going up to New Haven for *South Pacific.*" Irving watched them grimly. At the end of the day, Moss saw another tug pulling loaded barges downstream: "You know what's on *those* barges, don't you, Irving? That's the money coming down from New Haven to be put in the bank." Moss howled with laughter at Irving's stone face.

All these years later, I remind myself that the human tornado named Irving Berlin was born May 11, 1888, in Temun, Siberia, which means of course that he is ninety this month. Irving Berlin ninety! It is hard to digest. He looks, moves, and acts like a young man. He still writes every day—often some very funny novelty songs. I'm sure he still has at least three shows in him.

I won't hear from him for a year or so, and then one day he'll call and we'll talk for hours and laugh and brag. Like any good friend, I always know he's there. He and his wife have a beautiful woodland home in the Catskills and a handsome town house on Beekman Place in New York. Irving's room is on the top floor, under the mansard roof, overlooking the river. He spends his time playing his "Buick," writing or painting, turning out smallish, primitive portraits. If one of them happens to resemble one of his friends, he sends it to the person, suitably inscribed. One year he sent me a little flower painting with my wife's photograph pasted on it. It was inscribed, "To Josh from Irving," along with a couple of bars of music reading, "May all your Christmases be white." These little oils are full of excitement and therefore true to his spirit. They are as colorful and humorous as those of Bombois, Grandma Moses, or perhaps Chagall.

I always found Irving easy to work with. If for some reason I wanted a new song for a show or wanted one changed, he never objected. On the contrary, he loved the challenge. And I never knew anyone who more enjoyed writing for the theater or better understood how to write for it. "I can't resist a story conference," he said to me once.

Josh Logan and Berlin during rehearsals for *Mr. President*, Berlin's last Broadway show, in 1962. Photo credit: *Photofest*

In the three shows I did with him—and I hope there will be more—I was continually amazed at his almost mystical way of concocting a new tune or an idea for an entire show. There has always been in him a passionate, unquench-able enthusiasm, a powerhouse quality that sets anyone near him on fire. He is an encourager, a lifter of spirits who laughs loud and long at your jokes and makes you feel they are funnier than they really are. And he is *never* at a loss for ideas.

Perhaps that is the real cause of the violent jealousy that Berlin has often inspired. There seems to be a human tendency to view with suspicion, even fear, a prolific man with brilliant, inexplicable talent. Balzac's incredible out-put of novels and plays caused his furious competitors to accuse him of having a stable of writers in his employ. Scholars are still "proving" that another, better-educated subject of Elizabeth I must have written Shakespeare's plays. Rumors that Mozart was poisoned by a jealous rival found their way into the works of both Pushkin and Rimsky-Korsakov. And an article in last Febru-ary's *High Fidelity* described how Paganini's superb playing inspired tales that he was in league with the devil.

One wonders if, had Irving Berlin been born more than 200 years ago in Salem, Massachusetts, he would have been burned as a witch.

~~~~~~

| 29 |

Nancy Caldwell Sorel: First Encounters: Irving Berlin and George Gershwin

> Various versions of this tale exist. What is important is what they share: an ex-ample of Berlin's generosity, made all the more dramatic because that gener-osity was toward a young man who became one of Berlin's equals, George Gershwin. However the meeting went, whether Gershwin applied to Berlin and transcribed "That Revolutionary Rag" as a test of his abilities or, whether as told here, Berlin was wise enough to recognize Gershwin's genius.[1]

The Great War was over and the whole country seemed addicted to song. Who better to supply the national need than the King of Ragtime, Irving Berlin?

SOURCE *The Atlantic Monthly*, May 1988. Reprinted by permission of Nancy Caldwell Sorel.

1. See also the version of the story as told in *The Complete Lyrics of Irving Berlin*.

"Come on and hear (*boom! boom!*) Come on and hear (*boom! boom!*) Alexander's. . . ." That early hit had sold a million copies in a few months. Now Berlin, back from the Army, stopped by the T.B. Harms Co., in Tin Pan Alley to show the publisher Max Dreyfus his latest. "That Revolutionary Rag," Dreyfus read, "That was made across the sea/ By a tricky slicky/ Bolsheviki . . ." But the notes were a problem. Berlin's musical education had evolved from a battered piano in a Bowery saloon and remained forever locked in the key of F sharp. He needed someone to take the song down for him. Dreyfus said he had just the man—only a kid really, but showing great promise.

Enter young George Gershwin, glad to oblige. Harms was a big step up from Remick's where he had pounded a piano in a cubicle up to ten hours a day. He took down the song, made a lead sheet, and played it back to Berlin with extravagant improvisations that left it almost unrecognizable. Then, abruptly, he asked the composer for a job as his musical secretary. Berlin intimated he might be overqualified. What did he really want to do? Write songs, Gershwin said, tearing up the keyboard with his latest. "What the hell do you want to work for anyone else for?" Berlin asked. "Work for yourself!"

Gershwin took his advice, and within the year there was "Swanee." Then came "Stairway to Paradise." "Rhapsody in Blue" made him as famous—and almost as wealthy—as Berlin. They became friends—two hustlers of Russian-Jewish parentage making it big in America.

Gershwin was twenty that day they met in the Alley. Brash, confident, he seemed just at the beginning of his life, whereas in reality it was more than half over. Berlin, a more cautious thirty, would not have believed his own eventual longevity. Strike up the band. Alexander, Irving Berlin is 100!

~~~~~~

| 30 |

Mark Steyn: Excerpts from *Top Hat and Tails*

Berlin's one-hundredth birthday set off a string of tributes and other celebratory events, including a gala concert at Carnegie Hall. Mark Steyn of the London paper *The Independent* brought together an impressive list of Berlin's colleagues to comment on his work, from which a selection follows. Many of them focused on his lyrics, with each finding a different lyric which sums up

SOURCE *The Independent* (London), May 7, 1988. Reprinted by permission of the author and *The Independent*.

Berlin for them; Irving Caesar, for example, makes note of Berlin's ability to find subjects other than love as the basis of a popular song. The music is not neglected, though, in particular with comments by two fine composers, Burton Lane and John Green (who makes a reference to the "little colored boy"—even in 1988 the story was alive). Lane acknowledges Berlin outliving his copyrights, which was a sore point for Berlin (the law has been changed to life of the writer, plus 75 years, so it is now to the songwriter's advantage).

Green, Irving Caesar, Sammy Fain, and Ann Ronell are perhaps less well known today than they were in 1988. A quick glance at some of their song titles show that their work lives on, even if their names have faded from public awareness.[1]

Oh, ma honey / Oh, ma honey / better hurry and let's meander.

Hurry AND meander? Well, "meander" rhymes with "Alexander" and Irving Berlin has always been a practical man. But the moment that introductory verse hits its chorus, most of us are sold. "Alexander's Ragtime Band," in Alan Jay Lerner's phrase, [was] the alarm clock that awoke American popular music.

Berlin followed it with "Alexander's Bagpipe Band," this time borrowing a line from "Auld Lang Syne." Between them, the two "Alexanders" encapsulate Berlin's entire career—moments of brilliant inspiration alternating with Tin Pan Alley hackwork. Few people have written more bad songs, but no-one has written more good songs. Or more hit songs. He still writes the occasional song, but these days, sadly, he keeps them to himself.

Few entries to the *Oxford Dictionary of Music* (he's next to the Berlin Philharmonic) owe as much to chance as Berlin's. He'd probably be in retirement on a collective farm in Siberia had not some over-zealous Cossacks burnt down his home village and sent Israel Baline and his parents scuttling west. His Americanised name was nothing more than a printer's error on his first published song. And he only became a composer because a lyric he took along to a publisher's was assumed to be a complete song: asked how the tune went, Berlin made it up.

As a lyricist, he was one of the first to inhale the idiom of urban immigrant America, and to rhyme in American, even offering for the unrhymeable

---

1. Caesar wrote, as noted in the article, "Tea for Two" and "Swanee"; Ronell was one of the writers of "Who's Afraid of the Big, Bad Wolf?" but had a more artistic achievement with "Willow Weep for Me," which is now a jazz classic; Green wrote "Body and Soul"; Fain's "The Deadwood Stage" may now be forgotten, but he wrote two classic hits, "Let a Smile Be Your Umbrella" and "Love Is a Many Splendored Thing."

"orange" the ingenious "doorhinge" (which just about works in certain U.S. accents).

Asked in 1913 to assess "The Popular Song" he wrote: "Born just to live for a short space of time / Hated by highbrows who call it a crime," Irving Berlin went on to prove himself wrong. As for the highbrows, well, there's some things you can't teach. In the words of Annie Oakley, "You don't have to know how to read or write / When you're out with a feller in the pale moonlight / That comes natur'lly." And so, apparently, can songwriting.

IRVING GAESAR, LYRICIST OF "TEA FOR TWO" AND "SWANEE"
Irving's seven years older than me, but we both grew up on the Lower East Side like a lot of songwriters—Kalmar and Ruby, the Gershwins. Our parents arrived from Europe at Ellis Island and they'd just settle in the ghetto: those were the days before immigrants started moving north or out to Brooklyn. I've never known why so many songwriters came from the East Side, but I will say this. The Jewish immigrants always liked to rhyme, you'd call out to one, "*Izzy*," and he'd say; "I'm not busy." And most of us learnt from the little Jewish patter songs of those days.

Irving started as a singing waiter—he worked at Nigger Mike's in China-town. But it was "Alexander's Ragtime Band" that really got him going. I remember him introducing it at the old Burlesque Theatre in the Bowery. Irving sang—he had no voice but he was very effective—and there was a spon-taneous reaction. We all knew we'd heard something we'd never, ever forget. Today, a song can be heard in millions of places simultaneously, but in those days it could only be sung in one place at one time. Yet, within a few months, it was a hit all over the world.

Irving and I are very different. I'm an anti-militarist—I couldn't write a song about war—but Irving's more pragmatic, he's a survivor. And, when he joined the army during the First World War, he wrote songs that were not good, they were brilliant. I remember talking to some children, telling them all popular songs are about love, and one said to me "What about 'Oh! How I Hate to Get Up in the Morning'?" The kid had me by the throat. That song's about a soldier who's tired from marching, and only Irving could have made it a hit.

Irving's always been a loner—I mean, he's never around for the poker games, that sort of thing—but he called me a few weeks ago and told me this story. Some years ago, an interviewer asked him: "Mr. Berlin, can you write a hit song anytime you want to?" and he said, "No, only Cole Porter can do that." She giggled and told him she'd asked Cole the same question, and he said, "No, only Irving Berlin can do that." You know what? They're both right.

BURTON LANE, COMPOSER OF *FINIAN'S RAINBOW*

I was a teenager the first time I met Berlin. I'd placed a few songs with his publishing company. Those were the days when they were full of little booths, each with a piano, and Berlin would come and call me into his office to play me a new song. Like most self-taught pianists, he played on the black notes because he could pick them out easily—the three and the two—and he had special pianos with a lever that raised and lowered the pitch. His music secretary would make his piano parts and fill in the harmonies, and Berlin would say, "No, no. That's not what I meant." He could hear what he wanted, but he couldn't write it down.

He played very badly—everything sounded terrible—and it was the lyrical construction that let you know how good the song was. And you thought, "Gee, that sounds good, I'd love to hear it played properly." Mostly, he started with a lyric idea, which he'd work out very carefully. In "How Deep Is the Ocean?" (1932), every line except one is a question, and the questions are answered by other questions: "And if I ever lost you, how much would I cry? How deep is the ocean? How high is the sky?" He was a Tin Pan Alleyman, yet, without any education, he managed to write beautiful, honest songs that are never embarrassing. You know, you sometimes squirm when you hear a sentimental balled. But not with Berlin.

We've had great composers in this country, but, when it comes to songwriting, Berlin is head and shoulders above any of them. Under our laws, though, he's outlived the copyrights on his early songs, including "Alexander's Ragtime Band." He enlightens the world with his songs, and they're not even his anymore. They're public property. That's a tragedy.

JOHN GREEN: COMPOSER OF "BODY AND SOUL"

I'm very proud of the recordings I made with Fred Astaire of the songs from *Top Hat* and *Follow the Fleet* because I know that Fred was Irving's favorite singer—hands down, no question. But I'd known Irving since I was 14 years old. I was a pushy youngster, always hanging around stage doors and publishing houses, and that's how I met him. So although I love things like the release of "Top Hat," I go way back to "Pack Up Your Sins and Go to the Devil," which is rhythmically extraordinary. At that time, we'd heard nothing like it. Of course, Irving's definition of a good song is a hit song. He's not interested in the others—until, that is, somebody violates the copyright laws.

Irving has one of the most sophisticated senses of harmony of anyone I've known. He had an obligation to write four new songs for *Easter Parade* so, when his musical secretary was taken ill, I said I'd help out by taking down his music. He played one of the new songs—in F sharp, as usual—and I wrote it down and played it back to him. "What do you think?" he asked. "It's great," I said, "but in the third bar you used the third in the bass, and I think it sounds a little muddy. Why not use the fifth?" He said: "Play it your way," so I did. Then, he said: "Play it my way," so I did. And back and forth until finally he announced: "I think we'll have it *my* way." So anytime anybody says Irving can't write music or gives you that old story about the little colored boy in the closet who wrote all his tunes, you slug 'em in the teeth from me.

SAMMY FAIN: COMPOSER OF "THE DEADWOOD STAGE"
In the early '30s we all moved from New York to Hollywood because, with talking pictures, that was suddenly where most of the work was. You'd be under contract to a studio, and you'd go along for a while with no assignment, and then suddenly they'd say, "We're shooting Thursday. We need three songs." And they'd put your songs in other fellows' pictures. But Berlin was an exception. They respected him—not just because he'd written big commercial songs, but also because he was a powerful publisher. He never had interpolations from other writers in his films and the movie was always billed as "Irving Berlin's such-and-such."

He wasn't a brilliant pianist, but he played with his soul. Once, when I was living at the Beverly Wilshire Hotel, I had a new grand piano he wanted to try. He played a few bars of something, and said, "That's no good. I'm going to discard it." It sounded fine to me, but then he used to throw out lots of songs other writers would have kept.

Then he said, "I've got something new I'm working on," and he played, "Heaven, I'm in heaven, and my heart beats so that I can barely speak." "Cheek to Cheek" was one of his first film songs for Astaire and Rogers at RKO. It was a new kind of musical picture, more sophisticated, more intimate than the Buzz Berkeley spectaculars at Warners.

They say he can't write a bad song, which isn't strictly true. The best writers aren't always on top form, and he's had flops like *Miss Liberty*. One or two people, like Harry Warren, felt he got too much acclaim. For all his great catalogue, Warren was unrecognized, and he'd make a lot of sarcastic cracks that were deeply felt. I remember him in the war saying, "They bombed the wrong Berlin." But most of us have always felt Berlin deserves his special status. I call him the songwriters' songwriter. He likes that.

JULE STYNE: COMPOSER OF *GYPSY* AND *FUNNY GIRL*
I met Irving at 20th Century Fox. I was a vocal coach on *On the Avenue* (1937), which he wrote, and he used to take me to Chinese restaurants every night and pay the cook $100 to be allowed into the kitchen to cook me a meal.

Irving's early songs are great: "I love a piano . . . P-I-A-N-oh-oh-oh . . ." That's my favorite lyric of all time. Oscar Hammerstein said Irving was the greatest because he said, "I'll be loving you always." Most fellows couldn't do that; they'd try to be clever. But it's easier to be Larry Hart or Cole Porter than Irving Berlin, to be clever or cynical.

When Irving wrote "There's No Business Like Show Business," it was originally for the two guys. Then Dick Rodgers said, "That song's so good you have to let Merman do it." So after the two guys sang it to her, she went, "You mean?'—There's no business . . ." and she did the second chorus.

All of us who write for the theatre or popular music owe everything to Irving. He established the forms of popular songs. Little tricks—like putting a tag in the rest bars of the first eight ("In-ci-den-tal-ly"), he started those. People talk about these fellows like Scott Joplin. But Irving wrote better songs; he had better ideas. He changed popular music in England, too. Remember all those junky Edwardian things? You'd have lots of verses, and just a little 8-bar chorus. Irving changed all that. He realized the chorus counted for far more.

And he gave songwriters respect, too. He helped set up ASCAP to look after our interests, and, because of his reputation, people began treating us as a profession. That's why we put him on a pedestal above the rest of us. He's the Tower of London, the Statue of Liberty.

~~~~~~

| 31 |

Marilyn Berger: Berlin at 100: Life on a High Note

In 1916 the *New York Times* published an article drawing on what was already the standard biography detailing Berlin's career and life story. Seventy-two years later, the *Times* joined the hundredth birthday celebrations, with an article that is primarily a collection of entertaining anecdotes about Berlin by colleagues. Even at this late date, some of the errors of the Berlin biography persist, in this case the enduring legend that he played only on the black keys of the piano [see the introduction to "The Boy Who Invented Ragtime"]. Among the tales, the brilliant agent Irving "Swifty" Lazar confirms that Berlin was always his own public relations man. Finally, the closing story about Cary Grant

SOURCE *New York Times*, May 8, 1988. Reprinted by permission of the *New York Times*.

is one of those wonderful show business tales that would be scoffed at if had been written for a film rather than being true.

In the 1950s, when Irving Berlin complained that 20th Century Fox had paid more to Rodgers and Hammerstein for *Oklahoma!* than it was offering him for *Annie Get Your Gun*, Joseph M. Schenck, the studio head, tried to reason with him.

"What do you care?" asked Schenck. "Half a million, $750,000. What difference does it make? You're so rich, and anyway you give 91 percent to the government."

"Joe," Mr. Berlin reportedly explained. "You don't understand. I came to this country from Russia and look what's happened to me. This country has been wonderful to me. I love this country. I *love* to pay taxes."

That one story, out of hundreds that have been told about him, best sums up Irving Berlin's century-long love affair with America. He is more than this country's poet laureate of song. He is a great—and grateful—patriot, and, despite his feelings about taxes, an astute businessman. He is also loving, sentimental, generous and competitive and a lifelong insomniac, which explains why he hates to get up in the morning. He is a painter and a poker player and one of the most private men in or out of show business. These days he talks to just a few friends, and then only on the telephone in the still-young, wispy, slightly foggy voice in which he first sang his elegant, simple songs.

On Wednesday he will be 100 years old, a birthday that will be marked by an ASCAP-Carnegie Hall celebration that evening starring some of the greats from show business, some of them on the way to becoming almost as legendary as Irving Berlin.

Though Mr. Berlin has become something of a recluse, the many stories about him—some of which may be accurate—are still making the rounds and have become part of the mythology, the oral history of his hundred years as songwriter to America.

Friends say that Mr. Berlin is not a man to stroll down memory lane, that he is more interested in what's happening today than in what happened yesterday. But with his birthday upon us, it seemed high time to get people who worked with him to reminisce, thereby to add to the lore. No great themes emerged, just stories.

It is reported that Mr. Berlin is fond of saying these days that from the neck up he's still in great shape and that new tunes are still running through his head.

When friends call and ask, "What are you up to?" he has been known to say, "I'm working on a score." In fact, Steve Lawrence, the singer, says that when somebody called a year or two ago to ask Mr. Berlin if he might use one of his songs, the answer was no. "I'm going to put it in a new show I'm working on."

But when Jerome Robbins asked not long ago if he might use the song "Mr. Monotony," which had been dropped from a show years ago, Mr. Berlin is supposed to have said, "I'll pay you to use it."[1]

Consider this. By 1924, Irving Berlin was the most famous songwriter in America, even though he could neither read nor write music. He could only give birth to it, Alexander Woollcott wrote. By 1925, Woollcott had already written a biography of the man he called "a creative ignoramus." Mr. Berlin, he said, "stamped a new character on American music" with the syncopated rhythms of "Alexander's Ragtime Band," which he wrote in 1911. That means that Irving Berlin has been famous for at least 77 years. In 1958 Gilbert Millstein wrote in the *New York Times* that Mr. Berlin could "safely, and sentimentally, be called the greatest popular songwriter who ever lived."

Sammy Cahn, no slouch himself when it comes to writing hit songs, said, "Here's a startling statistic. If a man, in a lifetime of 50 years, can point to six songs that are immediately identifiable, he has achieved something. I'll give you an accurate statistic. Irving Berlin can sing 60 that are immediately identifiable. Somebody once said you couldn't have a holiday without his permission: 'Happy Holiday,' 'Easter Parade,' 'White Christmas.'"

Songs seemed to have a way of just happening to Irving Berlin. Once, when Fred Astaire was waiting in the hospital while his wife was having a baby, Mr. Berlin played cards with him. In the middle of the game, as the story goes, he asked, "What do you think of this for a tune?" Astaire listened for a moment and said, "I like it." "Good," Mr. Berlin replied. "Gin."

Another time, as Mr. Cahn tells it, Mr. Berlin was in Los Angeles during the filming of the movie *Holiday Inn* and when Mr. Berlin was walking out of his bungalow at the Beverly Hills Hotel some words formed a verse in his mind:

The sun is shining, the grass is green,
The orange and palm trees sway.
There's never been such a day in Beverly Hills, L.A.
But it's December the twenty-fourth,
And I am longing to be up north.

---

1. "Mr. Monotony" was dropped more than once—it originally was performed by Judy Garland in *Easter Parade*, but was cut as it was too sophisticated for her character and made the film too long. Berlin later tried to place it in *Miss Liberty* where it was dropped out of town, and again in *Call Me Madam*, in which it was sung by Ethel Merman but even her talents could not keep it from being again dropped out of town. Some thought was given to placing it in the film *There's No Business Like Show Business* (perhaps for Merman again), but it did not survive beyond the planning stages.

"That verse became the introduction to the phrase 'I'm dreaming of a white Christmas,'" which, Mr. Cahn says "is one of the most important copyrights in the history of copyrights."[2]

Rosemary Clooney remembers working with Mr. Berlin on a later (1954) film called *White Christmas*. The title song had already become a standard, having been featured in the earlier movie *Holiday Inn*. It was recycled for the new film and, as Miss Clooney tells it, Irving Berlin was on the sound stage when she and Bing Crosby and Danny Kaye were recording. "He walked up and down and paced back and forth as though there had never been a recording and it wasn't already a hit. Finally, Bing said, 'Irving, go over there and sit down. Go to the dressing room. This is already a hit. There's nothing we can do to hurt it.'"

Like so many turn-of-the-century immigrants, Irving Berlin—then known as Izzy Baline—started out on New York's Lower East Side. He graduated from a paper route to a job as a singing waiter and soon was writing his own material, composing all his tunes on the black keys of a piano in the back of a saloon. In his 100 years he never learned to play in any key but F sharp.

But on those black keys he composed the music and wrote the words for songs that have become American classics, songs like "How Deep Is the Ocean," "Always," "Blue Skies," "There's No Business Like Show Business," "Cheek to Cheek," "This Is the Army, Mr. Jones," "Top Hat, White Tie and Tails," "Puttin' On the Ritz," "I've Got My Love to Keep Me Warm," "I Got Lost in His Arms," "It Only Happens When I Dance With You," "Isn't This a Lovely Day to Be Caught in the Rain?" "I Left My Heart at the Stage Door Canteen," "The Girl That I Marry," "They Say It's Wonderful," "What'll I Do?" "A Pretty Girl Is Like a Melody," "You're Just in Love." He was the first to admit that some of his songs were less memorable, including one of his first, called "Cohen Owes Me 97 Dollars."[3]

---

2. Verses sometimes were later additions to songs that were otherwise finished and may have already appeared in a show or film. Berlin did write the entire "White Christmas" before filming.

3. With Berlin "early" is a relative term. "Cohen" comes from 1915, by which time Berlin was an established figure on Tin Pan Alley and Broadway. Since it has been mentioned here, it is worth pointing out that "Cohen" is a fine example of the type of ethnic song Berlin wrote in the 1910s. During this period ethnic songs were popular and usually were demeaning of the ethnic group in question. Berlin wrote many of them, often playing on stereotypes but in a way that was not demeaning; in this case he is satirizing the stereotype as much as he is making fun of supposed Jewish parsimony.

Mr. Berlin is fond of saying that there are only six tunes in the world. Once, when George Abbott, the legendary director who is a year older than Mr. Berlin, said he liked one of his tunes, Mr. Berlin said, "I do too. I've used it lots of times."

No matter how successful he became or how famous, Mr. Berlin never gave up selling his own songs by the sheer weight of his personality. The moment he finished a song he couldn't wait to sing it to someone—often on the telephone. Hal Prince remembers that when he was a kid just starting out on Broadway he was in the middle of a casting call for *Call Me Madam*. Hundreds of singers and dancers had shown up and were pressing the barricades when the telephone rang backstage. As Mr. Prince remembers it:

"The voice on the other end said, 'This is Irving Berlin, who's this?'

"'This is Hal Prince, Mr. Berlin.'

"'Well, who are you?' And I said, 'I'm casting and I'm assistant stage managing; there's a chorus call today.'

"He asked for George Abbott, the director; he asked for [Howard] Lindsay and [Russel] Crouse, the writers, but no one was around. They couldn't take the multitudes that had shown up. Then he asked for Ethel Merman, the star of the show, and she wasn't there either.

"'Well, who are you?' Berlin asked once again.

"'I'm the assistant stage manager,' I said, whereupon Berlin sang an entire song to me over the phone.

"'What do you think of it?' he asked, and I said, 'I like it.'

"He said, 'Good, so do I,' and hung up."

Irving P. Lazar, the high-powered agent known to everyone in show business as Swifty, says he was there when Irving Berlin walked into Arthur Freed's office at MGM carrying a package under his arm. "It was obvious that he had a portfolio of music, so Freed said, 'What's that?' Irving Berlin said it was a new score. 'I've got to hear it,' Freed said.

"When Berlin said he didn't want anyone to hear it, Freed—who was one of the great producers of Hollywood musicals—was beside himself. He said 'I've got to hear it.' The problem was that Irving Berlin couldn't use the piano in the office—he needed one with a clutch that could change key, since he could only play in F sharp—but beseeched by Freed he finally took out one piece of music.

"The way Berlin sold a song was unique. He would lean his face within an inch of yours and sing it to you. Well, he sang that song and some others and Freed bought the score for a million dollars. He was the first to sell a score for a million."

The score was for a film that was supposed to be based on the life story of Irving Berlin—*Say It with Music*. But a script was never approved.[4] Irving Berlin got the score back and, according to Mr. Lazar, he got to keep the million.

Some time after that, Mr. Lazar recalls, he and Mr. Berlin went to lunch at Romanoff's. "I said to him, 'You're the biggest hero in America. Why do you go around selling your own stuff? Why don't you have me as your agent—it's more dignified. You don't have to sing it to anybody. That's so cheap, so second-rate. With your music what do you want to do that for?' So he said to me, 'Listen. If you were me would you hire you to be my agent?' I said, 'No.' So he said, 'So what are you bothering me for?'"

In Hollywood, Mr. Berlin was known as a fierce poker player, and, according to Mr. Lazar, the biggest winner. A lot of money that Irving Berlin won, and much that he earned in royalties from copyrights he held as publisher, lyricist and composer of more than a thousand songs, has been given away. A measure of the hundreds of millions of dollars he is believed to have earned in his lifetime can be seen in what he has given to charity.[5]

The entire proceeds from his World War II revue *This Is the Army*—just under $10 million in the final accounting—first went to the Army Emergency Relief Fund. When the fund was discontinued the royalties from those songs were added to the God Bless America Foundation, first established with the proceeds from one song, the song that has become an alternative American anthem. Those royalties still go to the Boy Scouts and Girl Scouts of Greater New York, and, according to the Foundation Center, grants from the fund in 1985 alone totaled $90,000. In 1982 the Scouts shared $110,000.

The office of the Irving Berlin Music Corporation gives out virtually no information about Irving Berlin, least of all about his charitable contributions, which extend far beyond scouting. But the figures contained in the God Bless America Foundation's publicly reported tax returns for only those two years give some indication of the amount given to scouting since the fund was established sometime after 1938. That was the year Mr. Berlin pulled an old song out of a file for Kate Smith.

Mr. Berlin had written that song, "God Bless America," years before, for his World War I Army revue, *Yip, Yip, Yaphank*. But he dropped it from the score

---

4. Berlin never allowed his life story to be dramatized, so that idea for the film was abandoned immediately. "Say It With Music" went through many script revisions, with one version being three separate love stories taking place at different times—1911, 1925, and 1965—told simultaneously.

5. Berlin's charity work was the subject of controversy in the 1990s when people intent on showing that he was unpleasant in his later years posited that he ignored Jewish charities. This simply was not true.

because he felt it was too patriotic, even for him, to have soldiers singing it in that show.

Musicians are notoriously ungenerous to each one another, and because of his enormous success, Mr. Berlin was the target of a lot of jealousy in Tin Pan Alley. Harry Warren, who wrote "42nd Street," is quoted as having said, "The trouble with World War II was they bombed the wrong Berlin."

Stories persist—stories usually whispered off the record—that even when he was at the top of the heap, Irving Berlin was not fond of seeing other songwriters succeed. Some say he suffered from a sense of inferiority because he had never been trained as a musician. But he was also capable of the generous gesture. When Cole Porter had a big hit on Broadway—nobody seems to remember whether it was *Kiss Me Kate* or *Can Can*—Mr. Berlin, in a reprise of his own song in *Annie Get Your Gun*, sent a telegram to his fellow composer. It said, "Anything I can do you can do better."

Leonard Gershe, the playwright, who is a friend of Mr. Berlin's, says, "Kern, Porter. He adored their work. He says, 'I can't hold a candle to what they do.'"

Irving Berlin was a charter member of ASCAP, the American Society of Composers, Authors and Publishers, established in 1914 to protect the royalties of songwriters over the decades. The first year that the annual ASCAP survey did not contain a new Irving Berlin song was 1958. But he returned to the list in 1966 with "An Old Fashioned Walk," a song he wrote for the revival of *Annie Get Your Gun*.[6]

Irving Berlin tried retirement but it didn't agree with him. He tried golf, and he hated it. He tried fishing, but it didn't interest him. He was a man of no hobbies until, fairly late in life, he found one suited to his temperament, a hobby for which the songwriter Harold Rome takes a measure of credit.

"I used to go to Central Park in the old days with my watercolors," Mr. Rome said. "One day, as I was coming out of the park on my bike I ran into Irving Berlin. He said, 'What are you doing? I showed him and he said, 'Gee whiz, that doesn't look too hard.' I said it is wonderful, a wonderful way to spend your time. He said he'd like to try it. He did and he became a painter."

Mr. Berlin has said that "as a painter I'm a pretty good songwriter." But his friends treasure his canvases, many of which are unusual collages of photographs surrounded by his oil painting. Jule Styne, who wrote *Funny Girl*, keeps

---

6. "Let's Take an Old-Fashioned Walk" was from *Miss Liberty*. The song in *Annie Get Your Gun* was "An Old Fashioned Wedding."

a copy of a painting Mr. Berlin did of Barbra Streisand, in which, Mr. Styne thinks, he painted Barbra Streisand with Fanny Brice's nose.

Americans have marched to war to Irving Berlin songs and fallen in love to Irving Berlin songs; they remember who they were and where they were by what Irving Berlin song was popular at the time. One of his perennial hits, in fact, is called "Remember."

Yet Irving Berlin himself can never seem to remember that he has become a legend. About 10 years ago, according to Leonard Gershe, Veronique and Gregory Peck hosted a musical evening. "Cary Grant sang 'Lazy' and he was very funny because he acted it out. But he got the last line screwed up, so the next day I called Irving and said he should send Cary Grant a copy of the lyrics because he had gotten them mixed up. Irving got all excited and said, 'You mean *Cary Grant* sang *my* song?'

"Well, Berlin sent the sheet music with a note and Cary called me and said, 'Can you believe I got a *letter* from *Irving Berlin*!' He said, 'This goes in the vault.' For the next three weeks Cary composed a letter to Irving and he kept calling me to read me the different drafts. They all sounded all right to me, but each time Cary said it wasn't good enough, it wasn't good enough for *Irving Berlin*. Now the phone rings and it's Irving. 'I got a letter from *Cary Grant* and the children are coming over to read it.'"

~~~~~~

| 32 |

Murray Kempton: Bit of Blues for Ballads of Berlin

A sour note on the hundredth birthday festivities comes in a critical commentary by political journalist Murray Kempton (1917–1997), who is clearly no Berlin lover. His early years in journalism were as a copyboy for H. L. Mencken, which perhaps explains his cynical tone. Once again a critic is underestimating Berlin's abilities (as did Brooks Atkinson in the review of *Annie Get Your Gun*). As has been noted by more perceptive observers, Berlin could write well-crafted, even sophisticated, songs which deceived by their apparent simplicity.

Mightn't one small and not too disrespectful cough be permitted in the clouds of incense smoking up from all these altars to Irving Berlin?

SOURCE *New York Newsday*, May 15, 1988. Reprinted by permission of *Newsday*.

He is, of course, an immensely old party, and too few of us can look at a sere and yellow leaf without surrendering to seductions toward gilding it. Ever since I commenced protracting my own sunset, the world has been larding me with forgivenesses unearned and even a few honors unmerited.

Not long ago, I wandered uncredentialed past a Secret Service barrier. One of my juniors asked how I had done it, and it popped into my head to reply that you can work hard and you might even be talented, but nothing helps like being old.

Still, useful as it is, old age cannot convey the clearest of titles to exemption from detached assessment, and it may indeed be subject to suspicion among the heavenly powers. If I flog myself through another 10 years before yielding up the ghost, I shall be unsurprised if the Recording Angel's opening question is, "Where you been so long? Dodging subpoenas?"

The coldest eye could not, to be sure, cast itself upon Irving Berlin's copybook without noticing several flecks of gold. A measure of glory must forever sit on the shoulders of any man who once drew a royalty from a Bessie Smith record.

"Easter Parade" remains a lovely tune undiluted with a trace of the vulgarities of the occasion of its inspiration. We tend to enshrine "Easter Parade" among Berlin's contribution to the secular hymnal from which we chant those "Magnificats" to ourselves that we might more fitly reserve for the Almighty.

But that song ought to be left to shine by itself for being so superior to the rest of the items in the Berlin psalter. I once suffered unexpected throbs of the heart at hearing "White Christmas" in New Guinea one December, but am disinclined to travel 12,000 miles to see if it would happen again. I shall pass over "God Bless America" except for saying that I hope He always will, particularly at those junctures when we might tempt Him to recall His youth as the Lord God Jehovah and deliver us to damnation and the Philistines.

I also omit mention of the finales in his musicals where all members of the ensemble, including such stagehands as are sober, arise to proclaim with patent insincerity that they are the happiest of living creatures. It is kinder and more just to run the mind back to "Isn't This a Lovely Day?," that not least enduring of the unforgettabilities of Fred Astaire and Ginger Rogers, or to the up-tempo Berlin tunes Bing Crosby recorded in the period when, as *Time* so wonderfully said, he sang every song as if it were the best he had ever heard.

But may the good Lord deliver us from those dreary ballads. "A Pretty Girl Is Like a Melody" is far short of what a pretty girl is about, particularly in the matter of melody. To think of what the Gershwins did with a ballad in the days when Berlin was doing his very best is almost to lapse from good manners.

But then his failure upon any such comparison may explain why the supreme art singers so seldom call upon Berlin. Frank Sinatra did an exhilarating "Blue Skies" when he was conscript to Columbia Records but, once his taste in the ballad was free to exercise full sovereignty, he preferred to explore the more adult profundities of Rodgers and Hart and the Gershwins.

And I think those lights and shades of grown-up experience are what we finally miss in Berlin.

He spares us the illusions of adultery but he cheats us of the bitter wisdom that follows the fall into it.

There is a want of the depths of emotion, and it may explain why, if he probably stole from others—as who hasn't?—so few others bothered to steal from him.

His is just not quite the stuff to inspire the improvisation of changes up to the ones Charlie Parker blew on "Embraceable You." None of us could ever imagine what Parker might draw out of a melody until he had set about it, but it is hard to conceive of even him draining Berlin of the treasures he pulled from Gershwin.

But that was Gershwin. Mercer Ellington tells of the day his father hired Ben Webster. Webster was one of God's chosen grouches and started right off complaining that there was too much in the Ellington book for him to learn.

"Don't worry," Duke Ellington assured him. "Just sit there and, whenever it's time for the whole band, just play 'I Got Rhythm.' Something will come up."

And something did. It was "Cottontail."

The reports that Irving Berlin is a sour old man are beyond my competence to judge. But I can understand how he might be. He had mourned—perhaps not unrelievedly—George Gershwin and Jerome Kern and along came Cole Porter, Ellington, Harold Arlen, etc. and etc., and then all of them were buried, and suddenly, when song seemed to have dried to dust, up rose "Let It Be."

Our betters simply won't go away. Do you think it's comfortable for me to trudge with my dim torch on a track better lit so often by Russell Baker and Jimmy Breslin? But all you can do is to accept the gods as the inequitable distributors of gifts they are, do what you can—as Irving Berlin so well did—with what you were given and not be bitter.

33

Josh Rubins: Genius without Tears

The *New York Review of Books* made note of Berlin's centenary in a lengthy, insightful article by Josh Rubins. Some of the songs he assesses have been discussed in previous articles, a testament to the enduring interest in these songs by critics of all kinds. Unfortunately he continues the misunderstanding of "Easter Parade" and its source in "Smile and Show Your Dimple."

Rubins points out the dangers of overexposure in some of the most famous Berlin songs. Any creative artist can become a victim of his own success. Many good Berlin songs are lost because of a few that are ubiquitous; the same is true for Richard Rodgers, and George Gershwin's orchestral music is almost totally eclipsed by the "Rhapsody in Blue." Rubins neatly reminds us of the qualities that made these Berlin songs overexposed, along with insight into how Berlin seemingly effortlessly made the unusual seem commonplace, both in terms of his music and lyrics.

It seems appropriate, if highly ironic, that a year celebrating George Gershwin—a new biography, concerts, recordings—has by now dovetailed into a year of tributes to Irving Berlin. Much of the irony, of course, lies in the lopsided juxtaposition of these "contemporaries," born only ten years apart. While 1987 marked the fiftieth anniversary of Gershwin's death at age thirty-eight, the 1988 festivities honor a living composer on his one hundredth birthday. (Berlin was born in Temun, Russia, on May 11, and came to America with his family in 1892[1].) Some whimsical Olympian dispenser of talent and life spans appears to have played a dark prank on musical history.

In creative territory, too, the forever-young composer and the grand old songwriter make a strange yet ineluctable couple, more complementary, even

SOURCE *New York Review of Books*, June 16, 1988. Reprinted by permission of *The New York Review of Books*, copyright 1988 NYREV, Inc.

1. Actually 1893.

polar, than twin-like. Gershwin, often in inspired collaboration with his brother Ira, reached from the theater song "up"—as cultural convention would have it—to concert works, operetta, and opera. Berlin, writing both music and words, stuck with the broader, downtown segment of musical life in America, the world of player pianos and dance bands and juke-boxes; in this realm the theater song (or its film-musical equivalent) was the upper limit of "serious-ness" and the thirty-two bar was the basic form, continually reexamined yet rarely expanded. Jerome Kern and Richard Rodgers created more ambitious and ravishing specimens of the romantic ballad and, in Broadway collabora-tions, made bolder contributions to the evolution of musical theater; much of the jazz and blues of Duke Ellington and Harold Arlen has greater depth. But, between them, more than any others, Gershwin and Berlin embody the remarkable range of distinctive American composition in the first half of the twentieth century.

For Berlin, admittedly, the 1988 celebration is largely a case of *déjà vu*. He first found himself famous more than seventy-five years ago, in 1911, when "Alex-ander's Ragtime Band"—a virtually unsyncopated march, far less Joplinesque than a dozen earlier ragtime songs (including several by Berlin himself)—triggered a world-wide "ragtime" craze. The twenty-three-year-old songwriter, an uninhibited eclectic from the start, had managed to distill a simplified, strutting pulse from the rhythms of urban black music, combining it with just enough harmonic sophistication (e.g., the way the second line unexpect-edly leaps up a fourth) to challenge and stimulate, but not alienate, a mass audience.

Two world wars later, as the source of such ubiquitous anthems as "White Christmas," "God Bless America," "Easter Parade," and "There's No Busi-ness Like Show Business," Berlin came to be regarded as an institution: a totem of patriotic values, a folk hero of sorts. And, in every decade since, there have been reverential salutes to the longevity of both the songs and the man. The week of the hundredth birthday itself predictably elicited the most extravagant testimonials thus far. Journalists and broadcasters echoed each other in invoking the same phrases: "America's songwriter laureate," "Mr. American Music," "genius," "beloved," "legendary," Kate Smith's ren-dition of "God Bless America" seemed to be on permanent televisual dis-play, frequently followed by a solemn anchorperson intoning "God bless Irving Berlin."

Yet, despite this adulation (or, to some degree, because of it), Berlin's work—especially its musical component—remains undervalued, only half-appreciated. For many urbane listeners, his name immediately, if somewhat misleadingly, calls up an off-putting knot of associations: simplistic refrains, conservative or jingoistic sentiments, popularity with (in Berlin's own ironic words) "the mob." Such an impression would certainly have been reinforced by most of those centenary paeans. (Even the coverage by PBS's *MacNeil/Lehrer Newshour* was embarrassingly superficial.) Similarly, musicologists—including the few who no longer treat Gershwin with condescension—have shown little inclination to take bar-by-bar interest in scores by Irving Berlin.

That academics would have a problem with Berlin is not surprising. He presents that baffling phenomenon: the thoroughly illiterate yet cultivated master who is impossible to dismiss as a "primitive" or "folk artist." From a far poorer family than Gershwin's, Berlin quit school at eight to sell newspapers and wait on tables (his father, a part-time cantor, had died). He never learned to read or write music. His by-ear piano playing—only in the key of F#, which keeps the fingers almost exclusively on the black keys—was energetic, ten-fingered, but rudimentary. He took a rigorously practical approach to the songwriting profession, shunning any "artistic" pretensions and cheerfully acknowledging his apparent technical limitations. (His purchase of a specially built piano, one that could mechanically change from key to key as Berlin continued to play in F#, was widely publicized.)

In *The New Grove Dictionary of Music and Musicians*, Berlin—though identified as "perhaps the most versatile and successful American popular songwriter of the 20th century"—receives barely two columns, with a single paragraph of appraisal: less attention than Gunnar Berg or Erich Bergel or Jan Levoslav Bella. The few attempts at a Berlin biography, beginning with Alexander Woollcott's 1925 *The Story of Irving Berlin*, have resulted in ragged personality sketches, devoid of critical ambition or musicological credibility. A reductionist notion of "tunesmith Irving Berlin" persists: on his ninety-ninth birthday, an affectionate but ill-informed and patronizing *New York Times* editorial presented the hackneyed image of folksy Mr. Berlin picking out melodies "on the piano with one finger."

The songwriter himself bears much of the responsibility for the dearth of reliable Berlin-iana. Not only has he allowed the image of an untutored street-kid composer to harden with time into caricature. He has aggressively opposed, since the 1920s, nearly all investigative efforts by would-be biographers, critics, and cultural historians. One could attribute this hostility—and Berlin's fiercely anti-intellectual posture—to defensiveness: the illiterate's fear of ridicule (even if Woollcott, who called Berlin a "creative ignoramus," reminded readers that Homer, too, was probably unable to write down what he composed). Or one could mention instead Berlin's more general antipathy for the press, apparently dating back to his 1924 courtship of the cable heiress Ellin Mackay; she became his second wife—but not until after news-hounds had pursued the couple from city to city, trumpeted the opposition of Mackay's father (an anti-Semitic tycoon) in headlines, and announced to the world that Berlin's recent ballads ("Remember," "All Alone," "What'll I Do?") were written out of a star-crossed lover's anguish. Berlin denied one story after another, ineffectually.

A few years later he was stung by the goading public discussion of a creative dry spell that preceded his 1930s resurgence. Thereafter, though always pre-pared to plug a new song or show with zeal, he reportedly remained suspicious of journalists' motives and skeptical about their competence. Not without rea-son: during just the past year the *New York Times* buried the composer (with a reference to "lawyers for the Irving Berlin estate"), declared that his last show, *Mr. President*, "closed out of town" (it ran on Broadway for eight months), and—in a hundredth-birthday piece—confused "An Old-Fashioned Wedding" with "Let's Take an Old-Fashioned Walk."

Fortunately, however, the true dimensions of Berlin's achievement have been kept in view by some of his most erudite colleagues. Stravinsky, who used the word "genius" far less casually than television news writers do, applied it to Berlin. Virgil Thomson wrote in 1947 that there are not "five American 'art composers' who can be compared, as song writers, for either technical skill or artistic responsibility, with Irving Berlin." Isaac Stern, in truncated interviews during the hundredth-birthday celebration, suggested how Berlin's long-lined melodies recall Mozart's and Schubert's. And, in a less subjective vein, the impeccably trained arrangers and orchestrators who took "musical dictation" from Berlin—Robert Russell Bennett and John Green, among others—testify that he never merely sang them a tune. All the harmonies, and often the *voicing* of those harmonies (the far subtler question of which notes in a chord are played high, low, or in a middle position), were clearly formed in Berlin's mind—even if he could not himself transcribe or fully play the precise chord sequences he heard in some inner ear.

In a landmark 1972 study, *American Popular Song: The Great Innovators, 1900–1950*, the late Alec Wilder, taking a scholarly yet unpedantic approach to the history of popular music, offered a fairly persuasive assessment of Berlin as "the best all-around, over-all song writer America has ever had." Wilder, a composer of chamber music as well as a gifted songwriter ("I'll Be Around," "While We're Young"), pronounced himself to be "frankly astounded" by the sophistication of many Berlin songs. He also concluded—somewhat reluctantly—that the harmonic complexities involved were unquestionably the composer's own work: "It is very nearly impossible, upon hearing some of these melodies, to believe that every chord was not an integral part of the creation of the tune."

Why, then, is Berlin still underrated by many sophisticated people?[2] The platitudinous lyrics for songs like "God Bless America" and "The Girl That I Marry" are one reason. Another, as Wilder pointed out, is that the numbing familiarity of a few Berlin songs has made it easy to overlook their quality. From even the most knowledgeable listeners, for example, "White Christmas" is more likely to summon up a blur of emotional responses, sentimental or cynical, than an appreciation of the bold chromaticism in its brooding opening phrase. In fact, though customarily embraced—or dismissed—as treacle, "White Christmas" captures, with remarkable economy and restraint, the thick mixture of moods stirred up by the Christmas and New Year holidays: nostalgia, anxiety, tenderness, depression. The melody, after several attempts to extract itself from that darkly chromatic rumination, does eventually make its way to the open-heartedness suggested by wider intervals (the gentle ascent on "merry and bright," the near-octave dip on "Christmas"); in the lyric, too, the singer moves from introspection to feelings of fellowship.

These textures were undoubtedly inspired, in part, by the specific circumstances of the song's creation, for the film *Holiday Inn*, in 1942: the warmth of Bing Crosby's lower register, the long-distance separations and heightened apprehensions of wartime. But, for innumerable singers and succeeding generations, the song's layers and subtleties continue to generate unmawkish sentiment (a Berlin trademark)—and help to explain, as does the tune's beauty, why "White Christmas" has survived incessant repetition, bland or inane performances, and guilt by association.

On the other hand, "A Pretty Girl Is Like a Melody"—one of Berlin-the-composer's best things—has been seriously damaged by overexposure and insensitive handling, though some might put the blame in this case on Berlin-the-lyricist. The consummate professional, always ready to write for occasion or function, Berlin sometimes lavished melodic and harmonic refinement on banal verse or trivial subject matter. (The music of "Easter Parade" was originally used for a song called "Smile and Show Your Dimple.") "A Pretty Girl Is Like a Melody" was a commission for the *Ziegfeld Follies of 1919*, the thirteenth edition of the annual revue—which always featured at least one procession of whimsically costumed beauties, serenaded by a preening tenor. In 1919's *pièce de resistance* each showgirl represented

---

2. Rubins cited here the Kempton article, "Bit of Blues for Ballads of Berlin."

a well-known classical melody—Offenbach's "Barcarolle," Massenet's "Elegy," Dvorak's "Humoresque"—and Berlin's mercifully little-known verse began: "I have an ear for music/And I have an eye for a maid."[3]

Within the limitations of the *Follies* format and sensibility, the lyric for the song's chorus is spare and elegant, elaborating on the basic simile with a series of precise, unforced images: "Just like the strain / Of a haunting refrain / She'll start upon a marathon / And run around your brain." But quickly identified as the paradigm of "girlie revue" tunes, "A Pretty Girl" was seized upon as the perfect musical accompaniment for every beauty pageant, fashion show, and striptease artist. After decades of coarse performance, the melody became known almost exclusively in exaggerated versions, and the song's first four chords devolved into a vaudeville gag: musical shorthand for any reference to overt female sexuality (or transvestism). By the 1960s "A Pretty Girl" was generally regarded less as music than as a cliché, a joke, or an irresistible target for parody. A *Mad* magazine "songbook" refitted the tune with a lyric beginning "Louella Schwartz describes her malady / To everyone in sight"—one of twenty-five song parodies that led Berlin, an obsessed guardian of copyrights and royalties, to sue the magazine, without success. (The ultimate Court of Appeals decision, endorsed by the U.S. Supreme Court, defined the extent to which a parodist may borrow from the work he attempts to burlesque: "We doubt that even so eminent a composer as plaintiff Irving Berlin should be permitted to claim a property interest in iambic pentameter.")

But the music itself—as arranged for piano and voice in a "Standard Edition" from the Irving Berlin Music Corporation, and cleared (to whatever extent possible) of seventy years of sociocultural encrustation—remains fresh. Like so many other Berlin songs, "A Pretty Girl Is Like a Melody" avoids the predictable structure, known to songwriters as "AABA," that would, by the mid-1920s, become the genre's most conventional form. (The AABA form, epitomized by Gershwin's "Somebody Loves Me" or Berlin's "Blue Skies," includes three iterations of the eight-bar "A" section.) The song presents a continuous stream of new musical ideas, with only a single repeat of a six-bar section. It combines, like the best of early Kern, European lushness with American jauntiness, a grand arc of melody energized by the irreverent bounce of a few eighth notes that arrive, unexpectedly, on the downbeat. Paradoxically, the alluring nature of this music (which foreshadows, among others,

---

3. I would argue that the verse of "A Pretty Girl Is Like a Melody" does not deserve to be dismissed as "mercifully little known." As with so many Berlin verses, it does effectively set up the chorus.

Gershwin's "A Foggy Day") is both the reason it has become over familiar—while dozens of lesser *Follies* parade themes are long forgotten—and the reason it deserves to be heard anew.

Other immoderately well-known Berlin "standards" also tend to be only partially, or superficially, known. Nearly everyone can bring to mind the child-like initial phrases of "Always": "I'll be loving you, / Always, / With a love that's true, / Always." The lyric is one of Berlin's homeliest or sappiest, depending on one's viewpoint. The music, too, in these first eight bars, is melodically and harmonically plain: a waltz that features the tritest chord change of all—from the tonic (F) to the dominant (C⁷) and back to the tonic. But of those who are roughly familiar with "Always" few would be able to sing or hum on through the remainder of the song, which is anything but commonplace. While the singer continues to pledge undying devotion in the subsequent twenty-four bars, in the most prosaic and untroubled words imaginable, the music tells another story. Disturbing modulations take the melody on a precarious journey; the song briefly threatens to leave its original key entirely, straying too far ever to return. Finally, when those bone-simple opening chords, F and C⁷, do regain control, they have a different, less cozy quality because of what has preceded them.

This degree of harmonic daring was unprecedented in the Tin Pan Alley of 1925, and the fact that "Always" was also a huge commercial success encouraged others, Kern especially, to expand the musical vocabulary of the popular song. Also influential, on a much less obvious level, was the song's suggestion, almost certainly not deliberate, of psychological complexity. The contrast between the complacent, blindly optimistic lyric and the restless, spasmodic music conveys (especially in an artful performance) an undercurrent of anxiety, a dislocation between what is said or thought and what is felt—perhaps unconsciously. In this connection, it should be noted that "Always" was Berlin's wedding present to Ellin Mackay and that his first marriage in 1912 ended after five months when his bride died of typhoid fever, contracted on their honeymoon in Cuba.

Indeed, the unique capacity of the song as a form to work on two distinct levels simultaneously is what probably explains the endurance of more than a few seemingly "uninteresting" Berlin chestnuts. "All By Myself" (1921) reverses the layers: an unrelievedly woebegone lyric is redeemed by musical charm and pluck; the self-pity is slyly aerated by a major-key, buoyant melody that eschews every sad-song mannerism. "Blue Skies" (1926) takes the subtextual shading of "Always" even further. The words assert total contentment with near-fatuous certainty:

Blue skies
Smiling at me
Nothing but blue skies
Do I see.

The music, however, clings to the mournful key of E minor, allowing only momentary glimpses of G major brightness (the ostensible key signature) to break, rather wanly, through the gloom. Then, when the song's "B" section turns downright jubilant—"Never saw sun shining so bright / Never saw things going so right"—the musical intensity builds as well: these eight bars, leaning heavily on the "blue note" effect of the G chord's raised fifth, is Berlin at his most atypically lamentational and Hebraic.

Tension between words and music, rarely perceived by the listener as such yet subliminally forceful, can reflect the tangled nature, the ambivalence, of most human emotion. This internal discord, intended or not, may account for the remarkable vitality of "Blue Skies" (revived every ten years or so, most recently by Willie Nelson) and for the durability of such other mixed-message ballads as 1932's "How Deep Is the Ocean?" (favored by jazz artists, memorably recorded by Ray Charles and Sarah Vaughan). Moreover, the joyous/mournful texture of "Always" and "Blue Skies" presages the similarly layered ambivalence of the very greatest ballads of the 1930s: the Gershwins' "Love Is Here to Stay," Kern and Hammerstein's "All the Things You Are," and Rodgers and Hart's "My Funny Valentine." (Rodgers and Hart had good reason to have "Blue Skies" on their minds. In 1926, just before the opening night of their early musical *Betsy*, Florenz Ziegfeld, the producer, secretly bought a new song from Berlin for the star of *Betsy*, Belle Baker, to have as a show-stopper. In his autobiography, *Musical Stages*, Rodgers writes: "It really didn't take a trained ear to appreciate that the Berlin contribution, 'Blue Skies,' was a great piece of songwriting, easily superior to anything Larry and I had written for the production, but at the time I was crushed by having someone else's work interpolated in our score.")

The excessive familiarity of all these plain-spoken ballads—others include "Marie," "Say It Isn't So," "They Say It's Wonderful"—have damaged Berlin's reputation in another way as well. The "old favorites," love them or hate them, have distracted attention from the unparalleled range of the entire Berlin catalogue. In the very early 1920s, before "Fascinating Rhythm" from *Lady, Be Good!* (1924) definitively captured the jagged, nervy essence of citified jazz, Berlin—a veteran popularizer of tricky dance patterns—was experimenting with the irregular accents that give the Gershwin tune much of its novelty.

"Everybody Step" (1921), in fact, sounds not unlike an early draft of "Fascinating Rhythm," with both its metrical unrest and its bluesy insistence on the
interval of the minor third. Berlin's melody and rhythm on the phrase "syncopated rhythm / Let's be goin' with 'em when they begin" are very nearly dupli-
cated in the Gershwins' "What a mess you're making! / The neighbors want to
know / Why I'm always shaking / Just like a flivver." (The Gershwin music
has an extra twist, though, in the piano accompaniment, which is always in
syncopated opposition to the melody.) "Pack Up Your Sins and Go to the
Devil," from 1922, is even more advanced than "Everybody Step." And while
"Fascinating Rhythm," after sixty-some years of Copland, Thomson, Afro-
Cuban jazz, and other unsettling rhythmic challenges, has come to seem pos-
itively congenial, Berlin's masterpiece in this manner, "Puttin' On the Ritz"
(1929), remains an unnerving provocation, wonderfully subversive in its metrical eccentricity—thanks, in part, to that uneven collaborator, Berlin-the-
lyricist. The words here underline the unpredictable stresses in the music
with witty insolence:

> If *you're* blue *and*
> You *don't know* where *to*
> Go *to* why *don't you*
> Go. . . .

The rhymes are placed precisely where they will jangle rather than fall comfortably into alignment. The ear wants desperately to match the stressed "blue"
with one of those unstressed "to"s: the frustration is part of the dazzle.

That Berlin began to come into his own as a stylish lyricist with "Puttin' On
the Ritz" has a certain rightness about it—because, although the song was
written for an early talkie starring the top-hatted crooner Harry Richman, it
was promptly recorded by Fred Astaire, who would give the number its definitive performance in the 1946 film *Blue Skies*. Astaire had been a fan of
Berlin material since his vaudeville years with his sister Adele; around 1915
they bought "I Love to Quarrel With You," for their juvenile act, from the
music publishing house of Waterson, Berlin and Snyder. (They never got to
see the famous young composer himself.) But by 1935 Astaire, teamed with
Ginger Rogers, was not only a dancing film star and a remarkable singer but
also the celebrated epitome of down-to-earth cosmopolitanism and relaxed
elegance. In his past, after all, were Broadway and Hollywood renditions of
the most refined Gershwin and Porter tunes. Inspired (like most songwriters of the period) by Astaire, Berlin produced—for three Fred-and-Ginger

movies—sleeker, worldlier songs, informed by the music in Astaire's background, yet vigorously original nevertheless.

"Cheek to Cheek," from *Top Hat* (1935), is probably the longest hit tune Berlin ever wrote, seventy-two bars of AABA (plus the tiny, surprising interlude that begins "Dance with me!"), rather than his customary, old-fashioned thirty-two. The way that each stanza starts off, as if in mid-thought, is lightly ironic, pure Astaire. The romantic exuberance that was flatly proclaimed in the early Berlin ballads has now become hesitant, a murmur that gently expands while the melody climbs up, little by little, through a full octave:

> *Heaven,*
> *I'm in heaven,*
> *And my heart beats so that*
> *I can hardly speak,*
> *And I seem to find*
> *The happiness I seek*
> *When we're out together dancing*
> *Cheek to cheek.*

Even after many hearings, most listeners are unaware of any technical devices at work in the "Cheek to Cheek" lyric; they notice only that the words glide by effortlessly, with a sense of inevitability, and provide almost tactile pleasure for those doing the singing. On close examination, however, one finds that Berlin is nearly always manipulating (perhaps more intuitively than consciously) alliteration and assonance, and has threaded this stanza with just the right number of "h" words, "s" words, and "ee" sounds ("beats," "speak," "seem," etc.) to create an irresistible momentum, both fluid and percussive. (Cole Porter achieved a similar sheen with a profusion of internal rhymes, a technique that Berlin—who recoiled from rhyming dictionaries— never cottoned to.)

For the same movie, Berlin wrote Astaire's signature tune from the 1930s onward, "Top Hat, White Tie and Tails." The main theme is merely good, but both the introductory verse and the "B" section of the chorus create such rhythmic excitement (in the same irregular, off-rhymed fashion as "Puttin' On the Ritz") that routine lyrics become mesmerizing:

> *I'm steppin'*
> Out, *my* dear *to*
> Breathe *an at*-mos-*phere*
> That *simply* reeks *with* class.

And *I* trust *that*
You'll *excuse* my *dust*
When *I step* on *the* gas.

"Isn't This a Lovely Day To Be Caught in the Rain?," also from *Top Hat*, has an unadulterated charm that is both musically and lyrically Gershwinesque— faintly recalling Astaire's triumphs in *Lady, Be Good!* and *Funny Face*, but also uncannily anticipating (and perhaps influencing) the songs that the Gershwins would write two years later for Astaire and Rogers's *Shall We Dance?*

Isn't this a lovely day
To be caught in the rain?
You were going on your way,
Now you've got to remain.
Just as you were going,
Leaving me all at sea,
The clouds broke,
They broke,
And oh what a break for me.

The scores for *Follow the Fleet* (1936) and *Carefree* (1938) were less imaginative. But, along with such ingratiating tunes as "I Used To Be Color Blind," "Let Yourself Go," and "I'm Putting All My Eggs in One Basket," they contained two other quintessential Astaire numbers in the high-stylish "Cheek to Cheek" manner. "Change Partners" lifts the conversational lyric to a new level of unadorned eloquence:

Must you dance
Every dance
With the same fortunate man?
You have danced with him
Since the music began.
Won't you change partners
And dance with me?

Especially fine is the song's middle section, which enhances Berlin's droll, gentle humor with a subtly alliterative procession of *w*'s and *t*'s:

Ask him to sit this one out
And while you're alone

I'll tell the waiter to tell him
He's wanted on the telephone.

The fatalistic, doom-shadowed "Let's Face the Music and Dance," however, may be the most impressive Berlin/Astaire song of all. The unique structure involves a suspenseful variation on the AABA form, with an odd-sized basic unit—an "A" section of fourteen bars, not the customary eight or sixteen— that keeps the listener on edge. Furthermore, when the opening section is repeated, it departs from the original tune for six rebellious bars: on the lines "Before they ask us to pay the bill / And while we still have the chance," the music suddenly rises in pitch and grabs at distant harmonies, giving in to anxiety, before it settles back down into its initial groove. The ambivalence here, unlike that in "Always" or "Blue Skies," is clearly premeditated, with a singer who keeps reaching for C major but always finds himself sliding back into C minor. Several Cole Porter songs generate this same sense of harmonic peril, but even the best of them ("I Concentrate on You," "I've Got You Under My Skin") do so less gracefully—and without Berlin's crisp evocation of gallantry in the face of ominous portents:

Before the fiddlers have fled,
Before they ask us to pay the bill,
And while we still have the chance,
Let's face the music and dance.

Still, though Berlin was much more versatile than his detractors realize, his work has distinct limitations. As a ballad lyricist, Berlin seemed to know a good deal about loss and devotion but very little about rejection, guilt, or lifelong insecurity; Lorenz Hart, Cole Porter, and Johnny Mercer (when writing with Harold Arlen) brought to the torch song a smoky tinge of after-hours regret, of been-around-the-block wisdom, that must have been alien to the creator of "Always." As a writer of comedy, Berlin could be broad or dry but never sardonic or brittle or daring. For better and worse, he wrote what was called for, with few imperatives of his own.

As a composer, on the other hand, Berlin was an adventurer who could do virtually anything he tried, occasionally taking his native brilliance on excursions shared by none of his contemporaries. (Despite extensive study of counterpoint, for instance, neither Kern nor Gershwin could concoct a "double" number—two independent melodies sung at once—with the captivating vigor and wondrous interplay of "You're Just in Love" or "Play a Simple Melody.") Berlin's openness to every kind of music in the air and on the street, especially black music, made him the mainstream's greatest pioneer. So when asked to write for Ethel Waters, in *As Thousands Cheer* (1933), he wrote not only "Heat Wave" and "Harlem on My Mind" but also "Supper Time"—one of the many exceptional songs that nobody mentioned much (if at all) during the centenary blurbs-a-thon:

> *Supper time—*
> *I should set the table*
> *'Cause it's supper time.*
> *Somehow I'm not able*
> *'Cause that man of mine*
> *Ain't comin' home no more.*

This is the lament of a woman whose husband has been lynched, whose children don't yet know that their father is dead. Its fiercely dramatic music foreshadows *Porgy and Bess* (especially "My Man's Gone Now") in a way that Kern's *Show Boat* does not. It also looks ahead, perhaps more strikingly than any bluesy love song by Ellington, Arlen, or Gershwin, to the overwhelming influence that gospel music and rhythm-and-blues would have on ballad writing in the century's second half.

Throughout the most active decades of his career, in fact, Berlin kept reinventing himself. Part chameleon and part lone wolf, he managed to inhale virtually everything around him—a star performer's personality, a public sentiment, the latest catch phrase or dance step—and expel it as pure Berlin air. The "signature tunes" he fashioned for Astaire, Bing Crosby, Al Jolson, Ethel Waters, and Ethel Merman (a good half of the *Annie Get Your Gun* score) retain the songwriter's own stamp as well. But most of Berlin's songs were intended—unabashedly, with none of the misgivings of a self-conscious composer "going commercial"—as signature tunes for average Americans in their better-than-average moments: the inarticulate wooer's charm in "It's a Lovely Day Today," the unforced enthusiasm of "I Love a Piano," the way that "White Christmas" (with its shifting interplay of yearning and reserve) rises above the maudlin. Thickly disguised as the "most successful songwriter" in history, or as a juke-box composite of national virtues, Berlin the dogged innovator and complex artist quietly tagged along, a genius without tears.

34

Arthur Maisel: Irving Berlin (1888–1989)

Arthur Maisel, in *The Musical Times*, places Berlin in relation not only to his contemporary Tin Pan Alley tunesmiths but also with some of the great composers of Western music. His final assessment that Berlin "was an average man" is true to a degree. In some ways he was, but added to his amazing "ability to make songs" he had remarkable show biz savvy, was always his own public relations man, *and* was a shrewd businessman. That is better than average.

The Nation magazine for 16 October had a charming tribute to Irving Berlin by cartoon artist Edward Sorel. Entitled "September 22, 1989" (the day Berlin died at the age of 101), the drawing shows the songwriter's arrival in heaven in mock-Baroque style. Schubert is shaking Berlin's hand as Mozart and Bach look on complacently; Gershwin is rushing in, arms outstretched; Wagner, in the foreground, looks over his shoulder with teeth clenched; and the *putti* are playing "Always" (what else?) in the background.

More than merely charming, the drawing is musically apt as well. Schubert the "melodist" greets a fellow craftsman, one of comparable fecundity (thus also the presence of Bach and Mozart, and their approbation); Gershwin is, of course, Berlin's *landsman,* not only as brilliant popular composer, but as a Russian Jew who is at the same time archetypically American; Wagner probably envies Berlin's ability to reach depths of feeling with concision or may just be annoyed that someone else is getting attention.

The subgenre of a celebrated composer among the heavenly host is not a new one, ultimately deriving pictorially from the genre of "assumptions." It is perhaps worth pondering why this seems right. Why should creators of music be thought of so often in relation to the empyrean—whether like Beethoven

SOURCE *Musical Times,* December 1989. Reprinted by permission of Arthur Maisel.

shaking his fist skyward or like any number of others with a direct line to the heights?

To a composer, it seems self-evident that people whose chief reason for being is to give pleasure to others deserve a heavenly reward. Wagner's presence is otherwise a mystery! But there is more: music itself gives us a picture of an ideal world where many independent actors (the individual voices) contribute to a higher unity (called harmony). Music teaches us to take a long view (dissonances are *passing* phenomena and will *resolve*) and thus constitutes a kind of wisdom.

Is it ironic, then, that Berlin did not harmonize his own songs, but paid a trained musician to do so? (According to Alec Wilder, who heard him play them on the piano, he was "inept" at keyboard harmonization.) No, for it is far more important to recall that Berlin had final say over the published arrangements, often sending the arranger away again and again to find another set of chords. As Robert Russell Bennett, the distinguished Broadway orchestrator, said to Wilder, this implies that Berlin had specific harmonies in his mind when he composed and was only technically incapable of rendering them with his fingers on the keys. So it is legitimate to speak of his genius. (If an "Irving Berlin" were to arise in contemporary popular music, one's tendency to sneer at its reliance on technology would lose most of its justification.) In any case, the melodies themselves are works of art without harmonization—see Deryck Cooke's *Language of Music* where examples by Berlin nestle comfortably with ones by Purcell—and Wagner.

Another aspect of Berlin's output is its sheer variety. Wilder, in his book *American Popular Song*, going through a sampling of the songs, can find no distinctive mannerisms, nor can he find a *typical* Irving Berlin song. Whimsically making a show of exasperation, Wilder asks, "Is Berlin's writing experience one of such enormous intensity that the song being written is totally isolated in his mind, to the exclusion of every other song he has written, resulting in a unique form and style for each one?" Perhaps this is why so many of them seem perfect, and also why we don't notice how unusual so many of them are—another proof of Berlin's genius. (Who notices, for example, the five-note segment of the chromatic scale in "White Christmas"?)

One element of Berlin's songs sometimes goes unremarked: his lyrics. Unlike most of his great songsmith colleagues, he wrote his own words. The only other composer/lyricist of similar stature is Cole Porter. On the one hand, the music is usually obviously Porter's—by its quality, but also by its mannerisms—in contrast to Berlin's. On the other hand, Berlin's words, while usually not as determined to be witty and sophisticated, are clever when the occasion demands, yet can express a range of emotion that Porter cannot match. One tends to agree with Wilder's conclusion that, as an all-round maker of songs, Berlin had no rival.

Speaking of words, there is no denying that Berlin's are sentimental. But though there are few things that become dated sooner, Berlin's sentiments still mostly ring true. For example, among today's hypersophisticates Berlin's patriotism (mainly represented by one song, "God Bless America") can seem an embarrassing joke—even to those of conservative bent, who are always willing to manipulate others by playing on such sentiments. No-one can deny the sincerity of Berlin's feelings, however. And with a stretch of the imagination (as unaccustomed as it is for such sophisticates) the feelings aren't hard to understand, for the US was very good to Berlin. Besides, his patriotism was neither jingoistic nor militaristic. Let us not forget that he also wrote the soldier's lament, "Oh, How I Hate to Get Up in the Morning," with its homicidal intentions toward the bugler, and the priceless couplet, "I'll seize upon his reveille/and stomp upon it heavily."[1]

Berlin's secret was that he was an average man in all other ways aside from his ability to make songs. He felt what the average person feels, at the same times and with the same intensity. Then, with his singular ability, he spoke for us all.

~~~~~~

| 35 |

Edward Sorel: Cartoon, "September 22, 1989"

The cartoon by Edward Sorel (see next page) mentioned in Maisel's article is a modern version of a once-popular device of depicting notables entering heaven to the greetings of their peers who have gone before. As Maisel points out, Berlin's place in the pantheon of musical greats is confirmed by the presence of a smiling J.S. Bach in the background, an admiring look from Wolfgang Mozart, and a welcoming handshake from Franz Schubert. Given Berlin's generosity to George Gershwin, it is no surprise to see the younger man welcoming him with open arms. The only cloud is a scowling Richard Wagner, whose anti-Semitic views can only be deeply offended by Berlin's arrival; ironic given that Wagner's name was often invoked by critics praising Berlin.

SOURCE *The Nation*, October 16, 1989. Reprinted by permission of Edward Sorel.

1. The line actually is "I'll amputate his reveille / and step upon it heavily." The image of "amputate his reveille" is a brilliant one and far cleverer than "seize upon."

September 22, 1989, by Edward Sorel.

Part IV

Irving Berlin in His Own Words

Introduction, Chapters 36, 37, 38, 39

It is inevitable that any successful songwriter will be asked the secret of his success, or the formula for writing a hit song. Berlin offered up his opinions, particularly early in his career when it helped keep his name in front of the public. In some instances he is credited as an article's author; it is not clear if he was the writer, collaborated with a ghostwriter, or—knowing the publicity value—simply allowed his name to be used. Intertwined with his thoughts on songwriting was his hope of writing a ragtime opera, sometimes mentioned along with his songwriting tips. Certain "rules" appear consistently in his thinking, though with some variations. Most consistent is the need for hard work to achieve a song which appeals to the masses: "easy to sing, easy to say, easy to remember, and applicable to every-day events."[1]

The earliest article in this group on songwriting dates from Berlin's trip to London in 1913. His basic rules of songwriting are set forth here and will be the core for all his tips on songwriting in subsequent articles. Of interest in this piece is Berlin's apparent defensiveness over his songwriting abilities; he makes sure to set the record straight.

"Song and Sorrow Are Playmates" dates from 1914 and offers a rare and interesting insight into the always guardedly private Berlin. The loss of his wife Dorothy may be a factor in this philosophy; he does make reference to "When I Lost You," but with no explication of how it came to be written. For the first time Berlin expounds on his theory of the "punch line," which will turn up in later pieces in relation to "My Wife's Gone to the Country." Here he uses "Alexander's Ragtime Band" as the example, noting that it is "perhaps the largest selling ragtime hit that was ever written," over two years after its publication—he always knew the monetary value of his work.

---

1. "Words and Music (How They Are Written)," Irving Berlin with Justus Dickinson, *Green Book Magazine*, July 1915.

The philosophy of song and sorrow stayed with Berlin. Later songs such as "Blue Skies" and "White Christmas," while dwelling on happy visions, have a sense of melancholy, too (see Rubins article in Part III).

"Irving Berlin Gives Nine Rules for Writing Popular Songs" gives the best distillation of Berlin's views. By 1920 Berlin had become a mature songwriter, and this article not only breaks down his philosophy into specific rules but also expounds on his own experiences. The rules are straightforward and Berlin does make it clear how difficult the creation of a song is, even following the rules. Berlin assesses his own improvements as a songwriter, in particular abandoning false rhymes. For someone who claimed not to have written autobiographical songs, his tale of "Oh, How I Hate to Get Up in the Morning" makes it clear that he considered it autobiographical. Here also is Berlin himself saying that "Alexander's Ragtime Band" started life as an instrumental for which he hastily retro-fitted words for a Friars Club event. (See articles in Part I on the song.)

At the time of *As Thousands Cheer* (1933/4) Berlin was interviewed again about songwriting. In this excerpt we see him discussing how he has matured as a songwriter; his self-critique is on the mark, including a great awareness of how his crafting of lyrics has improved over the years.

Across these articles there is some evolution in his thinking. What is constant, though, is that for Irving Berlin a song has to be what the public wants to hear or it will not sell.

| 36 |

Irving Berlin: How to Write Ragtime Songs

I am glad to have a chat with *Ideas'* readers about ragtime, for the reception given me in England was so spontaneous and hearty that nothing in the world has ever caused me keener pleasure.

And I would also like to take the opportunity of explaining that immediately after my arrival I gave an exhibition of how my ragtime songs were composed: and that although the press notices of the exhibition were almost too kind to me, yet in certain cases the wrong "angle" was put to the newspaper account.

SOURCE *Ideas*, circa 1913. Taken from the Irving Berlin scrapbooks at the Library of Congress.

One writer, for example, stated that after two hours I had turned out words and music which he himself could have done in five minutes, and that both verse and melody were in no way out of the ordinary.

I want to explain that the demonstration at my publisher's was merely to show how it's done, that is to say, the method I adopt when I set to work to write ragtime.

The theme, a very ordinary one, was suggested by the journalists themselves, and therefore I do not consider it was quite a fair test or criticism to discuss the quality of the song, for I merely set out to show how I worked, and did not for a moment guarantee that the method would produce, at will, a startling song and melody.

I think I have said enough to show where the mistake arose, but I should like to point out that even if you asked a genius like Wagner to sit down offhand and compose a masterpiece dealing with some commonplace subject, perhaps he wouldn't do it.

People have described me as the great American genius: it is not because I told them so. I am merely a song-writer who has enjoyed a few successes and many failures.

The majority of people like popular music, but certain persons attack me for composing it, and, I suppose, people for buying it.

I can give no more reason than a layman, by the way, as to why my songs are liked, but I keep plugging away and trying to please, and, as I have said, I learn much by my failures.

Sometimes I turn out four or five songs a night, so you can imagine how many bad ones I write. But there. I love it and breathe it.

There is a great deal to be said in defense of popular songs. Some American professors decry ragtime melodies in the most severe manner, but I don't know why. One of the national songs of America is "Way Down South in Dixie" which runs:

I wish I was in the land of cotton,
Old times there are not forgotten,
Get away! Get away!

And so on.

Every American all over the world knows and cheers it.

And look at these verses from "Alexander's Ragtime Band." Who, looking at it in cold print, would pick this out as something millions of people would buy to sing? and yet, words and music together, there is an unexplainable something which pleases and haunts.

Alexander's Ragtime Band

> Come on and hear, come on and hear, Alexander's Ragtime Band
> Come on and hear, come on and hear, it's the best band in the land
> They can play a bugle call like you never heard before,
> So natural that you want to go to war;
> That's just the bravest band that am,[2] honey lamb;
> Come on along, come on along, let me take you by the hand,
> Up to the man, up to the man, who's the leader of the band;
> And if you care to hear the Swanee River played in rag-time,
> Come on and hear, come on and hear, Alexander's Ragtime Band.

Kings and queens may or may not care to have popular songs on their programmes; but the masses do.

And I have learnt that the public will not sing if you have tried to get your music too classic. After all, it's not what you say, it's how you say it, and how you fit what you say to the melody to bring it out.

I don't claim that there is any great genius connected with writing a song. Anyone can sit down and write "rag—drag—moon—coon," but to turn out a success, that is to say, a song which will sell by hundreds of thousands of copies, is not so easy a task as it looks in print.

In America we have thirty different publishing houses, each with four to twelve writers on the staff; and throughout English-speaking countries some five to ten thousand songs are composed every week.

With all these songs written, if there are twelve natural successes in a single year in England or America, then it has been a great year.

I myself receive fifteen to twenty songs a day, and probably two a year are acceptable from a commercial point of view.

As I have before remarked, a great deal is to be learnt from our failures, and, further, practice makes perfect. If a certain little effect has pleased an audience I note it down; if a certain phrasing does not pan out so well as anticipated I remember it—so as to avoid it in the future.

But the composer of a popular song is confined to certain rule. Since the song is to be sung by an average singer, the compass should not range beyond an octave. That is why some melodies sound ordinary.

And the composer must be careful of his phrasing. He must be prepared to sacrifice a good rhyme, or even a whole line, to get an open vowel or an easy syllable, with the result that in cold print the words sometimes read like "piffle."

---

2. The correct line is: It's just the bestest band what am.

The whole art of a good ragtime song lies in giving it a rhythm that is snappy, and in making it so simple that the artiste can sing it, a baby can sing it, anybody and everybody can sing it. Its appeal is to the masses—not to the classes.

My readers will perhaps smile when I tell them that I am writing an opera in ragtime; the whole of the libretto as well as the music. The idea is so new and ambitious that it may be a great big failure and certainly such a thing has never been tried before.

My reception in England was wonderful, and touched me deeply but nothing has ever made such an impression on me as a little incident that occurred after I reached London and was on my way from the station.

We met a crowd of little boys marching along the street, and there they were singing "Dixie" for all they were worth.

I guess that was a welcome, and the cheeriest welcome a fellow ever had.

| 37 |

Irving Berlin: Song and Sorrow Are Playmates

Song and sorrow are playmates. They began their never-ending association soon after civilized man began to realize that he possessed the power to think. For expressing thought in some form of song has always been more natural than speech. That's why the simple mother's lullaby existed long before accepted forms of music were dreamed of; and the sweet, sad song at the cradle, though crude in form and execution, convinced the first song-loving audience the world has known—and carried baby to the realms of slumber-land.

Sorrow is the one emotion that must find some form of expression. Joy may be contained; but sorrow longs for a terse expression of feeling. Such expression finds its best form in a poetic outburst. The human mind is so constructed that no brief expression of poetic sentiment can be conveyed without introducing some element of the epigrammatical. And when you arrive at this form of expression you have the first and final form of song. Meter, melody and everything else that relates to the construction of song are secondary. All that is necessary is to have something to say and to say it as quickly as possible.

SOURCE Appeared in an unidentified journal in 1913. Taken from the Irving Berlin scrapbooks at the Library of Congress.

I hope I am not becoming too didactical and that I have made my first thought clear without assuming the pose of a college professor addressing a graduating class. But, in order to show the relation of song to sorrow (which is the whole secret of songwriting), I had to find some argumentative base and, because I know the average reader wearies of philosophical discourse, I have tried to wade through the first and hardest part of this article as quickly as possible.

There is nothing quite so funny as a tale of woe. The person who experiences sorrow doesn't think so, but the rest of the world does. It is hard to express sorrow without exaggerating feelings. And this very exaggeration is what the world finds so amusing. If you doubt this, glance at the person reading a morning newspaper containing the account of some startling occurrence, and reflect whether any other form of entertainment (for that's what it really is) could make that person half so happy. Doesn't the average kid get real enjoyment out of the blood-curdling dime novel? If you require any further illustration go to the corner moving picture show and see what an edge the serio-comic film has on all the comedies that may be produced. Unless tragedy is pure and brings tears of sympathy, the sadder the story the greater the mirth aroused.

And, instinctively realizing this, since the time when song originated, no minstrel has been foolish enough to paint a song of sorrow without some redeeming point of happier sentiment that would make the spectator see the contrast—and throw the coins at the needy minstrel. Perhaps songs of absolute woe have been written, but how popular did any of them ever become? From "The Rosary" to my own "When I Lost You" no ballad has met with real success that did not contain some sunshine interspersed with the account of sadness. For pathos devoid of contrast readily descends into the ridiculous.

No greater fallacy has been nursed by the public mind than the idea that the music of ballads or sentimental songs is intrinsically sadder than the melodic base of ragtime songs. As a matter of fact, the metre of ballad songs is too regular to express any sentiment that is not conveyed by the words.

On the contrary, ragtime had its birth in sadness. The southern type that found its home in popular music invariably originated in strains conceived by people held in slavery—the Negroes. They instinctively felt the futility of trying to express sadness without the lining of sunshine and this accounts for the fact that the words of the saddest southern songs always spoke of happy conditions that existed, while the indescribably appealing music told of the contrast between the sorrows of the present and the joys of the past. Since the roots of these songs constitute the basis of ragtime, it will be seen that ragtime of today is possessed of a native sadness and cannot be separated from this touch of the appealing without losing its best elements.

The point I am trying to get at is, in an ideal song, the words should express the joy while the music conveys the underscore of sadness. In my own songs I have followed this self-evident rule and I attribute no small degree of their success to this fact. In all modesty, I challenge anybody to produce a more rollicking song than "Alexander's Ragtime Band" or "Ragtime Violin," the first of which was really a shout-song of the "ballyhoo" order, and yet I defy any composer of standard ballads to produce melodies more intrinsically sad. And please remember that the millions of people who eagerly welcomed these songs from the time of their first release would have passed them by without approval had they possessed words as sad as the melodic strains.

This may be considered my reply to the critics who have maintained that I should have built my hits around more substantial themes. I could have done so easily, but, if my music did not sell, I could not remain in the publishing field and, in order to produce music that will sell, I must provide songs that will require little or no mental gymnastics in mastering the lyrics. Few performers require long rehearsals in order to master my lyrics and I try to make the melodies so strong that they will haunt people into wanting to use, wanting to hear and wanting to buy my music.

I like to hear original melodies (though I seldom do), and I like to write them. But I know the danger of writing melodies that are too original. I prefer to concentrate on the construction end of a song in order to order to produce my original effects. The introduction of syncopation and metre chopping, in order to get full space for the surprising concluding lines of a song, professionally termed "punch-lines," will produce melodic shifts that never could have been secured under the straight metre system of writing. I attribute many failures in the song-writing world to the writer's inability to express via syncopation.

Because the real originality in song writing consists in the construction of the song rather than in the actual melodic base it can readily be seen that there is no real objection to incorporating a standard melody in a song if the work is done artistically. I adopted this plan in "Alexander's Ragtime Band," perhaps the largest selling ragtime hit that was ever written, by quoting "Way Down Upon the Swanee River" for a "punch finish." Unfortunately when the song became a terrific hit other writers, in endeavoring to ascertain the cause, forgot the originality in construction and attributed its success to the employment of the quotation. After that the music market was flooded with songs embracing similar quotations, so many of them appearing at once that it is now the height of folly to attempt a melodic interpolation near the end of a song.

However, the real secret of my construction has never been found out, or, at least, it has never been successfully imitated, though it is hard for me to understand why, as my method seems as natural as child's play to me. I do not stop to consider rules, but devote all my time to estimating the effect the completed song will have on the performer. Perhaps it is because others are trying to find the wherefore and the why in what I do that they do not successfully produce that kind of songs I have originated. A writer surrounded by rules is afforded little opportunity to unbosom his soul in a way that will appeal to the supreme judges of all rules—the general public.

Most writers make the mistake of putting their thoughts on a single hit song that the market happens to be favoring instead of trying to get at the conditions that brought about the hit. When our marines were ordered to Vera Cruz I did not immediately come to the conclusion that the United States would absorb Mexico (as some of our newspapers predicted), but I examined the real facts underlying the situation. I found, however, that our soldiers were going to Mexico, and saw in this fact enough reason for a popular ragtime song. I entitled it "They're on Their Way to Mexico." Of course the market was soon deluged with all kinds of war songs pointing to impossible deeds of valor, and intimating that the United States would soon conquer the world. Perhaps I am lucky, as some of the boys claim, but I think there are other reasons why my war song proved successful. An examination of this number will disclose my favorite "stunt" of providing a light lyric for a sympathetic melody. The fact that a war song may be written in a light, easy manner, with its background of patriotic sentiment, is a splendid example of my argument that song and sorrow are playmates. Popular music meets its heartiest support during war time, for nothing else tends to show that we may have sunshine at home, despite international complications. It is a pity that most publishers abuse the confidence of the public by endeavoring to boost songs that deal with impossible conditions. Besides, I don't think it is the height of good taste to call attention to the horrible aspect of the wars by publishing songs detailing the horrors of the battlefield, illustrated with three-colored pictures of dying soldiers. This seems as bad an exercise of taste as was the publication of horror-songs immediately after the Titanic disaster.

This kind of music publishing is another aspect of sorrow that music must encounter. But, fortunately, the public is not compelled to buy inferior music forced out of an inconsiderate mill. It must be remembered that the public is the final and supreme judge of song merit. It is getting wiser every day regarding the caliber of songs it desires. The time will come when this indirect censorship will produce a song that will express real human emotion in the way such emotion should be expressed—in other words, a proper blending of song and sorrow. For it must be remembered, above all, that song and sorrow always have been and always will be playmates in the truest, farthest-fetched interpretation of the word.

| 38 |

Frank Ward O'Malley: Irving Berlin Gives Nine Rules for Writing Popular Songs

Irving Berlin is past master of several big fundamentals: He is of the crowd, and has a genius for knowing what the crowd wants. To his innate gifts he has added a comprehensive knowledge, gained by thoughtful study of his own and other's failures and successes, and by close observation of the public's likes and dislikes. Out of this knowledge he has evolved certain rules which, he insists, must always be followed by the writer of *popular* songs.

High on his list of ideas is the truism which he quotes so frequently: "inspiration is ninety per cent perspiration."

"I feel certain I've written more failures than any other song writer on earth," he says. "But I write more *failures* because I write more *songs* than anyone else does.

"And nobody appreciates more than I do how bad some of my lyrics are in the matter of technical details. I've rhymed 'Aida' with sweeter. I've done worse than that, especially back in my inexperienced days. The lyric of the biggest money maker of all, 'Alexander's Ragtime Band,' is simply terrible! Some of the biggest hits I've written were songs I was so ashamed of that I pleaded with the heads of music houses not to publish them. But none of my technical errors have been due to laziness or slipshod methods. My job is writing *popular* songs, not writing models of technical perfection. I'd like to 'put them over' in forms pleasing to the high-brow as well to the general public, if for no other reason than the practical one of adding all the high-brows to the rest of my music-buying public. But, first of all, I must make my songs *popular*.

SOURCE *American Magazine*, October 1920.

"Almost everybody—your ice man, butcher's boy, the grocery clerk, any-body!—has in him the making of some sort of lyric, which, if properly developed, would not only make him independently rich, but would keep a song-publishing house going successfully, on the earnings of just that single song, for a whole year—and a song publisher's business expenses run often as high as forty or fifty thousand dollars a month.

"Everybody has the makings of a great song hit in him, because everyone hears sentences and catches phrases, or originates snatches of refrains, quite as good as those which the experienced song writer uses as the groundwork of a colossal hit.

"I estimate that there are to-day at least a quarter of a million Americans earnestly trying to write popular songs—but not earnestly and intelligently enough to win. What is the result of all this misdirected effort? Why, if a year brings five or six successes of the kind the publishers know as 'natural song hits'—the sort of song that just explodes into success without advertising or 'plugging'—the music-publishing world gives three rousing cheers.

"The whole trouble is that the ice man, the newsboy, *and* the highly technical writer of polished verse rarely know, or try to learn, the rules of the big game of writing *popular* songs.

"The would-be song writer *must* follow the rules if his song is to be popular. He must follow the rules till the sweat pours off him. There isn't a night in the year—I have the habit of working all night instead of all day—that I don't write all, or a great part, of a song, literally by the sweat of my brow.

"Ambitious lads ask me almost daily: 'What's the easiest kind of song to write?'"

"'A good song,' I tell them. A bad song is the hardest to write because the song writer, in his efforts to turn a failure into success, never is finished with trying to write and rewrite it."

In order that I might have writing facilities to take down the song composition "rules" Mr. Berlin was about to dictate to me, he led me back to a small working den, the chief furnishings of which were a wonderfully carved writing table and, directly opposite the table, a shabby upright piano that must have come into being about the same time young Mr. Berlin did.

The base of the humble "upright" rested upon pads of folded felt many inches thick. Also, no meticulous surgeon had ever bandaged a broken leg more thoroughly than Mr. Berlin had swathed the innards of the humble of old piano with more yards of thick felt. Furthermore, he had dumped and packed many pounds of downy white feathers above and below the piano strings and sounding board. The pedals had been permanently locked with small wedges.

The explanation of all these elaborate anti-noise arrangements is characteristic of the youthful song writer.

"I don't want to bother anyone who might be sick, or resting, or asleep, in the neighborhood," was his simple explanation. "I've tried hard to do my own sleeping at normal hours, but found myself, night after night, climbing out of bed at all hours to hammer out a melody or write down a lyric that was keeping me awake.

"So now I begin my work shortly after dinner every night, and keep at it until four or five o'clock the next morning. The strings of this old bird are muffled so they make only a faint tinkle when the keys are struck. The creak is out of the pedals. Instead of using them, I tap my toe on a floor pad to keep in physical swing with the rhythm. With these precautions I can go to bed around daylight without feeling that I've invaded my neighbors' rights."

Having cleared up this matter, Mr. Berlin took up the nine rules which he not only preaches to others, but also practices himself.

"A song writer may break the rules of grammar, of versification, even of common sense and reason," he said by way of brief preface, "and still turn out a song hit of the popular variety. He *cannot* ignore the rules of popular song construction and get away with his song. As in everything else, there have been song hits which were exceptions to some part of the code, but the rules *must* be followed in a general way or the song will certainly—not probably, but certainly—be a failure."

Here are the rules as Mr. Berlin thoughtfully dictated them to me:

First—The melody must musically be within the range of the *average voice* of the average public singer. The average-voice professional singer is the song writer's salesman, the average-voice public his customers. The salesman-singer cannot do justice to a song containing notes too high, too low, or otherwise difficult to sing; and the customer will not buy it.

Second—The title, which must be simple and easily remembered, must be *"planted"* effectively in the song. It must be emphasized, accented again and again, throughout verses and chorus. The public buys songs, not because it knows the song but, because it knows and likes the title idea. Therefore, sacrifice lines you are proud of, even sacrifice rhyme and *reason* if necessary, in order to accentuate the title line effectively.

Third—A popular song should be *sexless*, that is, the ideas and the wording must be of a kind that can be logically voiced by either a male or a female singer. Strive for the happy medium in thought and words so that both sexes will want to buy and sing it.

Fourth—The song should contain *heart interest*, even if it is a comic song. Remember, there is an element of heart-longing in the most wildly syncopated "Ah'm goin' back to Dixie" darky "rag" ever written.

Fifth—The song must be *original* in idea, words, and music. Success is not achieved, as so many song writers mistakenly believe, by trying to imitate the general idea of the great song hit of the moment.

Sixth—Your lyric must have to do with ideas, emotions, or objects known to everyone. Stick to nature—not nature in a visionary, abstract way, but nature as demonstrated in homely, concrete, everyday manifestations.

Seventh—The lyric must be *euphonious*—written in easily singable words and phases in which there are many open vowels.

Eighth—Your song must be perfectly *simple*. Simplicity is achieved only after much hard work, but you must attain it.

Ninth—The song writer must look upon his work as a *business*, that is, to make a success of it he must work and *work*, and then *WORK*.

Mr. Berlin elaborated at random on his fundamental rules.

"As in everything else," he said, "there is an easy, lazy, wrong way and a difficult, right way of building the attractive title idea into a song. The quarter million almost invariably insist upon going at it the wrong way. If you will pardon me for harping on my own song hits, I can demonstrate to you in a moment what I mean.

"Take the case of my first big success: One night, in a barber shop, some years ago I ran into George Whitney, a vaudeville actor, and asked him if he could go to a show with me. 'Sure,' he said; and he added with a laugh, 'My wife's gone to the country." Bing! *There* I had a commonplace, familiar title line. It was singable, capable of humorous upbuilding, simple, and one that did not seriously offend against the 'sexless' rule; for wives and their offspring of both sexes, as well as husbands, would be amused by singing it or hearing it sung.

"I persuaded Whitney to forget the theatre and to devote the night to developing the line with me into a song. Now, the usual and unsuccessful way of handling a line like that is to dash off a jumble of verses about the henpecked husband, all leading up to a chorus running, we'll say, something like this:

My wife's gone to the country,
She went away last night.
Oh, I'm so glad! I'm so glad!
I'm crazy with delight!

"Just wordy, obvious elaboration. No *punch*! All night I sweated to find what I knew was there, and finally I speared the lone word, just a single word, that *made* the song—and a fortune. Listen:

My wife's gone to the country!
Hooray!

"*Hooray!*" That lone word gave the whole idea of the song in one quick wollop. It gave the singer a chance to hoot with sheer joy. It *invited* the roomful to join in the hilarious shout. It everlastingly put the catch line over. And I wasn't content until I had used my good thing to the limit. 'She took the children with her—hooray! *Hooray!*'—and so on.

"Take just one more instance: Nothing could be more commonplace or bromidic than the line, 'You'd be surprised.' Every man, women, and child in the English-speaking world has said it and heard countless times.

"I know from the bales of unsuccessful songs I am constantly coming across exactly how the mentally lazy or the uninitiated would go about the work of building that line into a song. They would write a lyric concerning one or several of the innumerable surprising things of life. They would possibly—no, *probably!*—jumble up their song with *all* the surprising things they could think of, thereby losing simplicity. And the chorus would be just a noisy blah:

You'd be surprised! You'd be surprised!
I realized you'd be surprised!
I must say that I recognized
Surprised you'd be—you'd be surprised!

"No punch again. Just repetition, not *effective*," accentuating repetition. Words, noisy words.

"Now, I'm not vain about the way I made a song hit out of that line; there are probably lots of ways just as good as mine, or even better. But as my way turned out to be a smashing big popular and financial success, I shall use my way merely for purposes of illustration.

"In the first place, I consciously strove for simplicity by confining my lyric to a description of one surprising and amusing characteristic of one single fictitious person. The lyric describes the seeming backwardness and timidity of the 'hero' of the song. In order that either a man or woman could sing the song logically, I did not have the lyric describe the singer himself or herself, but someone always spoken of in the third person.

"Every line in the lyric was written with the conscious effort to build it up to a chorus, in which the title was to be repeated again and again, each repetition of 'You'd be surprised' carrying with it that 'punch' of unexpectedness which plays so important a part in humor. Then, to give added emphasis each time to the delivery of the title line, I stopped the singer for a full beat the instant before he uttered the line. And finally I tried for still more emphasis by sticking into the music an instrumental 'bang' as the singer paused a beat. Listen!"

No breathless, noisy clamor of a chorus beginning, "You'd-be-surprised-you'd-be-surprised," came from Mr. Berlin's lips. With the sheer artistry with which he always sings his own songs—his shoulders swaying almost imperceptibly, his tone and manner intimate, confidential—he began the lilting melody of the chorus slowly, softly:

He's not much in a crowd,[1] but when
you get him alone—
[Bang]
You'd—be—surprised!

And the effect was one to which cold type can never hope to do justice.

In view of his nighthawk habits, I suggested that doubtless the enormously successful song, "Oh, How I Hate to Get Up in the Morning"—words and music written by Sergeant Irving Berlin at Camp Upton during the early days of the war—was alive with personal feeling.

"You said something then, brother!" he barked. "There's a song called 'The Star-Spangled Banner' which is a pretty big song hit, too; but my answer to the question in the opening line of the national anthem is a loud 'No!' I can't 'see' anything 'by the dawn's early light.' My song about hating to 'get up in the mo-o-o-rning' was a protest written from the heart out, absolutely without the slightest thought that it would ever earn a cent.

"It insisted upon making a fortune. So did another of my 'accidental' songs, 'Alexander's Ragtime Band.' Once I heard General Bell say at Camp Upton that if the camp had about thirty thousand dollars he could provide a sort of community house and other equipment necessary for the comfort of the soldiers' relatives and other visitors to the camp. So I wrote *Yip! Yip! Yaphank!* partly with the hope that *Yip! Yip!* might earn at least a small portion of the

---

1. The actual line is "he's not so good in a crowd."

necessary thirty thousand dollars, and partly, perhaps chiefly, for the fun of writing it. Some of the boys and myself came up to Manhattan to 'plug' the words and music of *Yip! Yip! Yaphank!* and after a comparatively short visit here we want back to camp and handed the general the net profits—eighty thousand dollars.

"I go into these details only because apparently accidental successes of this kind bear out, perhaps paradoxically, my contention that every song hit has careful, thoughtful method as its groundwork. The music of 'Alexander's Ragtime Band,' for instance, lay in my desk unpublished for a year. One day a social organization, the Friars, got up a club show and asked me to sing a song in it. I hastily wrote a lyric, silly in the matter of common sense, that fitted the instrumental manuscript lying in my desk, and sang it, 'Alexander's Ragtime Band,' at the club performance. It turned out to be what the vaudevillians call a 'riot,' both here and in Europe.

"No one was more flabbergasted than I was at the smashing hit it made. I humbly began to study my own song, asking myself, 'Why? Why?' And I got an answer. The melody, I saw, could lay claim to importance of [a] kind, in that it had started the heels and shoulders of all America and a good section of Europe to rocking—had originated the still widespread craze for syncopation. And I found from analysis that the lyric, silly though it was, was fundamentally right.

"Its opening words, emphasized by immediate repetition—'Come on and hear! Come on and hear!'—were an *invitation* to 'come,' to join in and to 'hear' the singer and his song. And that idea of *inviting* every receptive auditor within shouting distance to become a part of the happy ruction—an idea pounded in again and again throughout the song in various ways—was the secret of the song's tremendous success.

"The point I wish to prove by all this detail is that even a seemingly 'accidental' hit, written comparatively in a hurry, has method in its madness, *follows the rules*. Hurried composition does not necessarily mean slipshod composition. Hurried work, if it is successful, merely means a tremendous amount of effective work crowded into a short period of time.

"'Oh, How I Hate to Get up in the Morning' made an unlooked-for but emphatic grand slam, not only because it followed all nine rules to the letter, but also because it was the exposition of a familiar idea which everyone *resents*. The best sort of comic song is one that treats effectively some idea or thing universally disliked. Ridiculing a particular man, or man in general, or any familiar phase of life, results in sure-fire laughs when properly handled.

"My ex-soldier song, 'I've Got My Captain Working for Me Now,' owes its success to methodical treatment of still another elemental idea that is effective in comic song-writing—the universal, human delight experienced in turning the tables upon arrogant authority. Expressing egotism, vanity, or any other human failing concretely, especially if sung in the first person—the idea, for instance, that 'all the girls are crazy over me'—immediately puts the singer and the audience in a happy mood."

I asked Mr. Berlin whether or not comic songs more easily attained wide success than songs of pathos.

"No," he answered promptly. "It's easier for people to cry than to laugh. The old home, mother, the wayward girl, the prodigal son—these and other certain tear-starters are always at the song writer's elbow. And the songs of serious sentiment, love songs, or ballads soggy with sobs, make a greater and more lasting success in direct proportion to the more lasting qualities and intensity of serious sentiment, heart interest, and sadness, as compared with hilarity.

"The greatest successes, therefore, have been scored by the sort of song most easily written, the song of pathos. When it comes to the most difficult kind of song success to write—the comic song hit—you have to dig and sweat until you have unearthed or invented a humorous situation. And then you have to sweat some more, until you have so built up your idea that even the death heads across the foot-lights, or sitting in gloomy corners of the room will cheer up."

"What effect," I asked, "would education have had on your work?"

"Ruin it!" was the instant and emphatic answer. "I don't mean for one second that a lyric to be popular, must be, or even *necessarily* profits by being, wrong from the high-brow viewpoint. If I did think that, I'd be refuted immediately by remembering 'Home, Sweet Home' or 'Ben Bolt' or 'The Last Rose of Summer.' But I do know that the price we pay for experience and technique is self-consciousness.

"As in the case of most high-brows, technical self-consciousness runs away with a man to the extent of making him believe that the *learned* mechanics of a thing are more important than the thing itself. As compared to an idea itself, the *way* the idea is presented doesn't amount to a tinker's dam.

"The grown-up mob, thank heaven, still retains some of the naturalness of little children. I write for the mob, and the mob does not want self-consciousness. The mob, like the children, prefers *natural* rhyme to technical merit. Even the high-brow, who gnashes his teeth loudest at my lapses in rhyme or reason, would call for a cop if someone took the 'Mother Goose' book away from that same high-brow's child and tried to change the 'Tucker-supper-butter' or the 'tree-top, cradle-will-rock' rhymes in the child's book, or attempted to 'improve' the awful kinks of both rhyme and rhythm of the 'Lady-bug' jingle—changing it, say, to something technically perfect, such as:

Lady-bug! Lady-bug! Fly away home,
Your house is on fire from cellar to dome!

"No punch! But 'home' and 'alone'! Why, the high-brow *teaches* his child that natural rhyming and then he faints when a writer of popular songs recognizes that it is infinitely more important to impart to the lady-bug the idea that her 'children are all alone' in the burning 'home' than it is to hand her polished rhyme as a substitute for the news that her fat babies are all burning with a clear blue flame.

"I know now that if I attempted to-day to 'improve' some of my old song hits by substituting correct rhyme and rhythm for the glaring technical errors in those earlier efforts, I'd kill the songs. I do not presume to speak for others; but I do know that in my own case acquired technical knowledge would have caused me to try for perfection in the superficial values of the way a thing is done, thus crippling the enthusiastic, spontaneous thought itself. Technical education of the bookish kind, of any kind, is a wonderful thing—when the one who has it is old enough and experienced enough to know that it is merely the means of stimulating or using thought, and that the thought itself is the all-important end."

~~~~~~

| 39 |

Isaac Goldberg: Excerpt from Words and Music from Irving Berlin

Mr. Berlin talks well and easily of his work. And, if it is possible to mark off ratios, he is even more voluable on the subject of his lyrics than on his music. To write songs means, of course, to write words as well as tunes. What is more, Mr. Berlin is just as eager as ever the irascible Gilbert was to hear his words. They are part of his conversation, sung to you instead of being spoken, yet retaining much of the quality inherent in talk. He strives to make these popular ditties first of all communicative. Evidently he has that secret. And part of the secret, I am sure, is his own personality.

SOURCE Appeared in an unidentified journal, circa 1933/34. Taken from the Irving Berlin scrapbooks at the Library of Congress.

"I don't rhyme *m* with *n* anymore," he will tell you. Time and divine, queen and supreme, no longer satisfy his ear. Yet, such near rhymes as these, he recognizes, have a certain justification in popular song, much as—one might add—double negatives have a psychological value often more important than the stolid grammar that denies them. Looking back over his early songs, Berlin almost becomes a double personality. Half of him smiles at their naive vocabulary; the other half at the same time, wags an indulgent head and almost regrets that such things can no longer be. "I don't want to go high-brow on myself," says this troubadour. "I look at the old things and blush with shame. Yet I know in my heart that they should have been done in just that way, and I'm not sorry that they were."

Writing lyrics for songs today is not the snap that it appears to be. Most persons secretly believe that they could toss off a couple of "wows" between supper and bedtime. Reading the words in cold print, dissociated from the music to which they must be as organically close as flesh to blood, it is easy to minimize, or to miss altogether, the special skill required for this aspect of popular song. Mr. Berlin, as I have said, turns away from cleverness, excessive self-consciousness, toward simplicity, or what he calls "honest-to-goodness" language. He believes that mere cleverness in the music, too, is on the wane. He was never able to work with a rhyming dictionary, and has less use for such devices now than he ever had. Rhyme, in itself, he deliberately casts out of his thoughts when he sets to work, on a new song. What he is after is the fundamental power of simple rhythms—simple phrases that embody not only in their words, but in their very sound, the rock-bottom experiences of the average man and woman. He "sweats" over his lyrics with the biblical sweat of the toiler.

| 40 |

Irving Berlin: Selected Letters

Irving Berlin left behind a voluminous file of business letters. What follows is a very small selection, arranged chronologically, covering a range from business details such as dealing with a plagiarism suit, to settling card-playing debts with Samuel Goldwyn, arranging for a piano to accompany him on an Alaskan

SOURCE Excerpts of letters written by Irving Berlin used by Permission of Mary Ellin Barrett, Linda Emmet, and Elizabeth I. Peters, daughters of Irving Berlin.

cruise, retelling the background stories of some of his songs, and a few fan letters to the performers of his songs. As a lyricist Berlin was always working with words, so it is no surprise that his letters are well written and interesting. In being so well written they are a testament to the quality of education offered in New York public schools during the short time he attended school. Some of these letters illuminate stories told earlier in this book, while others cover some new ground.

The story of Berlin encouraging the young George Gershwin is a fairly well-known one, but he was also supportive of other up-and-coming songwriters, as seen in this excerpt from a letter to Max Winslow.[1]

July 17, 1933 [Excerpt]

Columbia Pictures Corporation
Hollywood, California

Dear Max:

I was especially pleased to hear from Saul [Bornstein] that you have signed Harold Arlen and Ted Koehler[2] to do a musical. I think they are the best of the new boys and I think it's wise of Columbia to think seriously about doing a good musical before it's too late.

Berlin was the defendant in a number of plagiarism suits during his career. The following letter makes the story clear: he was not accused of stealing lyrics or music from another song, but rather a concept.

October 3rd, 1933

Mr. Dennis F. O'Brien[3]
New York City

Dear Cap:

I have your letter, with copy of Arno's[4] claim. The facts are as follows—

---

1. Winslow helped give Berlin his start as a songwriter and later was a business partner for many years. At the time of this letter he was head of the music department at Columbia Pictures.
2. Arlen (music) and Koehler (lyrics) were the writers of such hits as "Get Happy," "I Gotta Right to Sing the Blues," and "This Time the Dream's On Me."
3. Berlin's lawyer.
4. Cartoonist Peter Arno, who felt that Berlin had plagiarized from his cartoons.

Irving Berlin in the mid-1930s, around the time of the films *Top Hat* and *Follow the Fleet* starring Fred Astaire and Ginger Rogers. Photo credit: *Photofest*

I wrote the Society Wedding number as one of the first songs for *As Thousands Cheer*. The idea is based on any one of four of the oldest stories there are.

The phrase, "They married and went right back to bed," and the line "I told my fiancée about it and she nearly fell out of bed laughing," have been going the rounds long before Peter Arno was born. The story of the blushing bride, which was current during the war and, if I am not mistaken, appeared in one of the American newspapers, was that of a doughboy in bed with a French girl, and she says to him, "By God, it's twelve o'clock! I must be going, as I'm getting married at one."

Boiling it down, there is nothing particularly new about the idea that my song is based on. It is the way we do it that makes it different. I never saw Arno's drawing until last Friday, when it was said that the actual set the number is played in resembled his drawing. Both Hassard Short and the artist who painted the set saw the drawing with me, and everybody agreed there was no resemblance at all.

Arno, no doubt, based his drawing on the same old stories, and if it is possible for a cartoonist to illustrate *Joe Miller's Joke Book*[5] and copyright them, then he probably has a very good case. If he and his lawyer intend to go to the bat for this, I have some information for you that will be very valuable.

I neglected to mention that, in a revue called *Hey Nonny Nonny* which was produced about two years ago there was a number called "Wouldn't It Be Wonderful," and that number, too, was based on the same stories.[6] As I remember, in that show they too had a bed with a couple dressing, and going off to the gag line of "And when we are married, wouldn't it be wonderful."

I hope you liked the show, and as you probably know by now, we really have a smash and it looks like it will there for a long time.

I am leaving for Boston today to see *Let 'Em Eat Cake*[7] and will be back tomorrow in case you want to see me about this matter.

This letter concerns the use of a song in the film *On the Avenue*.

December 2, 1936

Memo to Darryl Zanuck, Twentieth Century Fox Film Corporation

---

5. *Joe Miller's Jest Book: An Immense Collection of the Funniest Jokes, Quaint and Laughable Anecdotes, Mirth Provoking Stories, Brilliant Witticisms, and Queer Sayings, As Told by the Original Joe Miller* was a pirated version of *The Jest Book* as compiled by *Punch* editor Mark Lemon in 1864. So, the jokes were old ones.

6. The show ran at the Shubert Theatre from June 6, 1932, to July 2, 1932. A number of people contributed to the show, including Herman Hupfeld (best known for "As Time Goes By") who wrote "Wouldn't That Be Wonderful," E. B. White, and Ogden Nash.

7. George & Ira Gershwin show.

Dear Darryl:

Seymour Felix told me today that Ebele sent him a note to hold up "I've Got My Love to Keep Me Warm" until the last number. After our discussion about this yesterday, I suppose you feel it wise to see whether you will need "Love to Keep Me Warm" after the picture is finished. I again want to tell you how strongly I feel about this number remaining in the picture. To take it out, in my opinion, would be just the same as if they decided to take "Let's Face the Music and Dance" out of *Follow the Fleet*, which easily could have been done as there were seven numbers in that picture. However, without it the score would have been skimpy.

I am sure that Del Ruth[8] can so direct "Love to Keep Me Warm" to tie it in with the story, as he did today with "This Year's Kisses." It is the only song in the score that has the quality of "Cheek to Cheek" and "Let's Face the Music and Dance." I consciously constructed it along the same lines, and after the picture is released, I will guarantee that the band leaders will prefer to play it to any other song in the score. It gives the score body. Taking out the number will not only harm the score, but it will leave Powell[9] with only two numbers to sing—the "Police Gazette" and "You're Laughing at Me." I do not consider the reprise of "You're Laughing at Me" as a vocal for Powell.

I know your sense of story values is much better than mine. However, I think my judgment on the value of the songs for this picture is pretty good. You know that we were both quite satisfied with the score when I left last April, still I felt that I could do better than "Swing Sister" and "[On the Steps of] Grant's Tomb."[10] I think you will agree that the "Rhythm"[11] number and "This Year's Kisses" are better for the picture. I am getting all this off my chest to you in the form of a letter because I feel sure you will keep an open mind and give my feelings in this matter serious consideration. After all, it can't harm the picture to any great extent and I feel definitely that it will greatly hurt the score.

In 1937 the Berlin family, with Sammy Goldwyn (producer Sam Goldwyn's son), went on an Alaskan cruise. Berlin wanted to bring along his piano but encountered some difficulties when it would not fit through the ship's

---

8. Director Roy Del Ruth.
9. The film's star, Dick Powell.
10. Two songs originally intended for the film.
11. "He Ain't Got Rhythm" which is the film's opening number.

entryways.[12] This exchange of letters and telegrams tell of his efforts to secure a piano for the cruise.

Day letter dated July 19, 1937

> Cruise Director
> Seattle, Washington

My piano twenty-seven and a-half inches wide and fifty-five inches high. Very important to have it aboard with me so please see if something can't be done about it. Personally planning to be in Seattle Friday the thirteenth family arriving Saturday.

Wire dated July 21, 1937

> Irving Berlin
> Care Twentieth Century Fox Studios PFO Hollywood California

Have exhausted every possibility and find it impossible to put your upright aboard. However can accommodate grand of any size by removing legs. Suggest you bring grand instead of upright. Or if you prefer can rent fine Aldrich grand here from Sherman and Clay and may be able to rent new Steinway or Chickering for you please advise by wire.

Wire dated July 21, 1937

> Cruise Director
> Seattle, Washington

Please try and rent small Steinway grand very soft tone.[13]

In his younger days Berlin was an inveterate poker player. In later years his game of choice was gin rummy and, as seen below, for money. Producer Sam Goldwyn was one of his regular card-playing buddies.

January 17, 1942

> Mr. Sam Goldwyn
> Hollywood, California

---

12. Mary Ellin Barrett tells the story of this trip in *Irving Berlin: A Daughter's Memoir*. She relates that until Sammy Goldwyn heard Berlin working at the piano he had no idea that "Mr. Berlin did something other than play cards."

13. A "new Steinway Grand piano" with "a very soft tone, as you requested" was found.

Dear Sam:

Enclosed is my check for $155.00, which I think is the correct amount of what I owe you for our last gin-rummy session. There may be a difference of a few dollars one way or the other. If so, let me know.

I am leaving for New York tomorrow, so this is goodbye.

I expect to come back in about five weeks and will look forward to seeing you again.

Best to Frances.

Wire dated October 29, 1942

Mr. Deems Taylor[14]
c/o ASCAP Dinner
Hotel Astor
New York City

Sorry I can't be with you tonight. Understand I was scheduled to sing "Oh How I Hate to Get Up in the Morning." If you still feel that song should be sung by someone without a voice, why not sing it yourself. My best to everybody especially our customers. It's a fine day for ASCAP when we can all sit and break bread together and have a good time. Here's for many such dinners.

A March 1, 1943, letter from a student at the Graduate School of Journalism at Columbia University asked Berlin, as the composer of "Oh How I Hate to Get Up in the Morning" to tell how he managed to rise and shine every day ("perhaps your method might be the answer to a sleepy-head's prayer"). Berlin's views on the matter had not changed since 1918.

March 4, 1943

I have your letter and wish you luck in trying to get to the bottom of the nasty business of getting up in the morning.

It's difficult to tell you how I "rise and shine" without going into several intimate details, which may prove embarrassing to young Columbia University graduates. I will just sum it all up by saying that I don't like getting up in the morning any more than you or your fellow students do.

---

14. Composer, musical commentator, and six-year president of ASCAP, now best remembered as the host on the Disney film *Fantasia*. He was also a good friend of Berlin's.

April 13, 1943 [excerpt]
    Mr. Irving Hoffman[15]
    New York, New York

Dear Irving:

By the way, they shot me in "Hate to Get Up in the Morning" last week[16] and I've just seen the rushes. Wallis[17] thinks it's okay. I shall reserve judgment until I read the notices. A wonderful crack was made on the set the other day while we were shooting. They were playing a recording I made of "Oh How I Hate to Get Up in the Morning." It was the same Berlin voice, full of bugs and anything but good. An electrician standing on the sidelines cracked, "If the man who wrote that song could hear that guy sing it, he would turn over in his grave."

In May 1943 Berlin was invited by T. B. Costain of Doubleday Doran to write an autobiography.

June 3, 1943

    Mr. T. B. Costain
    Doubleday, Doran & Co.
    14 West 49th Street
    New York, N.Y.

Dear Mr. Costain:

I have your letter of May 20th and wish to thank you very much for your kind offer. Your $5,000 advance is very impressive, even to one who has rubbed elbows with Hollywood figures. I know how great an amount it is for the advance on a book.

However, I am afraid I cannot take advantage of it. Frankly, writing an autobiography is completely out of my line. Then again, I have dodged having one written [about me] for quite some time.

I appreciate your very generous and flattering offer, nevertheless.

July 20, 1943

    Mrs. Joel Pressman[18]
    West Los Angeles, 24
    California

---

15. Broadway columnist and friend of Berlin's.
16. For the film *This Is the Army*.
17. Producer Hal Wallis.
18. Actress Claudette Colbert

Dear Claudette:

Your secretary telephoned today and wondered whether I walked off with one of your napkins the other night. I will hunt through my clothes. It is quite possible that as I sat there admiring you, I unconsciously put it in my pocket. Usually I get away with a tablecloth. Seriously, though, I will look and if I don't find it, I suggest you keep your eyes open the next time you go to the Goetzes[19] for dinner.

Goodbye—and love to you and Jack.

Wire dated August 10, 1944

Mr. Gilbert Seldes
Columbia Broadcasting System
15 Vanderbilt Avenue
New York City

Dear Gilbert: Am flattered by your invitation for television interview but am afraid I must beg off for many reasons least of which is my face. Seriously let's get together and maybe we can arrange something else. Best to you.

October 24, 1944

Mr. Dave Dreyer[20]
Irving Berlin Music Company
799 Seventh Avenue
New York City, N.Y.

Dear Dave:

I couldn't hunt up the story about the old piano that was written here in one of the studios, so here in a nutshell are the facts and you can have someone write this up into newspaper form.

I bought the piano from Weser Bros. in 1909 when I started writing for the Ted Snyder Company. It was then a second-hand piano. In those days transposing keyboards were the common thing in all publishing houses because few pianists who worked for the different publishers could read music and transpose.

---

19. Producer William Goetz who produced the film *Sayonara*; his wife was Edith Mayer, daughter of Louis B. Mayer.
20. Dreyer was Berlin's chief song plugger and a successful songwriter.

In writing a song I liked to play the tune as I set the lyric. With this piano I was able to transpose into my singing key, or rather to keep it within the range of my voice. I also found, as the years went on, that the worse the piano, as a piano, became the better it served my purpose to work on it.

This piano has had a varied and exciting career. I used to take it to Palm Beach with me when I went there in the early 20s. It has been to Hollywood and back and forth half a dozen times. I took it to Nassau[21] when I went there with Moss Hart to write *As Thousands Cheer*. It arrived at Hamilton Pier with half the hammers out of place and a British piano tuner sweated over it for a week before he could get it into working condition. He had never seen what he called "an American piano with a gadget." The longest trip it ever took with me was when Moss Hart and I went on an Italian cruise boat for a trip around the world to work on a show. It was fastened in the stateroom and would be shaken out of working order every time the ship rolled. I took it on another cruise when Ellin and I went to the West Indies.

The piano has become a personality because it has been written up so much in the past. It has gotten a great deal of publicity. There isn't an interview in which this famous piano doesn't become a part of.

I have kept it all these years, not alone for sentimental reasons, but because it is really the most practical piano for me to work on and to demonstrate my songs when I have to play them myself. Somner Bros. made a copy of the piano for me in 1921, which I have at home. I had another copy made by the Weser Company, who originally made this one, but theirs did not work out.

I can truthfully say that all my earlier songs were written on this piano and most of the latter ones. It was particularly useful in the writing of "Alexander's Ragtime Band" where the chorus was in another key, one-fourth above, and in demonstrating this song I would play the verse in one key, and then put my foot on the middle pedal, turn the lever, and switch into another key without interrupting my singing of the song.

April 22, 1945

Mr. Ted Collins[22]
New York, N.Y.

---

21. Actually to Bermuda.
22. One-time vice president of Columbia Records who discovered Kate Smith. He later became her manager.

Dear Ted:

I was so rushed leaving for California that I overlooked sending you the story behind "Heaven Watch the Philippines." Here it is.

When I arrived in Leyte about six weeks ago during my tour with *This Is the Army* in the Pacific, I heard the Filipinos singing "God Bless America"—only they were singing "God bless the Philippines." This touched me very deeply and I felt they might like to have a song of their own. I tried to combine the spiritual quality of "God Bless America" with their feeling of friendship for America and desire to be free in "Heaven Watch the Philippines."

I taught the school children of Leyte to sing this song and when *This Is the Army* opened in Leyte I sang it there for the first time as the finale of our show, backed up by 150 Filipino school children dressed in their native clothes. It was a very effective finale. A few days later we had a public singing of the song on the steps of the capital of Leyte, where General MacArthur made his famous speech when they recaptured the Philippines. There were about 1,500 children and townspeople gathered in the rain singing it.

When I went to Manila I made a formal presentation of the song to the Philippine Commonwealth and told them that if they ever decided to sell the song in the Philippines for profit, I would like them to give the proceeds to the Filipino Boy and Girl Scouts. I did this because, as you know, "God Bless America" has been given over to the Boy and Girl Scouts of America, and I thought it was appropriate to do the same with "Heaven Watch the Philippines" for their Scouts.

The song is dedicated to General Douglas MacArthur in commemoration of his liberation of the Philippines.

I hope you get this in time

On May 15, 1945, Abel Green, editor at *Variety*, asked Berlin for "a brief anecdote on the Inspiration Behind Your Biggest Song Hit, or the song with the best human-interest story attendant to it," drawing his inspiration from the story that Rodgers & Hart had come up with the idea for "My Heart Stood Still" when they were in a near-accident in a taxicab in Paris.

May 21, 1945

Mr. Abel Green
Variety
154 West 46th Street
New York 19, N.Y.

Dear Abel:

I have your letter asking for some anecdote behind one of my hits.

The most well-known is "Easter Parade," which was an old song called "Smile and Show Your Dimple" written in 1917. It was the kind of cheer-up song that civilians wrote for the boys who were going to do the fighting. The song was plugged by the Waterson Company but got nowhere. In 1933 when I was working on *As Thousands Cheer* with Moss Hart, I wanted an old-fashioned tune for the rotogravure section. After trying to write one it occurred to me that taking a melody that was written years ago might do the trick. So I dug up "Smile and Show Your Dimple," that is the tune, and wrote up the "Easter Parade" lyric to it. Of course there were some slight changes to make, but the melody was practically the same.[23] A funny side line is that "Smile and Show Your Dimple" was published in England by Feldman, and when "Easter Parade," which was published by Chappell, became a big hit Feldman dug up my old song and started a lawsuit suing Chappell and me for having taken one of my own melodies. The case was settled by Chappell giving Feldman sheet-copy royalty.

Another is the "God Bless America" story which is well known. I wrote it for *Yip, Yip, Yaphank* in 1918, but it was never used in the show. I felt it was too obviously patriotic for a soldier show. However, in 1938 after the Munich pact, we didn't take our patriotism as much for granted as we did in 1918. You know the result after Kate Smith introduced it on Armistice Day, 1938.

There's a story behind "A Pretty Girl Is Like a Melody." I had agreed to write one act for the *Ziegfeld Follies of 1919*. After I had finished it, Ziegfeld called me into his office and asked me to write one more song. He needed a spot to show off his famous Ziegfeld show girls. This was the so-called Ziegfeld Girl number in every *Follies*. He had some cos-tume plates for this number. This was John Steel's first appearance, and having him in mind I thought of an idea to have each girl represent a famous classical number like "Träumerei," Mendelssohn's "Spring Song," Schubert's "Serenade," etc. There were five of these melodies, each representing a girl. I wrote a special lyric for each classic, so Steel could sing it. I then found it was necessary to have some kind of a song that would serve as the springboard for these old classics. The result was "A Pretty Girl Is Like a Melody." It is interesting to note that the last

---

23. Berlin himself clearly is responsible for some of the confusion about these two songs. As shown in Chapter 14, he did a major rewrite of the tune when "Smile and Show Your Dimple" became "Easter Parade."

thing I thought of was this song. In other words, I had no idea that it would be anything more than a "special material" song.

There is an interesting story behind two other songs, "Say It Isn't So" and "How Deep Is the Ocean?" I wrote them during a period of my career [1932] when I felt I was all through. It was right after I had lost almost everything in the market, along with everybody else, and I had gotten rusty as a songwriter. I hadn't been working at my trade for quite some time. I developed an inferiority complex. No song I wrote seemed right. I struggled to pull off a hit. I became very self-critical. I'd call in anyone to hear a song and my uncertainty seemed to give them the right to be over-critical. The result was that I was afraid to publish any song. I had written "How Deep Is the Ocean?" but didn't like it and convinced everyone in the office it wasn't good enough. Soon after, I wrote "Say It Isn't So," which I also discarded. While I was in the Adirondacks, someone in the office let Rudy Vallee hear "Say It Isn't So" and he sang it on his broadcast. The reaction was good, so Max Winslow went after it and the song became a hit. I think these two songs are important because they came at a critical time and broke the ice.

You asked for anecdotes and it suddenly dawned on me that I am giving you case histories of the story behind the song, which may not be what you want. I have no particular one-line story behind any song such as the Rodgers & Hart near-accident taxicab "My Heart Stood Still" story. There is, of course, some kind of a tale behind every song, but mostly songs are written because one is a songwriter and there is a reason to write particular songs. Sometimes the situation out of a musical comedy book or a picture will suggest a theme. Sometimes a world condition or personal experiences. Sometimes there is a phrase in the air, such as "You'd Be Surprised," "This Is the Life." But most times it is because, as I said, one is a songwriter and writing songs is his business. I am sure if the incident in the taxicab didn't happened, Larry Hart would have thought up "My Heart Stood Still" as a wonderful phrase for a song.

Here is one more story that I think is necessary. Many years ago Wilson Mizner[24] told me of a famous will that was made by one Charles Loundsberry. He was an attorney and after giving away his

---

24. Mizner was a colorful character, raconteur and playwright, and with his brother Addison, an entrepreneur. Their exploits were the basis of a Stephen Sondheim musical, *Road Show*.

law books, which were his only possessions, he proceeded to give away the stars, the moon, the Milky Way for children to wonder at, and "all the best things in life that were free." This was the inspiration for a song I wrote many years ago called "When I Leave the World Behind." I believed there had been a Charles Loundsberry so dedicated the song, and all copies bear this inscription: "Respectfully dedicated to the memory of Charles A. Loundsberry." You can imagine the great shock and disillusionment when I found out that the will had been written by someone to be included in a pamphlet for an insurance company! This story is included in the Alexander Woollcott biography.

I hope something in the above will be useful. If not, let me know and I will send you along some others.

Wire dated May 16, 1946[25]

> Mr. Irving Berlin
> Imperial Theater, West 45 Street

> Thanks.
> Ethel

May 18, 1946

> Miss Ethel Merman
> New York City

Dear Ethel:

I tried to tell you last night how touched I was by your one word wire, and this note is to tell you that I still can't express how pleased I was to get it.

I'm going to the Coast for a week but will look forward to seeing you when I get back.

March 28, 1947

> Mr. Al Jolson
> c/o Columbia Pictures
> Hollywood, California

---

25. Opening night of *Annie Get Your Gun*.

Dear Al:

Jack Kapp let me hear your and Crosby's recording of "Alexander's Ragtime Band" and "The Spaniard That Blighted My Life." They are simply terrific, especially "Alexander." I never heard such vitality in a recording nor have you ever been in such good form. That goes for Bing, too.

You must be a very happy mug these days. Isn't it wonderful to reach up and find it's still there? I can't tell you how pleased I am for you, and when I see you next week at the Crosby broadcast recording, I will tell you more.

September 5, 1952 [Excerpt]

Mr. Joseph Schenck
20th Century Fox Film Corp.
Beverly Hills, California

Dear Joe:

I'm dictating this letter to you over the telephone from the Catskills where I've been since I left Hollywood.

First let me tell you that I feel just great. I've had several nights of good sleep without too much help. Also, for the first time in a long time, the work is coming faster and better.

I'm enclosing a lyric of a song I finished here and which I am going to publish immediately. That is, after I get some good recordings. You have always said that I commercialized my emotions and many times you were wrong, but this particular song is based on what really happened. The story behind the song is in its verse,[26] which I don't think I will publish. As I say in the lyrics, sometime ago, after the worst kind of a sleepless night, my doctor came to see me and after a lot of self-pity, belly-aching and complaining about my insomnia, he looked at me and said "speaking of doing something about insomnia, did you ever try counting your blessings?"

When I come back to the coast I'll sing the song for you. I think you'll be crazy about it. Personally, I feel it's the best song I have written in a long time and should be a hit. I would have saved it for one of the pictures, but they're too far off and I need a song for the publishing company.

In his column Walter Winchell reported that "Irving Berlin is fighting hard to stay well. His ticker . . ." Berlin wrote Winchell the following letter.

---

26. The song is "Count Your Blessings Instead of Sheep"; the verse is reprinted in *The Complete Lyrics of Irving Berlin.*

February 18, 1947

>Mr. Walter Winchell
>Roney Plaza Hotel
>Miami Beach, Florida

Dear Walter:

Who is the stinker

The low wishful thinker,

Who told you my "ticker" is bad?

Insomnia—yes. "Composer's stomach"—yes, but "ticker" *definitely no*!

On the contrary, I know you will be glad to hear I'm feeling particularly well these days.

Incidentally, I would view with suspicion any further items from this source of information.

Winchell wrote a retraction saying that Berlin's "'ticker' beats in rhythm."

February 14, 1957

>Mr. Irving Hoffman
>c/o Taft Hotel
>New York, N.Y.

Dear Irving:

Here is a copy of the demonstration record of "Sayonara" I sent on to Josh Logan and Bill Goetz sometime ago.

As you know, I wrote this song when Josh and I were planning to do a musical version of *Sayonara*.

I was called from Japan the other morning at seven o'clock with Josh on the other end saying that the butterfly line had to be changed. Enclosed is a copy of the cable I sent him.

I made my usual good business deal with Bill Goetz to use this as the theme song if Josh could fit it in. I told Bill I had two prices—what it was worth and nothing—and suggested that he accept the latter which he did.

April 8, 1958

>Miss Ella Fitzgerald
>Algonquin Hotel
>59 West 44th Street
>New York, N.Y.

Dear Ella:

I tried to call you at the hotel but you were out.

I wanted to tell you that I had the most thrilling afternoon yesterday listening to your new album which Norman Granz brought to my office.

There are so many high-spots and your conception of singing these numbers is simply marvelous.

Congratulations and a million thanks.

My best to you always.

~~~~~~

| 41 |

Irving Berlin: Irving Berlin's Insomnia

In 1996 the *New Yorker* ran a short piece by Berlin that he had written (by hand rather than by his usual habit of dictation) in 1945, as part of a projected memoir. It is a witty view of his first days in the Army during World War I.

The story behind *This Is the Army* is as good as the show itself. The story should be written, and I wish I could do it. Wilson Mizner, speaking of my limited vocabulary, once said, "Irving is a man of few words, but he keeps repeating them." Wilson might have added, "And he assembles them so they don't always make sense." That, however, hasn't stopped me from writing lyrics. But writing a book is quite different—as the mere thought scares me, and for a very good reason: it's not my racket. I haven't the tools, to say nothing of the talent. But I have the material for such a book. So this is an attempt to set down the bits and pieces of that story.

When I received that little card from my draft board, in the early part of 1918, I was surprised—I had gone through two physical examinations, because the case history I gave them of my state of health called for a double checkup. Much has been written of my early struggles, when I was a singing

SOURCE *The New Yorker*, August 26 and September 2, 1996. Used by Permission of Rodgers & Hammerstein: an Imagem Company, on behalf of the Estate of Irving Berlin.

waiter on the Bowery and in Chinatown. True, the life I led then was not one a family doctor would have prescribed for a growing boy, but my health was good. Not until after I became a successful songwriter did I develop all sorts of ailments—insomnia, indigestion, and all the by-products of what was known in the trade as composer's stomach. Many kinds of medicines were prescribed, which I would buy but never take. I kept going to one doctor for days and finally convinced him I had ulcers. He sent me to bed, where I was given a strict diet—the whites of eggs and cream at ten-minute intervals. After two weeks, he pronounced me cured; I got up feeling no better and no worse than I did before. Of course, my ills were mostly imagined, but I managed to leave the impression that a nervous breakdown was just around the corner. So when my draft board assured me there was nothing to worry about where my health was concerned, I was surprised. Joe Schenck was indignant. "It's ridiculous," he said. "What does the Army want with Irving?"

I arrived at Camp Upton and was put through the usual routine of questions and checkups before they gave me a uniform. I remember little of that first day, but I will never forget that first night. Ten o'clock found me lying on an army cot in the dark. The large wooden barracks was filled with dozens of men who would soon be asleep. As a civilian, I never went to bed before two in the morning. Up to then, I had taken it all in my stride. All day I was so busy being agreeable and doing what was asked of me in a manner that assured them I was going to be a good sport. Everyone was so nice and polite—this wasn't going to bad at all. But lying there that night listening to the strange sounds that came from the other cots made me realize for the first time that I wasn't going to like Army life. My cot was in a corner, next to a window. I got up and looked out. A guard holding a rifle on his shoulder was pacing back and forth. I went back and stretched out on my cot again. The next few hours were the longest I ever spent in my life. Suddenly, I got very hungry—I knew it was one o'clock, because I always get hungry at that hour of the morning. I thought of my apartment in New York. The night before, some friends had been there for a farewell dinner. What was left of a turkey was still in the icebox. Nothing could have brought home the seriousness of my position more than the fact that I couldn't be in my kitchen at one in the morning. I have no idea what time I fell asleep, but I woke with a start and heard for the first time the bugler who was to become my pet aversion and the inspiration for "Oh, How I Hate to Get Up in the Morning."

| 42 |

Lead sheet for "Soft Lights and Sweet Music"

"1st lead sheet ever taken down by Irving Berlin, August 15, 1932." After twenty-five years of song writing Berlin did learn to read and write music. He found it easier, though, to continue using a musical secretary, so this is a rare example of music in his own hand.

SOURCE Courtesy of Rodgers & Hammerstein: an Imagem Company, on behalf of the Estate of Irving Berlin.

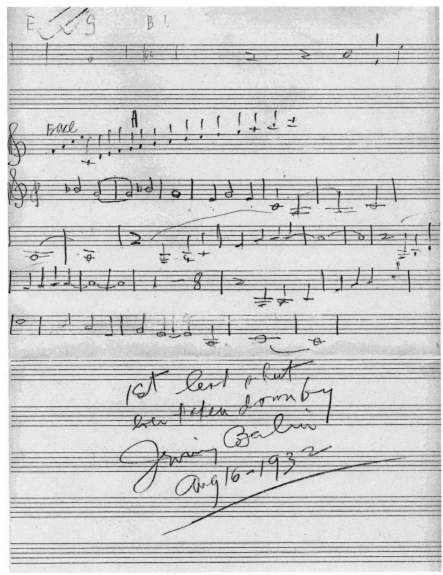

Lead sheet for "Soft Lights and Sweet Music."

Biographical Highlights

May 11, 1888—Born Israel Beilin in Russia; parents are Moses Beilin and Leah Lipkin Beilin. It is unclear where in Russia Berlin was born, and the actual day is also uncertain due to the Russian use at that time of the Julian calendar.

September 23, 1893—The Beilin family arrives in New York having sailed from Antwerp, Belgium, on the S.S. *Rhynland*, and the family name becomes Baline.

1901—Death of Moses Baline. Young Israel leaves home and supports himself singing on the streets.

1905—Becomes a songplugger for composer and publisher Harry von Tilzer, working at Tony Pastor's Music Hall.

1906—Starts work as a singing waiter at Mike (Nigger Mike) Salter's Pelham Café in New York's Chinatown where his lyric-writing begins as he caters to the customers' delight in parodies of popular songs.

1907—First song published, "Marie from Sunny Italy," lyrics only with music by Mike Nicholson. The publisher credits the lyrics to I. Berlin, leading to a new name, Irving Berlin.

1908—First song with both music and lyrics, "The Best of Friends Must Part."

1909—Berlin becomes the company lyricist for Ted Snyder, Co. He also has two hits with "My Wife's Gone to the Country (Hurrah! Hurrah!)" and "That Mesmerizing Mendelssohn Tune," the first of which Berlin often cited as an example of how to use a good "hook" to create a popular song—the adding of "Hurrah! Hurrah" to the lyric. This year he begins to have songs interpolated into Broadway shows.

1910—"Call Me Up Some Rainy Afternoon" is Berlin's first "number one" song, based on sales.

1911—"Alexander's Ragtime Band" takes the world of popular music by storm. Berlin begins his association with Florenz Ziegfeld, contributing songs to the *Follies of 1911*.

1912—Joins with Ted Snyder and Sam Waterson to create the publishing firm Waterson, Berlin & Snyder. In February he marries Dorothy Goetz, who dies in July from typhoid fever caught during their honeymoon in Cuba. Her death inspires Berlin's autobiographical song, "When I Lost You."

1913—Makes his first trip to London. Later in the year he is feted by the Friars Club, a unique honor for such a young songwriter.

1914—Creation of ASCAP with Berlin as a founding member. He creates his own company, Irving Berlin, Inc. in December to handle his scores. This came in conjunction with his first complete Broadway score, *Watch Your Step* which opened at the New Amsterdam Theatre. This is the first time a Tin Pan Alley writer goes "uptown" to write a complete Broadway score. His first "counter-point" song, "Simple Melody," is a highlight of the score.

1915—Berlin's second show, *Stop! Look! Listen!* opens at the Globe Theatre. "I Love a Piano" is one of the show's hits.

1916—Writes his first revue, *The Century Girl*, for the Century Theatre, sharing songwriting duties with the legendary Victor Herbert.

1917—Dissolves the original Irving Berlin, Inc., and opens a second firm, this time a partnership with Saul Bornstein, with the same name; this begins a move away from Waterson, Berlin and Snyder which will eventually dissolve.

1918—Becomes a U.S. citizen. He later is drafted into the army and finds a way to put his talents to good use by writing the army show *Yip, Yip, Yaphank!*, which raises funds for the community center at Camp Upton, where he was stationed. The show featured another autobiographical song, the comic "Oh! How I Hate to Get Up in the Morning," a clever reflection on Berlin's insomnia and late-night work habits.

1919—Leaves the army. "A Pretty Girl Is Like a Melody" is written for the *Zieg-feld Follies of 1919* and quickly becomes the theme song of the series. Berlin does not write the entire score, but contributes the major portion, a first for the *Follies* series.

1920—Joins with Sam Harris to build the Music Box Theatre, the first, and still only, time a songwriter built a theater for his own shows.

1921—The first *Music Box Revue*. "Say It with Music" becomes the theme song of this series and that phrase remains closely identified with Berlin.

1922—Second *Music Box Revue*; with another counterpoint song, the complex "Pack Up Your Sins and Go to the Devil." Berlin's mother, Leah, dies.

1923—Third *Music Box Revue*.

1924—Fourth and final *Music Box Revue*. Two Berlin classics, "All Alone" and "What'll I Do?" come from this year. He meets Ellin Mackay, who will become his second wife.

1925—First biography, Alexander Woollcott's uncritical *The Story of Irving Berlin*, is published. *The Cocoanuts*, a Marx Brothers musical mayhem, opens. One of his finest "waltz ballads" is written, "Always."

1926—Berlin marries Ellin Mackay in January; their first child, a daughter Mary Ellin, is born on Thanksgiving Day. In December, Berlin's "Blue Skies" is interpolated in the Rodgers & Hart show *Betsy*, outshining the rest of the score.

1927—Berlin becomes the first songwriter to write a complete score for the *Ziegfeld Follies*. The film *The Jazz Singer*, with Al Jolson singing "Blue Skies," proves that sound films are here to stay.

1928—Birth and death twenty-four days later, on Christmas day, of his only son, Irving Berlin, Jr.

1929—Films with Berlin songs, *Hallelujah*, *Mammy* (another Jolson vehicle featuring "Let Me Sing and I'm Happy"), and *Puttin' on the Ritz*, with the "Harlem" version of the title song.

1930—The ill-fated film *Reaching for the Moon* is produced. It became an unmentionable dark moment in Berlin's career.

1932—*Face the Music*, Berlin's first Broadway show since the *Follies of 1927*, opens. Berlin's second daughter, Linda Louise, is born.

1933—A revue, *As Thousands Cheer*, opens at the Music Box Theatre. The show has an interracial cast with the presence of Ethel Waters, for whom Berlin writes one of his greatest songs, "Supper Time." Also in the score is "Easter Parade."

1935—*Top Hat*, the first of three scores Berlin will write for the RKO Fred Astaire and Ginger Rogers films. For each film Berlin writes a song about dancing, in this case "Cheek to Cheek." He also gives Astaire a signature tune with "Top Hat, White Tie and Tails."

1936—*Follow the Fleet* is his second Astaire/Rogers score, with "Let's Face the Music and Dance."

1937—Another all-Berlin film, this time without Astaire and Rogers, *On the Avenue*, is released.

1938—Various events surround Berlin's fiftieth birthday, in particular a coast-to-coast radio tribute which is also a promotional event for his first "catalogue" film, *Alexander's Ragtime Band*. Berlin was always unwilling to have a biographical film made about him but did agree to select songs from his catalogue, along with some new ones, around which to build a story. *Carefree* is the final Astaire/Rogers score by Berlin; the dance song here is "Change Partners." Kate Smith introduces "God Bless America."

1939—A less successful film, *Second Fiddle*, is released.

1940—Berlin makes another return to Broadway with *Louisiana Purchase*.

1941—The film of *Louisiana Purchase* is released, Berlin's first Broadway show to be filmed.

1942—World War II show, *This Is the Army*, opens in New York. Berlin's rendition of "Oh! How I Hate to Get Up in the Morning" during the show's national and international tours marked his final stage appearances. He would also perform the song in the show's film version. He writes his fourth score for Astaire and first for Bing Crosby, *Holiday Inn*, which introduces his second holiday song, "White Christmas."

1943—"White Christmas" receives the Oscar for Best Song in a film. The film version of *This Is the Army* is released.

1944—Ends his business relationship with Saul Bornstein and dissolves Irving Berlin, Inc. In the settlement Bornstein continues as publisher of all titles except Berlin's; Berlin creates Irving Berlin Music Company as his new publishing company.

1945—Berlin is awarded the Medal of Merit by President Harry Truman for his war service. When composer Jerome Kern dies unexpectedly, Berlin steps in to write the score for *Annie Get Your Gun*.

1946—*Annie Get Your Gun* opens in New York at the Imperial Theatre starring Ethel Merman. A second Astaire/Crosby film, *Blue Skies*, basically another "catalogue" picture, is premiered. Berlin buys a home on Beekman Place where he will live for the rest of his life.

1948—Another "catalogue" film and his last score for Astaire, *Easter Parade*, is released.

1949—*Miss Liberty*, telling of the creation of the Statue of Liberty, opens at the Imperial Theatre.

1950—The film version of *Annie Get Your Gun*, with Betty Hutton in Merman's role, is released. However, Berlin follows up his success with Merman with a second show tailored to her style, *Call Me Madam*.

1951—*Call Me Madam* garners Berlin a Tony.

1953—*Call Me Madam* film is released, with Merman as star.

1954—Two last major Berlin films, both "catalogue" pictures, are released—*White Christmas* (again with Bing Crosby), and *There's No Business Like Show Business*, which gives Merman a chance to sing that title song (from *Annie Get Your Gun*) on the screen. Berlin is given the Congressional Medal of Honor.

1955–1961—Berlin works on many projects, none of which were ever finalized.

1962—His last Broadway show, *Mr. President*, opens at the St. James Theatre. It is successful financially, but disappointing artistically.

1963–1966—Again he works on various projects, but none to completion. *Annie Get Your Gun* is revived at Lincoln Center and starred Ethel Merman. Berlin contributes one new song, his last "counterpoint" song and final hit, "An Old Fashioned Wedding."

1977—Receives the Medal of Freedom.

1986—Receives the Liberty Medal.

1988—Berlin's one-hundredth birthday is celebrated with a gala televised tribute at Carnegie Hall. Death of Ellin Berlin.

1989—Death of Irving Berlin at the age of 101.

Suggested Reading

Over the past twenty-five to thirty years the interest in the popular music of the first half of the twentieth century—Tin Pan Alley, Broadway, and Hollywood—has exploded with many books being written about the era, the songwriters (including a now impressive collection of Complete Lyric books), and the performers. Irving Berlin played a major role in that period and as such is a figure in many books on the period, be they studies of the times or biographies of Berlin and his fellow songwriters, performers, and others. To select just a few is a difficult task, and this list makes no claim to completeness.

Not all these titles are currently in print, but many (if not all) can be found in libraries. The biographies of Berlin cover a range of viewpoints. Two, those by Alexander Woollcott and Edward Jablonski, are by people who knew him personally; Woollcott is fawning in his portrayal while Jablonski is able to take an objective view. Laurence Bergreen views Berlin as cranky and unpleasant, particularly in his later years. Mary Ellin Barrett paints a picture that only a family member can provide in a lovely portrait of both her parents. Another more intimate look at Berlin comes from Alan Anderson who worked closely with Berlin on the tour of *This Is the Army*. More scholarly, but always accessible, work comes from Charles Hamm and Philip Furia.

Some general interest books round out the list—these were perhaps the hardest to single out.

Much more is waiting to be written about Berlin. As noted in this book, certain periods of his life, such as that of the *Music Box Revues,* are still waiting for attention, as are wider overviews of his Broadway and Hollywood work.

BOOKS ABOUT BERLIN

Anderson, Alan. *The Songwriter Goes to War.* Montclair, NJ: Limelight Editions, 2004.

Barrett, Mary Ellin. *Irving Berlin: A Daughter's Memoir.* New York: Alfred A. Knopf, 1994.

Bergreen, Laurence. *As Thousands Cheer.* New York: Viking, 1990.

Freedland, Michael. *Irving Berlin.* New York: Stein & Day, 1974.

Furia, Philip. *Irving Berlin: A Life in Song.* New York: Schirmer Books, 1998.

Hamm, Charles. *Irving Berlin: Songs from the Melting Pot: The Formative Years, 1907–1914.* New York: Oxford University Press, 1997.

Jablonski, Edward. *Irving Berlin: American Troubadour.* New York: Henry Holt, 1999.

Kimball, Robert, and Linda Emmet, eds. *The Complete Lyrics of Irving Berlin.* New York: Alfred A. Knopf , 2001.

Leopold, David. *Irving Berlin's Show Business.* New York: Harry N. Abrams, 2005.

Rosen, Jody. *White Christmas: The Story of an American Song.* New York: Scribner 2002.

Whitcomb, Ian. *Irving Berlin and Ragtime America.* New York: Limelight Editions, 1988.

Woollcott, Alexander. *The Story of Irving Berlin* New York: G. P. Putnam's Sons, 1925.

GENERAL INTEREST

Barrios, Richard. *A Song in the Dark.* 2nd ed. New York: Oxford University Press, 2009.

Brahms, Caryl, and Ned Sherrin. *Song by Song: 14 Great Lyric Writers.* Bolton, Egerton, UK: Ross Anderson Publications, 1984.

Crawford, Richard. *America's Musical Life.* New York: Norton, 2001.

Forte, Allen. *The Great American Popular Ballad of the Golden Era: 1924–1950.* Princeton, NJ: Princeton University Press, 1995.

Furia, Philip. *The Poets of Tin Pan Alley.* New York: Oxford University Press, 1992.

Furia, Philip, and Laurie Patterson. *The Songs of Hollywood.* New York: Oxford University Press, 2010.

Gottlieb, Robert, and Robert Kimball. *Reading Lyrics.* New York: Pantheon, 2000.

Hamberlin, Larry. *Tin Pan Opera: Operatic Novelty Songs in the Ragtime Era.* New York: Oxford University Press, 2011.

Wald, Elijah. *How the Beatles Destroyed Rock 'n' Roll: An Alternate History of American Popular Music.* New York: Oxford University Press, 2009.

Wilder, Alec. *American Popular Song: The Great Innovators, 1900–1950.* New York: Oxford University Press, 1972.

Index

GENERAL INDEX